MORE PRAISE FOR *SEX* CATHOLIC, PROTESTANT JEWISH, MORMON AND OTHER COMMUNITY LEADERS:

"*Sexual Wisdom* is clear, well documented, and should be useful for everybody from parents and educators, priests, and young adults."
  – **Cardinal Alfonso Lopez Trujillo, President of the Vatican's Pontifical Council for the Family**

"*Sexual Wisdom* is an eye opening and thought provoking book about a subject that our society thinks it understands but really doesn't. Dr. Wetzel clears away a number of popular (and dangerous) misconceptions about sex and replaces them with guidance that is both profound and practical."
  – **William Kilpatrick, author of *Why Johnny Can't Tell Right From Wrong***

"In *Sexual Wisdom*, Dr. Wetzel has provided a compelling road map to the treacherous terrain through which America's bewildered stagger."
  – **Rabbi Daniel Lapin, *Toward Tradition***

"Dr. Wetzel's innovative and sensible approach to misconceptions about sexuality is bound to reinvigorate our national discourse."
  – **Joe McIlhaney, M.D., President of the Medical Institute for Sexual Health**

"All Latter-day Saints should read this volume. With permissiveness rampant we finally have a book that makes sense out of an important subject that affects us all. Though not written from a theological base, and wisely so, the ideas herein are consistent with Latter-day Saint theology and practice. *Sexual Wisdom* — aptly named."
  – **Douglas E. Brinley, author of *Strengthening Your Marriage and Family***

"Ugly realities about sexual anarchy have forced our society to take a fresh look at our sexuality. As member of this society, we (Muslims) must be part of the debate, and Dr. Wetzel's book offers us the incentive, the data, and the backup we need to do just that."
  – **Minaret**

more...

"Congratulations to Dr. Wetzel for having hit a central nail on the head with a very factual and unarguable hammer."
— **Peter Kreeft, author of** *Back to Virtue*

"Writing in a clear, readable style, Dr. Wetzel addresses a complex group of attitudes and misconceptions which has helped produce the sexual aspects of our current cultural crisis. I believe that this book will be of assistance not only to parents but also to all of those who concern themselves with the proper sexual formation of young people today."
— **Most Reverend John Myers, Bishop of Peoria**

"Dr. Wetzel has taken up the challenge of providing a guide for all interested parties in this critical field. He combines a knowledge of medicine and psychology with philosophy and theology; the result is a marvelous inter-disciplinary manual."
— **Rev. Peter Stravinskas,** *The Catholic Answer*

"This is a terrific book that speaks from the experience of a doctor, husband and father. Dr. Wetzel's use of testimony from his patients is a perfect way to blend the scientific and practical wisdom that he has to offer. He explodes some myths that dominate our thinking – such as that people have a need for genital sex. We need many weapons to fight the out-of-control sexual chaos of our culture. This is a powerful one."
— **Janet E. Smith, University of Dallas**

"One on the most valuable books I have ever read."
— **Judie Brown, President of the American Life League**

"Casual, recreational, experimental, and exploitive sex is profoundly dangerous physically, emotionally, and spiritually. It is also the 'hub' social problem of our age, spinning off everything from teen pregnancy to teen suicide and undermining society's basic institution, the family. America stands in dire need *of Sexual Wisdom.*"
— **Richard and Linda Eyre, authors of Teaching Your Children Values, 3 Steps to a Strong Family, and How to Talk to Your Child About Sex**

"Most impressive!"
— **Eugene Diamond, M.D., Past President of the Catholic Medical Association**

Sexual Wisdom

A GUIDE
FOR PARENTS,
YOUNG ADULTS,
EDUCATORS,
AND PHYSICIANS

www.sexualwisdom.com

Richard Wetzel, M.D.

Sex Education for Advanced Beginners, Inc.
Huntington Beach · California · USA

Sex Education for Advanced Beginners, Inc, P0 Box 5574, Huntington Beach, California 92615

Printed in the United States of America

Fourth Printing

Publisher's Cataloging-in-Publication
(Provided by Quality Books, Inc.)

Wetzel, Richard, M.D.
 Sexual wisdom: a guide for parents, young adults, educators, and physicians/ Richard Wetzel. -- 1st ed.
 p. cm.
 Includes bibliographical references.
 Preassigned LCCN: 98065068
 ISBN: 978-0-9795402-0-2 (previously ISBN 1-882792-59-9)

 1. Sexual ethics. 2. Sex instruction. 3. Hygiene, Sexual.
 I. Title.   II. Series.

HQ32. W47 1998   306.7
                         QB198-171

Cover design by Rachel McClain

Contents

Part V: Approaches to Sexuality

Part VI: Sexual Morality

Part VII: Teaching Sexuality to Children

Preface

In discussions of sex, one often encounters two kinds of people. One type operates negatively – concentrates on avoiding AIDS avoiding unintended pregnancies, and avoiding such situations as having one's boyfriend sleeping with someone else. The other type works positively to achieve the most fulfilling sexual experiences.

This book offers the best of both worlds in that it explains the best way to avoid problems related to sex by focusing on achieving the best that sex has to offer. This book even goes so far as to offer a path to excellence – a path that will challenge many, if not most, people. Fifteen years ago, I, too, would have been greatly challenged by it. But after examining my previous convictions, I know that I have grown and changed, and now invite others to change also.

One of the most commonly expressed sentiments about sexual behaviors is that they are a matter of personal conscience. I agree. We must clarify, however, what conscience means. Conscience is not a gut feeling, what "feels" right at the time, or an urge or a whim. Conscience is most accurately considered a judgment of reason, and like any judgment of reason, it must be informed. The more one understands about sex, the more reliable one's basis for prudent decisions will be. This book offers information toward this end from the perspective of the family physician.

Lastly, such terms that I have used in this text might be defined in different ways by scholars of various disciplines – terms such as "good," "love," and "freedom." But I expect all such terms to be understood in their colloquial or commonly accepted meanings. In this text their use has not been restricted to any philosophical, technical or theological sense.

Acknowledgments

With deepest gratitude to my family: Sheila Wetzel, Dan Wetzel, Glenn and Mary Wetzel, Mark and Laura Garmus, Joe and Margaret Rincon, Dean and Gail Rincon, Dale and Ann Rincon, and David and Denise Naaden, for their support, ideas, and criticisms. A special thank you to my father, Chet Wetzel, and to Reverend Philip Smith, O. Praem, for their extensive editorial assistance.

A special thank-you is also extended to the following people for their assistance in developing the manuscript: Jeff and Erin Talbot, Jamie Lewis, M.D., Andrea Lewis, Paula Luber, M.D., Douglas Dennis, M.D., Jose DeSouza, M.D., Yasuo Konishi, Mark Wendley, Bill and Dawn Beigel, Katie Gates, John Drake, Anthony Bassanelli, M.D., Ray and Regeania Menard, and Paula Hunter.

Also, I wish to express my sincerest gratitude to Emi Wong for her enthusiastic research assistance, to Mel and Mary K. Keegan, Reverend Daniel Johnson, Paul and JoAnn Breen, and Paul Voida who had faith in me from the start, and to Barbara McGuigan for her inspiration and encouragement.

All proceeds from this book, which would normally benefit the author, are being directed to a nonprofit, educational corporation, Sex Education for Advanced Beginners, Inc. (SEFAB) in Huntington Beach, California. The sole purpose of this organization is to promote *Sexual Wisdom* and other educational activities of the author.

Dedicated

To Dominique, my wife, my "little friend," and chief collaborator, for my faith, the greatest gift of all.

To my parents who, through their example and guidance, taught me about love.

To my patients for their willingness to candidly confront me and themselves.

To my office staff for their encouragement, suggestions, and constructive criticism, and for ever reminding me of the essential relationship between the search for wisdom and humility.

And, most especially,
to my children and the children of my community
who are the ultimate motivation behind so much
of what we parents do.

Introduction

Toward Sexual Wisdom
After the Sexual Revolution

As a family physician I am always on the lookout for helpful books to recommend to my patients about the common problems they face: obesity, marital difficulties, stress management, etc. Many years ago the manager of a free clinic, at which I occasionally volunteered, asked me to teach sexuality classes to troubled teens living in group homes. Since then, while working with teenagers and adults in a variety of settings, I developed expertise in the field and a unique approach. During this time it also became ever more obvious, and frustrating, that there was no single book I could recommend to my patients and audiences on human sexuality. So I wrote a book, and here it is.

This book, then, offers a fresh approach to some of the most controversial topics in our culture. As has been said, most people think a lot about sex but few people reflect on the issues in any serious way. Most of the popular books on sexuality focus on what I describe as "sexual trivia." They titillate, but completely ignore the heart of the matter. It is time for our culture to move beyond titillation and take a broadminded, rational, and more sensitive look at the many escalating problems in our society related to sexuality.

Obviously, difficulties with sexuality are nothing new. Sexual misuse and abuse have existed for centuries. However, since the onset of the "sexual revolution" in the 1960s, an ever wider variety of sexual problems confronts us: these problems are more numerous and severe than ever before in human history.

Now, at the end of the last decade of our century, we are appalled to find that our problems are not being solved but are multiplying. In the United States today, the number of illegitimate births and abortions has increased dramatically; sexually transmitted diseases are infecting adults, teenagers, and newborns at record levels; new diseases and new manifestations of old diseases are surfacing at an unprecedented rate; debate over abortion is more impassioned than ever; censorship by those offended by increasingly sexually graphic works is bitterly opposed by the artists; hate-filled confrontations escalate in the battle over homosexual rights; women express outrage over sexual harassment and date rape; and the divorce rate has skyrocketed.

Throughout the country, family physicians like myself are seeing, among their regular patients, ever-increasing numbers of people with sexually related problems – problems not solved, but aggravated or even caused, by this sexual revolution. And beyond my office, I see deeply worrisome, frustrating cases reported in newspapers and medical journals. Even more painfully, I see them among my family and friends.

Let us consider two recent examples from my own practice. One, a young man who was concerned about a sore on his genitals, stated that he had been depressed during the few weeks prior and had sought consolation through sex. He had sexual intercourse with several women in one week, and now he was facing two of the consequences: an incurable herpes infection and deepening depression.

Another patient, a thirty-five-year-old woman, complained of lower abdominal pain. Her initial evaluation was normal. We discussed the likelihood that she simply had a bladder infection that would be cured with antibiotics. Because some sexually transmitted diseases can also cause abdominal pain, we also discussed her recent history of sexual activity. She and her boyfriend had lived together for a year and were soon to be married, a circumstance which seems quite ordinary today. But then, after further discussion, she asked to be tested for sexually transmitted diseases that are usually found among those with multiple sexual partners. I was struck by her apparent distrust of this man to whom she would soon be committing herself "until death do us part."

The remarkable thing about both of these people – one an entertainer, the other an administrator – is that they exemplify an extraordinary number of likable, intelligent people whom I regularly see as patients. Such people could just as well be your next door neighbors, the nice couple you met at a wedding reception, or people with whom you work. What is so disturbing is that painful consequences of sexual behaviors can and do affect such a large proportion of the population.

Recently, an affable young man who was experiencing his first outbreak of herpes came in to confirm his diagnosis and obtain medical advice. He was noticeably distressed; and as he departed, he said that while discussing his infection with his mother, she had commented that it was "just a consequence of growing up in the 1990s." She is wrong in the sense that one does not "just get herpes" from breathing the air or drinking the water in this decade. No, it is specific, identifiable misconceptions or mistaken attitudes about sexuality which are so prevalent today that lead inevitably to widespread suffering. Today, these harmful consequences of sexual behavior are increasing at an alarming rate among the young, the old, the single, and the married. Most people are rightly ambivalent about what our nation has just lived through. They are afraid for their children, their relatives, and their friends, in this time of sexual crisis. But through all this some of us still believe that sex can and should be a source of great pleasure and human joy.

Some of us believe that sex can bring inordinate good into people's lives. For example, as physicians we witness the tears of joy that often follow the diagnosis of pregnancy to a hopeful couple. The potential positive results of sex include the gift of new life, tender affirmation, passionate encounters, and more. To achieve these positive results, however, requires some forethought, which is what this book has been written to encourage.

The best and ultimately most healthy attitudes about sex do not come naturally to most of us. My own attitudes have changed dramatically since my days as an inquiring teenager and single adult. Now, as a husband, father, physician, and sex educator, I feel that I have come a long way, and I now most earnestly wish to share with others what I have learned.

In the early decades of this century, many people were dismayed with what they saw as repressive, "Victorian" attitudes toward sex. They were hoping and working for a sexual revolution that would liberate and free them from outmoded moral and social constraints. They were right that we needed a revolution, but what we now have is the wrong revolution. Mistaken ideas of the past have, in large measure, been replaced with worse ideas. Our society desperately needs a fresh approach, and that is what this book has to offer. This book is an invitation to experience sexuality on a level different from the one we have witnessed becoming the norm in our society. This book reviews the ways in which society went wrong, examines the consequences we are facing today, and explores the best means of encouraging positive, healthy attitudes about sexual relationships.

In my practice, when I encounter patients with conditions that are the result of unhealthy attitudes about sex, I can sometimes interest them in a different approach. A case in point is the twenty-seven-year-old man who came in to my office for evaluation of a sexually transmitted disease. He was a handsome, seemingly rough and ready sort, who had been dating his current girlfriend for a few months. He said, "When I told my friend about my problem, he told me to go to the doctor and have him fix me up" – a quick cure and back out to cruise the scene. My initial impression was that it would be imprudent to attempt a serious discussion about sexuality with this apparent womanizer.

After offering my usual medical advice, we wound ourselves around to a discussion of condoms, abstinence, and other issues. Somewhat to my surprise, he did not dismiss my introductory comments on these issues and the conversation rapidly advanced to some highly controversial, difficult areas. Fearing that I had overstepped a bit, I became somewhat hesitant but he urged me to continue: "Just get on with it," he told me, "I want to hear what you have to say." He was more sensitive, insightful, and open-minded than I had at first assumed and was anxious to hear more. He was also aware that I hadn't much time to offer him in a busy office setting. Later, he called me from home with a few more questions, one of which was how to get a copy of the book I was writing.

In another case, as I concluded an office visit with a married couple, they asked me if I could recommend an urologist to the husband for a vasectomy (sterilization procedure). I asked about their feelings toward future children and the husband eventually explained that they were having a serious conflict – he desired more children but she did not. This admission led to a discussion about a range of trouble spots they were having related to sexual intimacy. As the discussion progressed, it became apparent that a vasectomy would not resolve their underlying conflict but in fact would more likely act to increase barriers between the two. The discussion left the couple with some food for thought about what constitutes a healthy sex life. Their difficulties were perhaps more basic than they had thought and would find resolution not through a procedure but by increased communication and intimacy.

A woman came into the office complaining of painful intercourse. During the course of the interview, she described a rather stormy career with men. She was raising her young daughter as a single parent and had been sexually involved with her current boyfriend for the past eight months. Her initial glowing portrayal of him diminished greatly as we discussed specifics about his attitudes about sex. He had risk factors for sexually transmitted diseases (a potential cause of her current symptoms) and had demonstrated, in some circumstances that he took more interest in his own sexual gratification than in providing her with basic levels of affection and affirmation.

We discussed what attitudes she might reasonably expect from men about sex and why she was willing to put herself at risk for once again being controlled or deserted by a man. We also discussed the risks she was taking for contracting diseases and the impact of her own attitudes toward men on her daughter. She mentioned how difficult it was for her to think through these issues, and how grateful she was for the opportunity to discuss them with a physician.

These are the kinds of conversations I believe the public needs to hear to allow individuals to choose the best course of action for themselves. But they are only one means, not the end, for which I am writing this guide for parents, young adults, educators and physicians. That end is to positively integrate the gift of sexuality into relationships to help make us most fully human, alive, and whole.

Part I

Sexual Relationships

Chapter 1

The Greatest Misconception

Healthy sexual relationships are the result of healthy choices, which must be based on reality. Problems arise when people base their attitudes on falsehoods and distortions. Therefore, while we will ultimately take a very positive look at human sexuality, we must begin somewhat negatively: we must investigate and clear away the serious false assumptions and distortions of sexual reality that have led us into a host of problems – before we can hope to find their solutions. For convenience, we catalogue seventeen "misconceptions" for discussion in this book. One of them stands out among the rest:

Misconception #1: People, especially men, have specific, genital, sexual needs.

This is the most important misconception about sex for three reasons: (1) it is the fundamental attitude underlying abuse of sex in society today; (2) it has supplanted strengthening a couple's relationship as the most important reason for sexual interactions; and (3) it is the basis for the addictive approach to sex that is so rampant in our society today, whereby the "need" for sex is analogous to the alcoholic's "need" for a drink. We will consider the first two reasons in this chapter and the third in Chapter 10.

The misconception that people have specific, genital, sexual needs is based upon the fact that people *like* to have sex. People *really like* to have sex because genital sexual intercourse is arguably the most intense physical pleasure one can experience. There are, however, other things besides physical pleasure that we should consider. Imagine two people at a table on which sits a delicious-looking chocolate-fudge brownie. Now imagine the same situation, except that the brownie has been replaced by a stalk of broccoli. Since the first case involves a treat, it is likely to lead to one person taking advantage of the other. How desirable and convenient it would be if one person can convince the other that he or she has a *need* for that brownie, so as to get more than one's fair share. It would be even better to convince *oneself* of this need in order to avoid any feeling of guilt for making off with the brownie.

Rationalizing "needs" gives people an excuse to take advantage of others. Highly enjoyable activities like sex, and eating brownies, encourage development of such rationalizations. This "needs" misconception, in turn, promotes tolerance of abusive attitudes and sexual practices in our society. It asserts that men, in particular, need to climax, need to fulfill fantasies, or need to have sex with a certain frequency, or in a certain position. It's as if men are addicts, in need of a sexual "fix." According to popular wisdom, "boys will be boys," men cannot control themselves ("men are animals"), and men must relieve themselves of sexual tension. A man sees a beautiful woman and thinks I *must* have her. It's as if his genitals will fall off or wither away if they are not put to regular use (an event conspicuously absent from recorded history).

But the notion that people have specific, genital, sexual requirements is false for a number of reasons. First, a person can be distracted from this "need" no matter how stimulated he or she is or how great the perceived need is. For example, a couple goes to bed early because both are feeling amorous. They become intimately involved, but just before climaxing, the telephone rings. The man is absorbed in "fulfilling his need" to climax and only halfheartedly listens for the answering machine. The message, however, catches his attention. It is the emergency room calling. The man's mother has just been involved in a serious traffic accident and may not live. She is asking for her son. Given such circumstances, one might well expect the man to be distracted from his once consuming *need*.

Other biological needs, such as those for food and sleep, can be deferred temporarily, but then recur more strongly. Genital sexual impulses, however, do not follow any such pattern, and can be deferred indefinitely. Frustrations that arise from unrelieved sexual desires may escalate temporarily, but if relief remains unobtainable, they eventually dissipate.

No one has ever died from sexual abstinence. It does not lead to any disease or even any psychiatric disorders. While all people have natural sexual urges, which may at times be powerful, they are distinct from life-sustaining needs, such as for food, water, and sleep. There is no biological necessity to climax. Not even nocturnal emissions are evidence for a biological need to ejaculate. These culminate not only intense sexual dreams, but also intensely violent or otherwise stressful dreams – dreams which include no sexual imagery at all. We will discuss (in Chapter 12) the difficulty in distinguishing between sexual tension and other forms of stress, but from what is known about nocturnal emissions, it is simplistic to consider them a specific response to sexual needs.[1] Even if nocturnal emissions were simply a release of pent up sexual energy, there is no tragedy in that. They are not pathological, but normal, natural events. The only real problem with these dreams is psychological distress created by the erroneous assumption that they are abnormal.

Furthermore, sexual desires do not follow a "use it or lose it" pattern. Such a claim is analogous to saying that one would lose the ability to enjoy strawberry cheesecake if unable to enjoy it regularly. The reality, as we all know, is just the opposite.

We find this "needs" misconception in an enormous variety of contexts. For example, on a television show about prostitution, a concealed camera caught a man propositioning an undercover policewoman. She told the man that she was sixteen years old and asked him if he "had a problem with that." He answered "no," and the cameras followed them up to a motel room where the film crew descended on the surprised man and interviewed him. As it turned out, he had two daughters, one of whom was sixteen years old. This man was such a slave to his sexual "needs" and fantasies that he could not see this prostitute as someone else's daughter. When he initially propositioned her, he did not see her as a human being, even though he had a daughter of the same age. He was willing to use a sixteen-year-old prostitute to satisfy his compulsion, his fantasy, his "needs." One might wonder, however, what had happened to his "needs" by the time the T.V. crew had finished interviewing him.

As another example, consider the man who came to my office on two separate occasions for the treatment of sexually transmitted diseases. He had had multiple sexual partners in the past, and we discussed what sort of approach he might consider in future dating relationships. He said that, after two infections, he was afraid to become genitally, sexually active again; therefore, he decided that, until he got married, he would just have to stimulate himself. Not wanting to be hurt again, or to hurt anyone else, he could see no other option. But there was an option he had not considered: he did not need any genital, sexual activity. I explained that since men have no *need* to climax, it was possible for him to manage without stimulating himself at all. This fact was news to him, as it has been to others.[2]

We must distinguish between what people *need* and what they *desire* – "I need" as opposed to "I want." Those denied a desire are frustrated; those denied a need are impoverished. People really do need friendship, companionship, and intimacy. Many people die of loneliness: it is not uncommon for the health of elderly patients suddenly to deteriorate following the loss of a cherished spouse.

We have had experience with this phenomenon in our own family. When my elderly grandfather died at home in his sleep, my father was contacted immediately and was with my then senile grandmother when she awoke. Realizing that her husband was gone, my grandmother sat on a couch in my father's arms and died, just a few hours after learning of the death of her spouse. The despair of losing her lifelong companion was too much for her to bear. People need companionship.

Along with companionship, we also need balance in relationships. As relationships become more intimate, socially, emotionally, and spiritually, they naturally become more intimate physically, whether by touching, hugging, holding hands, etc. A balanced relationship is one in which these actions reflect the level of intimacy otherwise enjoyed by the couple; an imbalanced relationship is one in which they do not. A surprising number of wives complain about husbands who only approach them physically to initiate genital, sexual activity. These women yearn to hug and to hold hands, without the pressure of having to culminate every physical interaction.

Animals, both human and non-human, have developmental needs, particularly during infancy and childhood. Psychologist Harry Harlow performed classic experiments on orphaned monkeys that demonstrated the dramatic positive influence of a cloth "surrogate" mother. Baby monkeys that experienced the warmth of the cloth were much more capable of integrating socially with other monkeys later in life than those whose only consolation came from a "mother" made of chicken wire.[3] Similarly, institutionalized children commonly suffer from psychiatric disturbances due to a lack of physical contact early in life.

People *need* companionship, a balance in relationships, and physical nurturing during childhood. However, beyond such general requirements, people do not have specific, genital sexual needs. Rather, the idea that people have such requirements often leads to one person taking advantage of another. When one person has a "need" and the other person has a conflicting "want" or preference, the question is who will win, which one will be satisfied? Because it seems that a person must satisfy his or her own perceived "needs" but not another person's "wants," the door opens to abuse. How could a woman deny her spouse or "significant other" something that he *needs?* There is the husband who demands daily sex to fulfill his "need." There is the boyfriend who "needs" to have sex in a particular manner, such as oral sex, when his girlfriend "just *wants* to snuggle." What a difference between these situations and one in which a couple strives to balance the *desires* of both individuals. If it becomes acceptable to use someone to fulfill a "need," then sex has become more important than the relationship, or as some people incorrectly maintain, "Bad sex is better than no sex."

How this "needs" misconception, with its profound implications, became so entrenched in our thinking is something of a mystery. Part of the answer lies in the subtlety of this falsehood. If it were more obviously wrong, it is unlikely that society would have so generally accepted it. The key to the success of the "needs" misconception is the often subtle manner in which it violates the truth: people do have intense sexual *desires*. Another factor is that, in the last few decades, increasing affluence has led to greater materialism and self-centeredness. Consequently, people are now more willing to magnify the nature of their self-interests. Lastly, one might expect this misconception to become more entrenched during the modem era due to the greater confusion over sexual matters. Bewildered people who are struggling to control carnal passions will more readily accept ideas that justify their own sexual abuse of others than those with clearer minds.

True sexual freedom is not possible if one is a prisoner to sexual needs, unable to control sexual urges. Rejection of this "needs" falsehood removes the chains that shackle us to self-serving behavior patterns. The freedom of the sexual revolution has been a freedom only to fulfill *contrived* needs. It has not freed us to be more loving of each other, but has only freed us from concerning ourselves with each other's welfare.[4]

It is this lack of concern for each other's welfare, this willingness to use others for our own selfish ends, which accounts for most of the misery in the world today. Floods and fires, disease and volcanic eruptions can account for measurable amounts of physical misery, but it's usually people who cause the human misery of incalculable proportions that we see all around. In this book, I am concerned with one particular kind of human misery – that directly attributable to our use and abuse of the sexual part of our nature – and I am most sincerely concerned about what we can do to alleviate that misery.

Throughout this book, we shall champion the view that to minimize this misery and to enjoy the healthiest sex, we must base our relationships first and foremost on love. This view is based on traditional teachings of natural law, which come to us from such formidable philosophers as Aristotle and Thomas Aquinas. Aquinas upheld that the first precept of natural law, or the most important rule for human fulfillment given the constraints of the natural world, is to do good and avoid evil.[5] To do good is to do what is virtuous or loving. Because love is the basis for doing good, it is the basis for the most natural, healthy approach to all aspects of life, including sex.

Among today's public, there exists considerable confusion about the various types of love. But in its most genuine form, love is a simple notion, familiar even to small children, and our society is in general agreement on its essence. Almost everyone can identify the purest form of love. It is compassion, consideration, kindness, unselfishness, altruism, thoughtfulness, extending oneself. Love is people going out of their way to give, with no thought for themselves – being nice, pleasant and courteous with no expectation of reward. Love is people at a Red Cross center donating their blood for nothing more than cheap cookies and punch. It is, according to Aristotle, to will the good of another.[6]

A great error in our modern approach to sexuality is to disregard the natural priority of love. Today, many people accept the valuing of other priorities as high or higher than love, especially in the search for sexual fulfillment. These alternative priorities include freedom (of expression, of choice, to "do your own thing"), pleasure, self-actualization, excitement, convenience, being "hip," and improving one's image. All of these priorities are valid, but none should be valued as much as love, because it is love which most readily leads us to fulfillment. When other priorities conflict with love, as they often do, love must be given preeminence.

In this book, we shall focus on five primary characteristics of love. These are: respect, responsibility, commitment, discipline (which enables one to sacrifice for others), and trust. We will use these characteristics to explore the truth about all manner of issues related to sex.

As we shall see, the natural supremacy of love is regularly questioned today. This occurs primarily through acceptance of misconceptions, such as the "needs" misconception, which distort the truth and act to support lesser priorities. Because of these distortions, other priorities are now readily allowed to encroach on the natural supremacy of love, and this in turn allows for radical changes in the perceived purpose of sexual interactions. The primary goal of sexuality should be to augment or enrich a relationship. Sexuality, whether genital or non-genital, should bring people closer together by adding a positive dimension to a well-rounded, supportive, nurturing relationship. *But, if people have specific, genital sexual needs which must be fulfilled, then the primary goal or reason for having sex is changed. The goal of sex becomes to meet those needs, instead of to enrich a relationship.* By emphasizing contrived needs (most commonly, the need to climax) the importance of pleasure is exaggerated. We lose sight of the highest priority and become focused on pleasure-seeking. The goal becomes to climax (or to achieve multiple climaxes), to fulfill fantasies, to "score," etc.

Our focus should be on relationships, not sexuality. One way of conceptualizing relationships is to liken them to a solar system. A solar system is made up of planets, each of which may represent an important aspect of the relationship. One planet might represent the physical (or sexual or sensual) aspect, another might represent the social aspect, another the spiritual aspect, and yet another the intellectual aspect. In each unique relationship, the planets (or various general components) differ in size or prominence. For relationships to maintain stability and harmony, the various forces created by the planets must remain balanced.

Genital sexual activity can be thought of as one moon circling the planet Physical. Other moons around this planet would include non-genital sexual interactions such as hugging, shaking hands, and kissing.

The function of each component, including sexuality, is to enhance the greater relationship – the solar system. The role of sexuality must be considered within the context of a relationship, rather than instead of one. This is the truly holistic approach to sexuality, or what has been called a cerebro-centric (versus a genito-centric) approach, and herein lies the wonderful potential of sexuality to affirm a sense of intimacy.

The common approach to sex in today's America gives genital, sexual activity inordinate attention. In the media, on bumper stickers, in magazines and books, in health clubs and in birthday cards there is a general preoccupation with sex. We are told to "Do it" (i.e., to have intercourse) in countless ways. "Secretaries do it from 9-5," "Nurses do it with patience," and "Teachers do it with class." Popular, self-help books carry such titles as *The One Hour Orgasm.*[7] To paraphrase chastity educator Coleen Mast, the goal has become to go as far as you can, or get as much as you can, with whomever you can, for as long as you can, and in as many different positions as you can.[8]

In addition to an increasing variety of avenues to pleasure and climax, we also face a growing acceptance of the idea that just about any method will suffice. For example, one study found that 27 percent of inner city youths attending an adolescent clinic had experienced anal intercourse.[9] We are encouraged to pursue a variety of partners and techniques so that we never become bored with our sex lives, and (for goodness sake) stop "doing it." Popular literature offers innumerable recommendations as to how to spice up "lackluster sex lives."

In summary, we must rethink our attitudes about the essential purpose of sexual interactions. We must ask whether genital, sexual activity is a part of a relationship or an end in itself. Since the populace has come to accept the "needs" misconception, the primary reason for sex has changed and become isolated. *For this to have occurred, individuals had to be willing to compromise on love, for only by maintaining the priority of love is the fallacious nature of the "needs" misconception revealed.*

Good sex does not require experiencing climax, the ultimate climax, multiple climaxes, or fulfilling one's or one's partner's wildest sexual fantasy. Any of these may be *a part* of good sex, but the primary objective of sexual experiences – genital or non-genital – is to enrich and validate a balanced, healthy relationship. Truly good sex is only possible within such a context. The difference between these two approaches may appear subtle, but the consequences of failing to distinguish between them are often profound. To focus on pleasure instead of on love is like directing all one's attention on dessert while ignoring a meal's main course – and it is equally unhealthy.

Chapter 2

Compromises On Love

Having discussed the primary reasons for the failure of the sexual revolution, let us now begin a tour of the most important topics related to sex. For each topic, we shall explore how our priorities and goals have changed as we investigate the elaborate set of misconceptions which has arisen to support these changes. We shall also see how lesser misconceptions reinforce the fundamental "needs" misconception. Understanding the misconceptions and how they have facilitated the breakdown of healthy attitudes about sex will enable us to understand what our attitudes should be.

Sex Without Love

Misconception #2: Sex without love is healthy, normal and natural.

This misconception is possibly the most extraordinary of all. The belief is that relationships based primarily on physical attraction are acceptable, or even, at times, preferable. It holds that sex should, at times, simply be for recreation, diversion, or escape. It accepts that sex with a stranger, without any strings attached, is a rational and potentially healthy alternative to committed, heterosexual monogamy. The bumper sticker says "Forget Love, Go for Lust," as if a contrived erotic interlude could somehow compare with the multi-dimensional experience of marital intercourse with one's beloved.

Sex without love is usually qualified by the comment, ". . . as long as it doesn't hurt anyone . . ." which leaves one to wonder, "How could it not hurt one or both partners?" Sex *with* love is sex with concern for others – partners, existing or potential children – because concern for others is inherent in the concept of love. But sex without love is unburdened by such regard. It is sex geared toward self, without serious concern for others. Such attitudes entice people to use others for their own pleasure and thereby abuse sex. It is no surprise that some of the greatest unhappiness related to sex is a consequence of this remarkable misconception.

During the discussion period following one of my lectures, a member of the audience described an unusual arrangement. A husband was obsessed with oral sex, but his wife did not share his interest, so they agreed that whenever he "needed" to have oral sex, he would drive to a neighboring state to have oral sex performed on him anonymously. Since no one got hurt and he had his needs fulfilled, this was posited as an ideal arrangement.

If we take a good look at the situation, however, we may discover a fairly long queue of hurt people taking shape. Obviously there is the wife, knowing that her husband considers her sexually inadequate, and that he gives his fantasies a higher priority than he gives his family. Then there is the anonymous oral sex partner in the next state, paid off and discarded. Neither she nor the man is likely to derive any heightened sense of dignity from the arrangement. But what the man may well bring home and give to his wife is one or more diseases and she is likely to have increasing apprehension about whatever other kinds of activities he may become involved in: genital sex, homosexuality and beyond. If he gives his physical pleasure such a high priority, his wife could never be sure what he would be doing when he was not right there with her. Finally, there is the rest of the family, the children, who may or may not learn the whole or even partial truth about their family circumstances. So many men complain about the little time they have to spend with their families – and then there is this fellow. This situation is likely to lead to more problems than this couple can imagine.

Sex without love cannot logically be considered natural. Consider how during the early stages of romance we hold hands with and sit next to each other. As emotional intimacy develops, we naturally hug, kiss and otherwise become more physically intimate. Healthy sexual interactions follow a natural progression. But advocates of the "sex-without-love-is-healthy" idea are, in effect, saying that to lie naked with someone and engage in wildly passionate, genital sexual intercourse, there need not exist any affection whatsoever!

It is truly astounding that anyone would want to separate sex from love. Only those who have declared immediate, physical pleasure as their highest priority could do so. Moreover, "sex without love" is essentially a lie, if not an outright contradiction in terms. A most obvious reality about sex is that people express affection through it. People naturally expect sexual interactions of all types to validate relationships, to add a physical dimension to the intimacy a couple is otherwise developing, and sex without love deliberately contradicts that expectation. When two people get involved in "casual" sex, they are, essentially, saying to each other, "By the way, I don't really care about you. I'm just doing this because it feels good." Yet the act itself says that they *do* care. If one can be involved in any sexual experience, from hugging to intercourse, without it being a demonstration of love, then how is one to know when such gestures demonstrate love and when they do not? Sex without love leads to confusing, misleading messages and so, again, is not compatible with healthy sex.

In summary, it is a misconception that genital, sexual interactions without emotional attachments create no harm. Dissociating sex from love leaves wide open the opportunity for selfish rationalizations and taking advantage of others. It promotes abuse, places people at risk for serious, unnecessary consequences, and confuses and creates unhappiness. To think that such an approach will not lead to harm ("nobody gets hurt") is to not think carefully enough.

Acceptance of sex without love is one of the peculiar consequences of succumbing to the belief that people have specific, genital sexual needs. When such needs are considered a given, the goal of sexual interactions becomes to fulfill those needs without regard to other basic considerations. Again, the way to avoid such illusions is to maintain the natural supremacy of love, a priority that many choose to abandon.

Premarital Sex

It is obvious to even the most casual observer that by the mid-1990s, premarital and extramarital sex have attained a level of acceptability previously unheard of. A wide range of publications provides statistical confirmation of this phenomenon. Studies on adolescents show a uniform upward trend. For example, sexual activity among sixteen year-old males increased by over 60% from 1982 to 1988.[1] Studies on college-age adults reveal the same pattern. In one study of unmarried university students, the rate of premarital intercourse increased from 38.3% to 64.6% during a five-year period.[2] Studies on life after college also reflect this trend. For example, the highly acclaimed University of Chicago sex survey published in 1994 offers ample evidence of a dramatic increase in promiscuity and premarital sex over the past few decades.[3]

Our paramount concern here is the effect of such activity on sexual relationships, i.e., the effect of premarital activities on attitudes and on future interactions between men and women. More specifically, the question is whether premarital sexual experiences strengthen or weaken a couple's underlying relationship.

In the course of discovering the answer to this question, we shall consider five more misconceptions.

Misconception #3: Premarital sex is acceptable if the couple loves each other.

This assertion ignores a whole spectrum of risks associated with premarital sex. When we love someone, we do not expose that person to foreseeable, unnecessary, serious risks. On the contrary, we *protect* our loved ones from such risks. Therefore, we should question how much true love can exist if two people will needlessly, willingly risk bringing serious harm to each other.

Some of the main potential consequences of premarital sex can be classified as physical, psychological, and social.

Physical Risks
- Sexually transmitted (venereal) diseases and their multitude of consequences.
- "Unwanted" pregnancies, or more appropriately, pregnancies in unwanted circumstances, i.e., without fully committed emotional, social, and financial support from the baby's father.
- Side effects of contraceptives.
- Complications following an abortion.

Psychological Risks
- Loss of self-esteem: Questioning if one is using sex in desperation to sustain a fragile relationship; wondering if one is allowing oneself to be used because of fear of unpopularity or other insecurities.
- Resentment over being used, over an "unwanted" pregnancy, or over acquiring a sexually transmitted disease.
- Fear of the physical risks listed above and the social risks listed below, of being caught. As a college student wrote to a newspaper: "My boyfriend and I are both very careful about birth control, but I'm well aware that no method is infallible. The possibility that I might get pregnant haunts me."[4]
- Guilt: Wondering if one is exploiting a partner or putting a partner at risk for selfish reasons; wondering how, if an "unwanted" pregnancy results, one is to explain everything when the child begins to ask questions, or how one would feel after an abortion.
- Loss of intimacy: use of sex to avoid rather than to express intimacy (especially in relationships already plagued with poor communication); substitution of activities based on external appearances for those which would create emotional intimacy.
- Embarrassment: worry of disapproval of one's parents or one's own children or friends should they find out; embarrassment over the possibility of public knowledge that one is pregnant or is being treated for a venereal disease.
- Distrust: Questioning why a partner is willing to put one at

risk for the problems associated with premarital sex; doubt-
ing that one is loved when there is no tangible commitment
or that the partner will continue to be supportive in case of
an "unwanted" pregnancy; speculating on whether a partner
would reveal that he or she had a sexually transmitted disease, or would be faithful after marriage, or is "doing it"
with, or thinking about, some other partner.

- •Stunted growth in personal identity and social skills: Premarital sex leads to an inordinate emphasis on the physical aspect of relationships and consequent loss of opportunities for
challenging and improving oneself academically, athleti-
cally, artistically, socially, and spiritually.

Social Risks (those affecting others besides the two in mutual consent)

- •Societal upheaval: Some argue that the greatest crisis facing
modem civilization is the abandonment of children, especially by fathers, through premarital sex, divorce and addictions. This abandonment is regarded as a primary causal factor in the development of adolescent and adult crime, depression, drug abuse, alcoholism, further illegitimacy, gang
violence, academic and employment failure, etc.
- •Economic burdens on society: for social welfare programs to
take care of illegitimate children; for treatment of abused
children; for treatment of sexually transmitted diseases
(AIDS, etc.).
- • Distrust within the family, because people are "sneaking
around" or are afraid of sharing their honest feelings.
- • Dysfunctional marriages (a common result of "shotgun"
weddings), with their effects on children, on relatives, and
on friends.
- • Diseases passed on to future children, partners or spouses,
diseases spread to the general population, for example, hepatitis and HIV contracted through the blood supply.
- •Imposition on relatives e.g., grandparents who are forced to
raise a second generation.
- • Tension among those involved in arranging for and carrying

out an abortion, or among friends of the same sex because of jealousy or suspicion about who is having sex with whose sometime partner, etc.

In the course of counseling patients, I am amazed that so many people who review this list suggest additions. The list is meant only to be representative, not exhaustive. So numerous and so serious are the risks inherent to premarital sexual activity that the assertion that people engage in it to show their love for each other is incongruous. In other circumstances, we make every effort to *protect* our loved ones from risks. We vaccinate our children and insist that they wear seatbelts and bicycle helmets; we take them to the doctor if they seem to be seriously ill. Why, then, are we so ready to expose "lovers" to avoidable risks, the magnitude of which we would not dream of exposing our immediate family to? The possible gain in pleasure from sex notwithstanding, what could the gain be relative to the risk? In a truly loving relationship, *restraint* and the *prevention* of exposure to these risks should be the expected course.

Some people would argue that almost all activities involve risks. A child riding a bicycle risks being struck by a car. True, but activities involving this kind of risk-taking are necessary – if children are to develop autonomy, self-confidence, physical conditioning, and coordination. Such activities are *necessary* to maintain health in the holistic sense. Premarital sex, on the other hand, fulfills no genuine need, and the risks associated with it are, therefore, unnecessary.

Men, in particular, downplay the reality of the risks associated with premarital sex with such comebacks as, "Life has risks. So what if you expose someone to more?" – a remarkably callous response in this age of sensitivity. This attitude sharply contrasts with the reaction of a sexually active teenager I was counseling who broke down in tears as we reviewed the risks listed above. While she had never been pregnant or contracted any venereal disease, she was well aware of the psychological price she had paid by compromising herself.

Chastity educator Pat Driscoll invites us to consider treating every date, girlfriend, or significant other as we would want someone else to treat our future spouses. She asks us to consider how the future spouses of our dates would want us to treat them. Sadly, such altruistic views seem the exception in contemporary thought.

I put the thought to sexually active couples: How can you know if having premarital sex truly expresses love to your partner? One way is to ask someone whom you know truly loves the partner. Ask his or her parent and see if the loving parent wants the two of you to have sex. Thus far, when I propose this scenario, I have only received acknowledgement of the reality that parents who are close to their children almost uniformly discourage them from having premarital sex.

Abstinence educators use a simple demonstration to open discussions of sex with adolescents. A boy volunteer is chosen and a strip of duct tape is firmly applied to his forearm. The tape symbolizes the bond between himself and a girl who gives up her virginity to him. The educator emphasizes the tightness of the bond, how with a first boyfriend the inexperienced and naive girl is capable of giving herself entirely. When the relationship breaks up, the tape is torn off the boy's forearm, representing the pain that the two experience from dissolution of the bond. The tape is then transferred to successive boy volunteers. With each transfer it loses some of its ability to adhere. This loss of adhesive power represents the decreasing ability of the girl to bond and form truly intimate relationships with each successive sexual partner. Finally the tape has no stickiness at all, and so its removal from a boy's forearm takes no effort and causes no pain. The now disillusioned and hardened girl is numb in her relationships with males and incapable of giving herself to them, incapable of fully trusting them and incapable of becoming deeply intimate with them. The same demonstration can be used for a boy and several girl partners.

Many, if not most, couples involved in premarital sex justify their actions to themselves and others with the idea that it is an expression of love. The truth is not so romantic, for the act by its very nature sends the message: "I don't love you as much as I could."

*Misconception #4: Premarital sex is the private decision of the
        two people involved.*

Intimate sexual behaviors do not occur in a vacuum but within a complex interpersonal and social context. What goes on inside the bedroom affects the couple and others outside the bedroom. In the preceding, we listed several social risks which result from premarital sex. The experience of a pregnant fifteen-year-old girl, whom I treated at a county clinic, illustrates the point. She was immaculately groomed, calm and well-mannered, and I was surprised to note an entry in her chart which stated that she had attempted suicide earlier in the pregnancy. When questioned, she said that her family had been terribly disgraced by her pregnancy and that her subsequent distress had been unbearable. If she had succeeded in committing suicide, one can only imagine how her death would have affected her family, her friends and all who knew this lovely girl.

All behaviors affect others to some degree, but for adult behaviors which carry such serious risks as sexual intercourse, the risk to others is often significant and sometimes dramatic.

*Misconception #5: Premarital sex is acceptable for consenting
        adults.*

The problem with this assertion is that a crucial word is invariably left out: "informed." If all of those consenting adults who have ended up in their physicians' offices had been *informed* ahead of time about the risks involved, premarital sexual activity would certainly decline. It is disheartening to see the surprised looks on people's faces once they learn how risky their behavior has been. The health care industry, the media and others fail to inform the public of the risks of premarital sex. Women know little about the risks they take and men, in general, know less.

An amiable young woman came to my office because she was concerned about a yellowish discoloration of her skin. She had hepatitis B, an infection which is often transmitted sexually. She had no risk factors except involvement in a serious, long term, sexual relationship. When she told her boyfriend about her diagnosis, he confessed that he had engaged in some homosexual behavior before meeting her but was unaware that he carried an infection. Homosexual relations carry a relatively high risk for hepatitis B. This woman had little idea that through her sexual activity she might be risking a possibly life-threatening liver infection. She was also unaware that a person can be infected with any sexually transmitted disease yet have no symptoms. She was mature, intelligent, experienced, and consenting, but uninformed, or at least not sufficiently informed to avoid serious consequences of her actions.

Witnessing the emotional anguish so often involved in these cases leaves one at odds with the notion that premarital sex is reasonable as long as both parties are "consenting adults." Premarital sex inherently entails serious risks. Couples can easily consent to it, but becoming thoroughly, or even adequately, *informed* about the risks they are incurring is a more complicated assignment.

Misconception #6: Premarital sex helps to establish a good sexual relationship in marriage.

This misconception ignores the fact that sexual intercourse is an inordinately simple act to perform. No strenuous preparation is necessary prior to marital relations. A basic understanding of reproductive biology is of benefit for all couples, but to experience arousal to climax with a member of the opposite sex prior to marriage has not been shown to benefit future marital relations. In fact, surveys indicate that premarital abstinence, not sexual experience, is associated with greater marital sexual satisfaction.[5]

With a holistic approach to sex, the priority lies not with having a good sex partner but with having a good lover in the fullest sense of the term. The advantage is not with those who have developed sexual prowess on their own, but with those couples who together develop their own unique pattern of interaction over the years.

Misconception #7: Premarital sex helps a couple to evaluate their compatibility before they commit to marriage.

Again, studies confirm just the opposite. Couples who engage in premarital sex[6] and couples who live with each other prior to marriage[7] have markedly higher divorce rates.

We have reviewed the main arguments used in defense of pre-marital sex and have found no credence to its supposed advantages. When we consider the advantages of waiting until marriage to have genital, sexual relations, however, the physical, psychological, and social implications are substantial. Consider the following advantages of waiting:

- Waiting encourages mutual respect and trust in relationships.
- Waiting makes it easier for spouses to be faithful as it conditions them to a restrained, disciplined approach toward sex.
- Waiting reinforces responsible attitudes toward sex.
- Waiting means that if a couple subsequently gets pregnant, they will have a more committed and therefore more stable partnership within which to raise children.
- Waiting motivates a couple to develop their relationship in other areas.
- Waiting means that sex plays an appropriate, and not an overblown, role in relationships with the opposite sex and, in particular, in the decision of whom to marry.
- Waiting means that sex is less likely to be associated with guilt, resentment, fear, or apprehension; therefore, sex can be more enjoyable.
- Waiting strengthens the marital bond, since sexual intercourse becomes something the spouses have shared only with each other.
- Waiting means no comparisons with prior sexual partners.
- Waiting means no risk, or a reduced risk, of sexually transmitted diseases.

In spite of the many problems associated with premarital sex, and of the many advantages of waiting until marriage to have intercourse, those who engage in premarital sex are not "bad" people. Most of us, at one time or another, make serious mistakes with regard to our sexuality and not one of us can know another's vulnerability in doing so. Our concern here is not with judging people, but with identifying attitudes and behaviors likely to lead to positive sexual experiences and those likely to lead to problems. The point is that premarital genital sexual activity is fundamentally unhealthy. It is demonstrably *the* sexual activity most commonly associated with subsequent unhappiness.

Does this mean that all sex within marriage is "good" or healthy? Unfortunately, no. Sex within marriage can be just as abusive, just as risky and just as dysfunctional as premarital or extramarital sex. Marital sexual intercourse, however, has a potential not found in premarital or extramarital relations. It has the potential to genuinely affirm the intimacy found within a healthy marital relationship. In contrast, sex outside of marriage creates obstacles to achieving this positive potential. Inherent in the decision to have premarital sex is the valuing of something – usually pleasure – more than love.

Behavior based on the acceptability of sex without love is a subset of premarital sexual behavior. Both rely heavily on the misconception that people have specific, genital, sexual needs. With premarital sex, the couple cannot wait for marital commitment. They love each other "so much" that they *need* to express that "love" through genital intimacy. The sexual tension becomes unbearable and *must* be relieved, even if the risks involved attest to the fact that true love is being compromised. Sex without love is justified because it achieves the goal of fulfilling a person's needs, even though it might mean degrading the sex act to the point of a detached exchange with a stranger. Sex without love is the extreme extension of the limitations and compromises placed on love by premarital sexual relationships.

Saying "No" to premarital sex means valuing oneself and one's date enough to refuse risking the possibility of using another or of being used. It means keeping one's sight on the heart of the relationship, maintaining the priority of love, and rejecting the "needs" misconception.

In a *Newsweek* magazine editorial,[8] a physician who specializes in the treatment of AIDS patients concluded, "Smart people don't use condoms." His point was that smart people don't have premarital sex. To expand on his thought: the smartest people keep their clothes on until they get married.

Chapter 3

The Victims of the Sexual Revolution

We have discussed the basis for the abuse of sex. Now we turn our attention toward the recipients of this abuse, four groups of people who are most harmed by the attitudes fostered by the sexual revolution: women, children, grandparents, and homosexuals.

Women

Women have borne and continue to bear the greatest burden of suffering from the abuse of sex. A popular misconception contradicts this fact.

Misconception #8: By removing the attitudinal barriers to pre-marital sex, the sexual revolution has liberated women.

When the sexual revolution of the 1960s brought us an era of acceptance of both premarital sex and sexual promiscuity, some people claimed that these "liberating" changes would benefit women. The reality, however is that such behaviors preferentially victimize women in four distinct ways: illegitimate pregnancies, sexually transmitted diseases, side effects of contraceptives, and psychological suffering.

1) Illegitimate Pregnancy (pregnancy among unmarried women)

From 1940 to 1990, the rate of illegitimate births has increased from 3.8 percent of all births to 28 percent of all births.[1] These pregnancies are a problem for all, but especially for pregnant, single women because, in the vast majority of cases, it is the woman who bears ultimate responsibility for coping with this problem. To solve it, she commonly has a choice among five options:

A. She may opt to raise the child herself, an often frightening prospect when she considers the challenges of single parenthood.

B. She may ask her parents or another relative to raise the child for her, or ask for an inordinate amount of support from them. Such a decision leads to a host of potential troubles including guilt for placing such burdens on others, worry that she will irreparably damage her relationship with her child, feelings of inadequacy, etc.

C. She may opt to give up the child for adoption. However, even those women who view this choice as the best option can expect it to involve a substantial psychological burden.

D. She may have an abortion. Although the medical and psychological consequences of abortion are controversial, it is clear that most women are in misery while they are considering submission to an abortion.

E. She may marry someone with whom she is less than enamored, and face a life of endless possible consequences.

While it is true that rare cases do exist in which unintended pregnancies occurring outside of marriage are resolved with minimal conflict, usually the woman is left to choose among these five difficult options. There is no easy way out. In most cases, the woman's distress far exceeds the man's.

2) Sexually Transmitted Diseases

The consequences of sexually transmitted diseases (STDs) are not distributed equally between the sexes. The female partner is usually the focus of attention when a clinician confronts these diseases because women suffer far more numerous and serious consequences from them than do men.[2] As one authoritative text states:

> Most STDs show a biological sexism. Women suffer more severe long-term consequences including PID (Pelvic Inflammatory Disease), infertility, ectopic pregnancy, chronic pelvic pain, and cervical cancer. Women are less likely to seek health care if infected because a greater percentage of their STDs are asymptomatic (without symptoms). Moreover, most STDs are more difficult to diagnose in women than in men. Additionally, due to the fluid dynamics of intercourse, women are more likely than men to acquire a sexually transmitted infection from any single sexual encounter.[3]

This topic is covered in greater depth in Chapter 7.

3) Side Effects of Contraceptives

All popular forms of contraception are "male friendly." Men assume no risk of side effects when their partners use oral contraceptives (commonly referred to as "the pill"), the IUD (intrauterine device), the diaphragm, steroid implants (Norplant) or shots (Depo-Provera), the cervical cap, or the cervical sponge. Every one of these, however, has potentially harmful side effects for women. Similarly, sterilization procedures for women are more involved than those for men and carry greater risks. The only male-oriented contraceptive, the condom, carries essentially no medical risk for either partner.

4) Psychological Suffering

A large base of literature addresses the differences between the ways men and women view sex. Overwhelming evidence verifies that women bring far greater emotional investment to sexual relationships than do men. Women are more likely to view sexuality as one aspect of an intimate, committed relationship, whereas men more commonly view sex as an emotionally uninvolved interaction meant to satisfy orgasmic, sexual needs.[4] Women, because of their disproportionate emotional investment, are less prepared for, and less willing to accept, the termination of sexual relationships. Therefore, women generally suffer greater psychological repercussions from termination of sexual relationships than do men.

In considering these four problem areas, it is apparent that women are far more vulnerable than men to the consequences of premarital sex, yet the sexual revolution was supposed to have liberated and created opportunities for women. While it is true that women have achieved valuable independence in some areas in recent decades, it is also true that the prominent call during this revolution for unrestricted premarital sex ("sexual freedom") has created far more problems for women than for men.

Feminist Response

Premarital sex and other forms of promiscuity (such as what is now euphemistically referred to as "serial monogamy") have become widely accepted in the wake of a sexual revolution aimed at satisfying men's "needs." Surprisingly, such practices have found little resistance among mainstream feminists, but instead are generally encouraged by their leaders.

Feminism is an umbrella term for several movements, each with its own agendas, but all feminists rightfully strive to invalidate the idea that women are inferior to men (a notion sometimes encouraged by traditionalists). It is disheartening, however, to witness the lack of concern among the most well known feminists over the consequences *for women* of premarital and extramarital sexual activity. Helen Gurley Brown, the editor-in-chief of *Cosmopolitan* magazine, states that according to the Cosmo philosophy, "it's alright to lust after men, not only lust after them but do something about it."[5] The pages of *Cosmopolitan* and other women's magazines openly defend "lustful" sex, devoid of love, and sex outside marriage.

Gloria Steinem, writing in *Ms.* magazine about premarital sex, admonishes "conservative religious authorities" for condemning "all sex outside marriage." She states that feminists should "stand clearly and publicly on the side of any consenting, freely chosen sexuality as a rightful form of human expression" and asks us to consider words like "lovers" and "sex partners" in a positive sense.[6] In the ever-popular book on sexuality, *The New Our Bodies, Ourselves: A Book By and For Women,* under the heading of "Virginity" there is no mention that premarital abstinence might be the best, or even one of the better choices. The text opts for neutrality, stating only that, "We must be free to have sex *or not* as we think best," and redefines virginity: "We are virgins with each new lover, sometimes with the same lover, and in each new phase of our lives."[7] Erica Jong, one of the world's most widely read feminist authors, refers to herself as the "patron saint of adulteresses."[8]Such attitudes on the part of feminist leaders seem incomprehensible to someone working in the trenches, seeing as a day-to-day experience the harm that comes to women through premarital sex. Many women are bitter about the abuse they have suffered at the hands of men. They complain with good reason about how men have exploited or used them. Yet the most prominent feminist leaders simultaneously encourage attitudes and behaviors that inevitably result in this bitterness. By allowing compromises on love and accepting men when they exploit women, these feminists place their own kind at peril.

It is an unfortunate reality in today's world that women themselves must ensure that men treat them with respect. For several reasons, many of today's men seem incapable of doing this on their own. First, many men know little about the risks at which they put women. Second, men are desensitized by messages to "go for it," which encourage disregard for the consequences of sexual activity. Third, of those men who acknowledge that risks are involved (e.g., of pregnancy), many also are well aware that they themselves are generally less threatened by them than women.

All true feminists should hold as a central tenet that they enthusiastically support premarital virginity, thereby encouraging women to take this practical first step toward liberation from the many serious risks associated with sex. The most grievous error in mainstream feminist philosophy on sex has been the emphasis on the priorities of freedom and power to the neglect of love and consideration.

Because the sexual revolution has promoted premarital sex, it has inadvertently fostered the abuse of women. The callousness of this revolution toward women can be appreciated by considering statistics on rape and other forms of abuse. In a study which polled 13–15 year old males in Rhode Island, eighty-six percent said that it is acceptable for a man to rape his wife! Twenty-four percent said that it is acceptable for a man to rape his date if he has spent "a lot of money" on her.[9] It is estimated that one in eight women now living in the United States has been raped.[10]

Rape is one of the most severe forms of sexual abuse, but when we discuss the sexual abuse of women in our society, rape statistics are but the tip of the iceberg. According to figures from the American Psychological Association twenty-eight percent of dating relationships contain some physical, emotional, or sexual abuse against the woman.[11] Most people agree that it is sexual abuse when a man forces his wife or girlfriend to have sex with him against her will. It is also abuse when he forces her to have sex in a position, or under a circumstance, or with a frequency to which she objects. A man who brings home to his wife a disease, which he acquired through an extramarital affair or from a prostitute, is abusing her, as is a man impregnating a woman and then absolving himself of responsibility, telling the woman, "You take care of it" or "You should have protected yourself better."

In a letter to a newspaper, a woman complained, "As for the pro-life minister who said that women have the choice 'not to go to bed with a man' who does he think he's kidding? Women learn early in life that in order to keep peace they must *give up control of their bodies*" (emphasis added). The tragedy here is that anyone would feel compelled to surrender in such a way! This woman's attitude is disheartening, but it seems to be a fairly common one. The real issues in this case are sexual abuse and marital dysfunction, not abortion. Women should not feel obliged to perform sexually for their husbands any more than men should "give up control of their bodies" to their wives.

As a final point on this subject, it is significant that women are often victimized through divorce, which has become even more common during the sexual revolution,[12] in part because of our changing attitudes toward sexuality. Here, too, women suffer disproportionately. Not that divorce is uncomplicated and painless for men, but, again, in comparison to women, the impact on them is less. Not only do women usually carry the responsibility of raising the children, but, under current conditions, they have fewer income opportunities than men. Given these facts, it is uncommon to find a divorced woman who is not struggling financially[13] or emotionally, or both.

Children

Forty percent of children in the United States go to sleep at night in homes in which their fathers do not live.[14] Along with women, children also have paid a high price for this revolution. Never before has our society witnessed such a decline in the standard of care for children as over the past few decades. The traditional priority of nurturing children has lost out to the priority of adult self-fulfillment. The worst consequence of this shift in priorities has been the widespread parental abandonment of children born as a result of premarital sex, or set adrift by divorce. Any breakup of the traditional nuclear family unit has its most devastating impact on children. Numerous studies document the extent to which children from broken homes suffer multiple consequences ranging from psychological and health problems through involvement in high-risk behaviors.[15]

Children also suffer from the current epidemic of sexually transmitted diseases. Not only are they contracting these diseases through sexual abuse, but also developing more congenital infections (during pregnancy and childbirth) than ever before. Data is sparse on the incidence of venereal diseases among molested children but is readily available on the incidence among newborns. The incidence of potentially life-threatening herpes infection in newborns continues to increase and now affects 1,500–2,200 babies per year.[16] A child who is exposed to venereal warts during birth may develop warts on his or her larynx (voice box), and treatment of this infestation may involve multiple surgeries.[17] Over 25 percent of infants who develop chronic hepatitis B eventually succumb to the disease as a result of liver cancer or liver failure.[18] Nearly 700 cases of syphilis occur annually among newborns, the highest number since 1949, the year when penicillin made control of the disease virtually certain.[19] These babies with syphilis may suffer serious complications or death from it. The United States Public Health Service estimates that 1,500–2,000 HIV infected children are now born in the United States each year[20] and HIV disease is now the seventh leading cause of death in children in our country.[21]

Children also pay a high price for being the result of "unwanted" pregnancies. Such pregnancies commonly lead to various forms of child abuse. When abuse is taken to the extreme, the woman may make her offspring the victim of an abortion.

When one considers the effects of the sexual revolution on women and children, it is clear that, had it exacted the same toll from men, it would not have spread so rapidly or so widely. Since men as a group are generally considered more powerful than women, they have more license to care for or to exploit. Unfortunately the revolution based on "needs" encourages many men to self indulgence, thereby reducing their ability to protect loved ones from the pursuit of their own selfish fulfillment.

Grandparents

Grandparents may seem unlikely victims of the sexual revolution, but in one area, they are indeed paying a heavy price. The steadily increasing numbers of "unwanted" pregnancies and the breakdown of the nuclear family have placed the responsibility of raising grandchildren on many grandparents. The number of children in this country who live with their grandparents now stands at 4 million, but is escalating rapidly.[22] It is striking to see the many small children brought to physicians by their weary grandparents, either because the single parent is unavailable or because the child has been abandoned to them. No doubt many grandparents shoulder this responsibility and give up their retirement freedom without qualm. But no doubt, too, some feel justifiable resentment. Even those who at one time accepted liberal notions about sex and drugs now acknowledge how much these put grandparents at risk of raising two or more generations.

Homosexuals

Because of HIV disease, male homosexuals bear a great share of the suffering from the sexual revolution. HIV has struck this population unmercifully and continues to take its toll. Due to similar causal factors, homosexuals also suffer from higher rates of other sexually transmitted diseases than do heterosexuals.[23]

Thus it is clear that many people suffer disproportionately from the abuse of sex. Healthy sexuality means avoiding the roles of either victim or victimizer. It does not put anyone at unnecessary risk of serious harm.

The sexual revolution has been geared primarily toward satisfying men's sexual "needs" at the expense of vulnerable population groups, including women, children, and grandparents. It is ironic that in the case of the male-dominated homosexual population, the revolution has, in such a tragic way, backfired.

Part II

Diseases

Chapter 4

Sexually Transmitted Diseases

Psychological or emotional distress probably accounts for the greater part of the suffering people experience as a result of their sexuality, but it is the hardest kind of suffering to quantify or document. It is virtually impossible to tabulate the distrust, guilt, insecurity, fear, anger, embarrassment or resentment associated with the abuse of sex. In contrast, an obvious and easily documented source of misery is sexually transmitted diseases (STDs). We know a great deal about the medical consequences of these diseases, but as devastating as these effects are, they pale in comparison with the psychological aftereffects of these diseases. Relentless depression resulting from herpes infestation is one compelling example.

STDs are analogous to having a cold in the genitals. When a person with a cold sneezes, the germs spread to others. In a similar way, when one person with germs in the genital area comes into intimate contact with another person, the germs travel from body to body. We can get some idea of how this phenomenon works from a list of 80 names of men and women believed to have been sexual partners, consecutively over the centuries, from Henry VIII to Prince Andrew and Sarah Ferguson. This list, published not long ago in *Harpers' Magazine,* includes names like Mme. de Pompadour, Napoleon, Sarah Bemhardt, and Edward VII. Such a list suggests the possible ramifications if Henry VIII was, indeed, carrying syphilis.[1]

Sexually transmitted diseases are fast becoming a major crisis for modern man. The United States experiences an estimated 12 million new cases of STDs each year,[2] and these are just one nation's share of the worldwide epidemic. It is estimated that one in five Americans is now infected with at least one *incurable* sexually transmitted disease.[3] The sexual revolution has seen not only an ever-expanding resurgence of old diseases, but has been fertile ground for the development of many new ones. There are now 50 types of STDs.[4] Among these newcomers are chlamydia, herpes simplex type 2, and HIV disease (Human Immunodeficiency Virus). AIDS (Acquired Immunodeficiency Syndrome) is the terminal stage of infection with HIV and usually develops after a latency period of from eight to ten years.[5] HIV and AIDS will be treated in depth in the next chapter.

Our current understanding about STDs is woefully inadequate. For example, in the case of bacterial vaginosis, scientists have yet to identify the offending organism, and it is even unclear whether or not this disease is sexually transmitted. Although it is seen in virgins, it is seen with much greater frequency among the sexually active,[6] especially those with multiple sexual partners.[7] One of the most alarming characteristics of STDs as a class is that the pathogens causing them can be carried by people who manifest no visible symptoms. Thus, incalculable numbers of other people can be infected by carriers who may or may not be aware of their power to spread disease. Even a brief overview of seven important STDs will suggest the enormous and increasing proportions of the physical, psychological, and social problems we face as a result of the sexual revolution.

Chlamydia and Gonorrhea

Chlamydia and gonorrhea are two of the most common STDs with a combined incidence of 6 to 7 million cases per year.[8] These bacteria are often considered together because the major syndrome associated with both of them is an infection of women's fallopian tubes, called pelvic inflammatory disease, or PID. As one text warns, "More important than the infection itself is the fact that at least one in four women who develop PID suffers serious, long-term health problems as a result of it."[9]

PID affects more than 1 million women in the United States each year.[10] Its long term sequela include infertility (in 21 percent of the cases) and chronic abdominal pain with painful intercourse (in another 21 percent). PID is responsible for up to one third of the estimated 2 million cases of infertility each year and is the leading cause of maternal death in the first trimester of pregnancy."[11] Women who have suffered a bout of PID are also at risk for a tubal (or ectopic) pregnancy, a life-threatening condition. PID is thought to be a major cause of the alarming increase in incidence of tubal pregnancies over the past few decades (see graph below).[12] [Note: According to the accompanying article, the decline in cases of tubal pregnancies in hospitals after 1989 was due to a "shift toward treating ectopic pregnancy in an outpatient setting." This shift was presumably due to economic pressures and technological advances.]

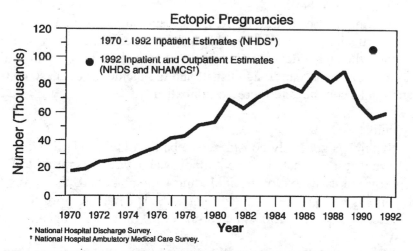

Figure 1: Number of ectopic pregnancies — United States, 1970 - 1992. Source: Centers for Disease Control, *Morbidity and Mortality Weekly Report*, 44, no. 3 (1995): 47.

PID exemplifies many of the dilemmas facing medical science with respect to STDs. Diagnostic tests are available for both chlamydia and gonorrhea, but currently there are no commercially available tests for the 25–50 percent of cases of PID caused by other organisms. Further, even the tests for these two known pathogens have limited usefulness and are negative in as many as 30 percent of cases where the bacteria are actually present.[13]

Diagnosis of symptomatic chlamydia or gonorrhea infections is not the only problem. As is characteristic of the other STDs, most people infected with these diseases have no symptoms and do not know they are infected. The same tests used to diagnose acutely ill patients are used to screen asymptomatic carriers for infections they don't know they have, and each type of test has serious drawbacks related to accuracy, timeliness and/or cost. It would be simple if all affected persons had symptoms, but 33 to 50 percent of males and 80 percent of females infected with gonorrhea have no symptoms.[14] Thus, when those infected are unaware of their contagiousness, they often unknowingly infect a sexual partner with gonorrhea or chlamydia, or both.

Development of antibiotic resistant bacteria is yet another problem, particularly in the case of gonorrhea. Since 1976, many strains of gonorrhea have developed significant resistance to the four antibiotics most widely used against it, and the incidence of these resistant strains continues to increase dramatically.[15]

Syphilis

Syphilis is generally considered to be the oldest STD. Historians believe that it originated in the Americas and was transported to Europe by the early explorers, including Columbus and his sailors.[16] Syphilis is responsible for the one great STD epidemic prior to HIV disease, when, in the 1500s, an estimated 10 million Europeans died of syphilis.

After introduction of penicillin in the 1940s, the incidence of syphilis declined by 99 percent.[17] This victory was short lived, however, because of the sexual revolution in the 1960s. Rates of primary, secondary and congenital forms of syphilis have now reached the highest levels since 1949.[18] No one predicts a replay of the epidemic of the 1500s, but the tragic consequences of the resurgence of syphilis for newborns is reason enough for great concern. Eighty to ninety percent of affected babies are born with skeletal abnormalities, and the brains of 40 to 60 percent are infected.[19]

Genital Herpes

Genital herpes was essentially unknown until a few decades ago, but 45 million Americans are now estimated to be affected.[20] The most feared complication from herpes is a disseminated infection, which is transmitted to babies from their mothers during birth. Persons with herpes are at greater risk of contracting HIV disease if they are exposed to HIV through sexual activity[21] yet incidence of this infection continues to rise despite publicity about AIDS.[22] Over half of the babies with disseminated infection die.[23] Physician consultations for genital herpes have increased fifteen-fold between 1966 and 1989. Symptomatic infections involving painful, recurrent outbreaks are, however, "merely the tip of the iceberg," since only one fourth of those infected have symptoms and the other three quarters of those responsible for new infestations had no evidence of infection themselves.[24]

Hepatitis B

Many people associate hepatitis B with intravenous drug use, but it is also commonly contracted through sexual activity. Most patients recover from the acute stage but that is only one aspect of the infection. Between 6 and 10 percent of those infected with hepatitis B become chronic carriers; they remain contagious, yet have no symptoms. Of these, 25 percent will eventually develop the most deadly form of the disease,[25] but the majority will live on as a reservoir for new cases.

Venereal Warts

Venereal warts are caused by over 20 different viruses[26] and are the STD most frequently associated with cancer. After a nearly tenfold increase between 1966 and 1987,[27] it is estimated that there are well over 12 million cases in the United States.[28] Again, only one tenth of those affected are symptomatic.[29] An estimated 32 to 46 percent of sexually active teenagers are infected with venereal warts.[30] Since venereal warts cause cervical cancer, the rates of these cancers have experienced a concurrent dramatic increase. From 1953 to 1986 the proportion of cervical cancer in women under 35 years of age increased from 9 to 25 percent.[31] Also, because venereal warts are caused by a virus, treatment is limited in much the same way as it is for HIV and herpes infections. According to a current medical text, available methods of treatment afford little hope of eradicating the infection or preventing its spread.[32]

Venereal warts can become so large that they obstruct the vagina (precluding the normal delivery of a baby), or the anus,[33] but most warts are microscopic. The physician cannot see them during a routine exam, and even with the use of an expensive magnifying instrument called a *colposcope,* the physician may miss 20 to 70 percent of infestations. Because of the seriousness of the disease and its high prevalence, some experts recommend that all adolescents involved in promiscuous sexual behavior be routinely screened by a full colposcopic exam.[34]

Difficulties in Screening Procedures

Inconsistency in the ways practicing physicians approach STDs should be of no surprise when we consider the large number of complicating factors: the general lack of medical information about these diseases; the expense, discomfort, embarrassment, and inaccuracies associated with many of the diagnostic tests; the fact that the majority of people infected with STDs are unaware of their own contagious state; the varying degrees of long term sequelae; the lack of effective treatment for many STDs; the dramatic recent increases in incidence for most of them; and the emotion-laden issues closely related to STDs, e.g., infidelity and sexual promiscuity. As a faculty member at the local teaching hospital, I have observed both experienced physicians and those in training, and have become aware of the great variety in their approaches to patients with STDs and treatment of these diseases.

Let us consider one common scenario in depth. Bladder infections are an extremely common problem encountered by family physicians. If a sexually active woman comes to her physician with

Disease	Symptoms	Effectiveness of screening Tests
Chlamydia	Discharge (pus) from the genitals, painful urination or pain in the abdomen or testicles.	Fairly good: 70-95%. [43]
Gonorrhea	Discharge (pus) from the genitals, painful urination or pain in the abdomen or testicles.	Fairly good: 70-90% for males.[44] 80-90% for males.[45]
Syphilis	First stage: Painless ulcer on penis, vagina or anus. Second stage: Rash. Third stage: Headaches vomiting, weakness, and other symptoms.	Good to excellent: generally well above 80%.[46]
Herpes	Recurrent, painful ulcers on the genitals, swollen glands in the groin.	Fair: Culture test accurate (77%) if timely.[47] Antibody (blood) tests are of limited value in making an early diagnosis.[48]
Hepatitis B	Jaundice (yellow eyes and urine) vomiting, dark urine, fatigue, abdominal pain seen in both acute and terminal stages.	Excellent, but test is often overlooked.
Venereal Warts (Condyloma)	Warts on the genitals.	Poor: 30-80% accuracy.[49]
HIV Disease and AIDS	Chronic cough, diarrhea, rash, fevers, swollen glands, weight loss.	Blood test usually positive within three to six months of acquiring infection.

cont. next page

Figure 2. Summary of sexually transmitted diseases.

Disease	Treatment	Complications
Chlamydia	Antibiotics. Possible hospitalization or surgery for females with severe cases. Permanent effects may persist despite appropriate therapy.	Women: infertility, tubal pregnancy, pelvic abscesses, chronic lower abdominal pain. Men: infertility and arthritis (both unusual).
Gonorrhea	Antibiotics. Possible hospitalization or surgery for females with severe cases. Permanent effects may persist despite appropriate therapy.	Women: infertility, tubal pregnancy, abscesses, chronic lower abdominal pain. Men: infertility. Both: arthritis.
Syphilis	Antibiotics are very effective. Hospitalizations for one week may be required if not diagnosed within the first few years.	If untreated, leads to dementia and death. In newborns: congenital defects, anemia, brain damage, death.
Herpes	Antibiotic pill or cream reduces symptoms and contagiousness. There is no cure.	Possibly associated with cervical cancer (infected women should have regular PAP smears). Potential life-threatening infection to newborn.
Hepatitis B	No cure. Immunization available to prevent infection of sexual partners or exposed newborns from known carriers.	Development of chronic carrier state (no symptoms but contagious to sexual partner or fetus), liver failure or death.
Venereal Warts (Condyloma)	Various methods used include freezing, burning, surgery, and laser. 20-100% success rates reported. May not be possible to cure but growth and spread can be controlled.	Strong association with cervical cancer (infected women should have regular PAP smears). Newborns may develop warts on voice box.[50]
HIV Disease and AIDS	There is no cure. Potent medications slow the progression of the disease. Without medication most die. With medications many survive many years.	Many unusual infections and cancers, dementia, death. Many serious side effects from medication. Infection can be passed from mother to newborn.

Figure 2, *cont.*

symptoms of a bladder infection, he typically will do a microscopic exam and a urine culture and give her an antibiotic pending the culture result. We know what kinds of bacteria cause bladder infections, and this knowledge determines the choice of antibiotic prescribed. Even though chlamydia can cause similar symptoms to a bladder infection, the antibiotics most frequently used to treat bladder infections are not effective against chlamydia. Not infrequently, the woman's urine culture result will be negative, i.e., no particular bacteria are found as the cause her symptoms. In one study, 65 percent of women who had symptoms of a bladder infection but negative bacterial cultures were found to be infected with chlamydia.[35]

The best course for the physician in this scenario is unclear. Chlamydia cultures could be routinely performed on all sexually active women whose urine cultures come back negative. However, obtaining a specimen entails not only a second office visit and the ever unpopular pelvic exam, but also requires that the physician probe inside the woman's urethra with a small swab. This procedure adds cost (for the second office visit, usually including extra charges for a pelvic exam and for the chlamydia test which alone runs about $35), discomfort (having one's urethra swabbed is uncomfortable), inconvenience and embarrassment to what is usually a relatively benign, inexpensive, single office visit. Then again, even if the physician puts the patient through all of the discomfort, inconvenience, and expense there is no guarantee that the test results will be accurate.

In my experience, women with symptoms of a bladder infection whose culture is sterile are usually well after a few days of treatment with antibiotics, even with antibiotics that do not effectively treat chlamydia. In light of current research, it is unclear what this means, and how many women are being undertreated for a potentially serious sexually transmitted disease.

For the sake of discussion, let us assume that we test our patient for chlamydia and the test comes back positive. The woman tells the doctor that she had broken up with her sexual partner of three years just four months before, and has recently become sexually active with another man. One question now is, which sexual partners should be treated? Most likely she was infected by her current boyfriend, even though he has no symptoms, but it is possible that she has carried the infection from the time of the former partner, and it has just now become manifest. It is interesting to consider whether the woman's history should be regarded as reliable at this point. The physician must attempt to determine which sexual partner is the more likely donor of the infection from a potentially biased history, i.e., it is likely that the woman would paint a better picture of her current boyfriend than of his predecessor.

Regardless of what history is obtained about each boyfriend's sexual past, clearly her current boyfriend should be treated. However, physicians would disagree about what to suggest for the former boyfriend. The situation is further complicated because the woman is usually not interested in being in contact with him again, especially under these circumstances. Nevertheless, both she and the physician have an obligation to protect him and the future women in his life from any infection he may carry. Further, if the woman tests positive for chlamydia, another question is whether she should be screened for other STDs. These infections tend to run in packs. If a patient has one, he or she is at risk for having others. Physicians disagree about which tests to order: sometimes they order no tests, or sometimes an HIV test alone.

Screening practices among clinicians vary widely. Some recommend chlamydia and gonorrhea screening for any sexually active teenager.[36] Others recommend an HIV test after diagnosing any STD.[37] Due to the many ambiguities, and different levels of training and knowledge among physicians, there are few recommendations that physicians uniformly follow.

To mention one final dilemma associated with our scenario, physicians also disagree over how to ensure that a patient who is treated with appropriate antibiotics is actually cured of his or her chlamydia infection. Antibiotics are almost always successful in curing an acute infection, but considering the consequences of a treatment failure, some physicians recommend performing the swab test again after the patient finishes a course of antibiotics to prove that the infection is gone. Again we are back to issues of cost, discomfort, test inaccuracy, embarrassment and inconvenience.

This is an example of the types of problems involved in even a most simple, common, clinical problem related to STDs. Medical science has few answers to these dilemmas. We are working with limited knowledge, inordinately complex cost/benefit analyses, a myriad of psychosocial issues, and various risk/reward ratios. Each decision must be made on an individual basis and based on consideration of a host of tangible and intangible factors.

Many misconceptions about STDs circulate but they can be reduced to one comprehensive but simple statement:

Misconception #9: STDs are not a serious problem because they are easy to screen for, diagnose, treat, and cure.

From the information we have just reviewed about seven STDs and the example of diagnosing, treating and following up on a case of chlamydia, it is obvious that this is a misconception on all four counts. By downplaying the seriousness of the risks of genital sexual activity outside of marriage, this misconception has created the illusion that such practices do not lead to serious harm. We find numerous examples of this misconception in print. For example, in the popular, public reference, *Our Bodies Ourselves,* the section on gonorrhea states only that, "As the infection spreads, it can *affect* the Scene's [on each side of the urinary opening] and Bartholin's glands"[38] (emphasis added). The article does not go on to explain that, according to a standard gynecological text, "The most common problem with Bartholin's gland, which brings patients to the physician's attention with acute symptoms, is a Bartholin's gland abscess. This abscess is typified by acute onset of pain, swelling, exquisite tenderness, and associated cellulitis (infection) of the vulva. Dyspareunia (painful sexual intercourse) is frequently reported, and the patient often has difficulty walking."[39] The complications of a Bartholin's gland infection include disfigurement of the vaginal area and chronic painful intercourse.[40] Gonorrhea is the most common bacteria to infect the Bartholin's gland. The "understatement" found in *Our Bodies Ourselves* is a classic example of deceit by failure to tell the whole truth.

In a handout published by a medical journal for patients with genital herpes, we read the statement that, "Herpes, although troublesome, is generally not a serious disease."[41] Parents of infants who die of disseminated herpes and those who suffer frequent, recurrent bouts of painful genital ulcers, however, have good reason to argue that herpes is serious.

Particularly disturbing, because the target audience is teenagers, are such popular books as *The What's Happening to My Body Book for Girls*. The author of this guide answers the query, "What should you do if you think you might have an STD?" with "Most STDs can be treated quite easily – usually with antibiotics – provided they are treated right away."[42]

A raft of falsehoods has concealed the serious nature of sexual risk-taking behavior, particularly sex outside of marriage. A 22 year-old patient told me of her experience when she was treated by laser surgery for venereal warts. Laser surgery requires general anesthesia and superficially burning large areas of the woman's genitalia over a period of a half hour or so. It takes weeks to recover from the procedure, and there is no guarantee of a cure. One can only wonder about her fear and apprehension before surgery and resentment and embarrassment following. How different her life might have been during that period if she had had more realistic forewarnings about STDs.

Chapter 5

HIV Disease and AIDS

We can understand much about current unhealthy attitudes about sex by considering society's response to HIV, the most serious sexually transmitted infection. For the benefit of those not yet overwhelmed by statistics on HIV and AIDS, let us review some recent figures.

- It is estimated that by the turn of the century, forty to one hundred million people throughout the world will be infected with HIV.[1] One in 100 people of reproductive age worldwide are now HIV-positive.[2]
- AIDS is currently the eighth leading cause of death in the United States[3] with 92 people dying of it each day,[4] and it is expected to be the third leading cause by the year 2000.[5]
- AIDS is now the leading cause of death for women aged 20-24 in major cities of the Americas, Western Europe and Africa.[6] The number of American adolescents with AIDS is doubling every 14 months.[7]
- 20 percent of South Africa's population is expected to be HIV-positive by the year 2000.[8]

- 65 percent of those who have developed AIDS have died of it thus far.[9]

Much has been made about recent statistics showing a reversal of the inexorable upward trend in AIDS statistics. This trend is as welcome as it is overdue. Yet, the reader should take note that what is being reported is the trend of AIDS and not of HIV infection. Because homosexuals account for the vast majority of HIV infections in this country there has been great concern about protecting the identity of HIV patients. Federal policies have therefore prevented the collection of accurate data on the spread of HIV infection, even though such information is more useful than data about AIDS. Unfortunately, the apparent decline in incidence of AIDS in recent years likely represents more the attainment of a saturation point among high-risk groups than progress. The incidence of AIDS continues to rise among lower risk groups including heterosexual adolescents and young adults.[10] Equally disturbing, recent increases in gonorrhea rates among homosexual men may "presage a new explosion of AIDS cases" according to federal authorities.[11]

Obviously, HIV disease is an enormous problem. Nowhere has minimization of STDs been so dramatic as in the case of this infection. We know that most of those afflicted with it imminently face chronic debilitation and death, yet our response to this calamity has been shortsighted, misguided, and ineffectual. Thus far, the response has been in the areas of research, education, and some public health measures.

Research

Funds and research resources have been allocated to the development of treatment and to basic research. While financial backing was delayed during the first few years of the epidemic, funds are now available. Over the past decade, the federal government has spent billions of dollars on HIV treatment and research.[12] The National Institute of Health spends over $31,000 per death on AIDS compared to $1,297 per death for prostrate cancer and only $815 per death for lung cancer.[13] Medications have recently been developed that clearly slow the progression of the disease (accounting, in part, for the recent reduction in death rates from it) but still no cure and no preventive vaccine appears likely in the foreseeable future.[14]

Safe or Safer Sex and Condom Education

While awaiting a cure or vaccine for HIV disease, the thrust of prevention efforts has been directed toward educating the public about "safer sex," with particular emphasis on the use of condoms. Leaders in the political, medical, and entertainment arenas have, with great uniformity, endorsed "safer sex," a term which is essentially a euphemism for the use of condoms. Examples of these endorsements are numerous and ubiquitous. *People* magazine reports that kindergartners in the remote hamlet of Tung Mon, Thailand, answer the question, "How do you prevent AIDS?" by shouting in unison, "With a condom!"[15] Elizabeth Taylor has been promoting the use of condoms through the media. Her message is seen everywhere from billboards on the freeways to magazine covers.[16] One professor of obstetrics and gynecology, who lectures regularly to college students on AIDS, argues that, "If you want to cut down on STDs, you want to sell patients on the subject of condoms as fun."[17]

Former Surgeon General Joycelyn Elders is an outspoken advocate of condom use in response to the HIV epidemic. Her enthusiasm for promoting condom use among schoolchildren had few limits, as she said, "Well, we're not going to put them on their lunch trays, but. . . ."[18] A Stuart Pharmaceutical Company booklet entitled *AIDS – You and Those You Care For* states, "Certainly AIDS patients and those at high risk for AIDS must not engage in any [sexual] activity without the protection of a condom."[19] According to a medical journal article entitled, *Condoms (not Diamonds) Are a Girl's Best Friend,* "Today, it is the obligation of all obstetrician/gynecologists and primary care physicians to explain the need for condom use to every patient . . . Until the STD epidemic is controlled medically, the condom will play a major role in protecting both women and men."[20] Guidelines from the Public Health Service on how to educate high schoolers about AIDS include the recommendation, "If persons are infected [with AIDS], they should . . . take precautions to protect sexual partners from becoming infected," i.e., use a condom.[21] "Protection" and "precautions" are also euphemisms for condom use.

Homosexuals appear on television news promoting the necessity of using condoms when having oral sex. *Awareness*, a patient education handout, answers the question, "Can an HIV-positive person safely have a sex life?" with ". . . you needn't deny sexuality. Risks are reduced by limiting the number of sexual partners. . . . Always use a latex condom." The handout does not mention the option of abstinence.[22] An article on how family practitioners should counsel patients requesting HIV testing states, "When appropriate, patients should be given information about sexual behaviors that increase the risk of HIV infection . . . . A thorough explanation of the role of condoms in risk reduction, their proper use, and their limitations is imperative." Again, no mention of the option of abstinence.[23] My own neighborhood claims a chain of stores whose name, *Condom Revolution,* reflects the current craze.

Public Health Measures

Besides "safer sex" education, few preventive public health measures have been put into effect. Screening of donated blood products has reduced the spread of HIV through transfusions, but a variety of other prevention strategies have been uniquely disallowed. Many potentially useful measures would entail possible public disclosure of the names of those infected with HIV. The prohibition of such measures is based on the not unfounded fear of subsequent harassment, political retribution, isolation, and civil rights violations. This fear has led to special confidentiality laws and to other restrictions which have further hampered implementation of containment measures.

The fact that there is no cure and, until recently, no adequate treatment for HIV infection has left us with prevention as the only means by which to limit its devastation. Since we have disallowed most other public health measures besides screening blood products, we have only education as a means of curtailing the transmission of HIV. So, through nearly two decades of increasing horror stemming from HIV disease, we have relied almost solely on the condom and a few other "safer sex" recommendations to contain it.

Future Campaigns against HIV

Few of our political, social, or medical leaders seem willing to seriously consider some of the risk statistics for HIV infection. When one does, four facts stand out:

1) Those who do not use intravenous street drugs and who do not engage in genital sexual activity have an extraordinarily low risk of contracting HIV.
2) No matter how well informed people are about high-risk behaviors, some continue to engage in such behaviors.
3) According to Public Health Service figures, from zero to thirty percent of adults who rely on condoms for protection from sexual partners infected with HIV will themselves become infected.[24] Even more alarming, teenagers are expected to have much less success than adults at preventing HIV infection with condoms.
4) If an HIV-free person is having sexual intercourse with a partner infected with HIV, and the condom slips, breaks, or leaks, that once "safe" person may become infected with HIV and die.

These are not the only facts we know about HIV, but they provide a reasonable basis for discussion of what we should be doing to stop this epidemic. "Safe sex" or what might more accurately be called "sort of safe sex" is an interesting term. It implies (1) that sex outside of marriage can be safe, and by downplaying the risks, it subtly sanctions premarital sex; and (2) that premarital and extramarital sex have only recently become risky. The fact is that they always have been, but now we must add one additional, spectacular consequence: the threat of imminent death. The term "safe sex" epitomizes just how insensitive we have become to the serious consequences of premarital sex. According to this approach, only the threat of death itself qualifies premarital sex as "unsafe."

A Planned Parenthood pamphlet entitled *Sex and Disease: What You Need to Know*, lists the "Seven Steps to a Healthier and Safer Sex Life." The pamphlet does not mention the option of abstinence, but assumes sexual activity as the norm.[25]

Step #1 reads, "Be selective when you choose a sex partner . . . Be sure you know your partner's *name* and *phone number*" (emphasis added). Step #2 counsels us to "limit" the number of sex partners, but does not specify the number. Step #3 states, "Use latex condoms every time"; this message is repeated twice on the page. The condom, as we have noted, typically gets center stage in "safer sex" education materials.

Step #4 counsels the reader to "Find out about your partner's health and sexual history" and to "watch out for the 'smooth talker.'" No means are provided, however, for insuring that one's partner is telling the truth. Medical studies indicate that accurate sexual histories are not easily obtained. For example, one survey of college students found that 32 percent of the men and 23 percent of the women said that they concealed from a partner their sexual involvement with someone else. Fully 20 percent of the men said they would lie to a partner about having tested positive for HIV.[26] In a study of male patients at a Los Angeles clinic for people infected with HIV, nearly half reported that they continued to have sex after their diagnosis, and more than half of those kept their infection secret from one or more sexual partners.[27] In a 1992 study of partners of HIV-infected patients, only 7 percent had been informed by their infected partners.[28] Dr. Robert C. Noble, an infectious disease expert, writes, "At our place we are taking care of a guy with AIDS who is back visiting the bars and having sex. 'Well, did your partner use a condom?' I ask. 'Did you tell him that you're infected with the virus?' 'Oh, no, Dr. Noble,' he replies, 'it would have broken the mood.' You bet it would have broken the mood."[29]

Step #5 urges, "Have a checkup for STDs at least once a year . . . . . *Eat well, get enough rest* and limit your use of alcohol, tobacco, and mood-altering drugs" (emphasis added). Diet and sleep patterns have not been shown to affect the transmission of HIV. Such a platitudinous recommendation in the face of a deadly disease is ridiculous. Step #6 proclaims, "If you think you have been exposed to an STD be responsible . . . Do not have sex until you and your partner have been *tested* and considered *cured*" (emphasis added). The reality is that HIV infection has no cure, and testing for HIV is an inexact science – a person can be infected and yet test negative for months. Finally, Step #7's warning that people should not "let alcohol or drugs jeopardize" their self-control is clearly the most sensible advice in the publication.

Such is the prescription for practicing "safer sex" according to Planned Parenthood, the organization which rightly claims to be the nation's foremost agent of social change in the area of reproductive health.[30] And this is the prescription we have been relying on to contain the HIV crisis.

According to the Centers for Disease Control, 311,381 deaths in the United States have been attributed to HIV.[31] In contrast, there are 58,183 names on the Vietnam Memorial in Washington, D.C. We can only imagine an enormous wall, many times larger than the Vietnam Memorial, inscribed with the names of the hundreds of thousands of people worldwide who have died of AIDS, and with the names of the hundreds of thousands or millions of family members who have suffered as a result of the premature death of a loved one with AIDS, and with the names of the millions of people still alive but infected with the HIV virus, and of their loved ones. Imagine this panorama of countless names, and then consider the fact that the lowly condom is the focal point of our society's response to the HIV tragedy. Multiple studies in a variety of settings have also specifically measured the impact of "safer sex" education on attitudes and behavior. These studies point to the same conclusion: the *best* "safer sex" education can do is produce clinically insignificant change.

A study of homosexual and bisexual males in New York City found that 48 percent continued to engage in high-risk sexual behavior, i.e., unprotected anal intercourse with multiple partners. The study, which was published in a journal with a consistent pro-homosexual bias, states, "Most of the men . . . were highly educated, mature adults. All were well informed about the transmissibility of AIDS through sexual activity and could describe the specific measures necessary to protect against infection. Yet *even under these relatively ideal conditions*, the majority of these informed men did not adopt and maintain behavior to the extent necessary to prevent HIV infection in themselves and others. The campaigns [to educate ho-

mosexuals] have succeeded in accomplishing considerable behavioral changes . . . yet, ultimately we must acknowledge that *these
campaigns have failed to accomplish sufficient change."*
[32](emphasis added).

Perhaps most disturbing is that this study population consisted of
the highest risk group in one of the highest risk cities in the world.
Homosexuals have more to gain from practicing preventive measures than anyone else. On the September 4, 1994 *60 Minutes* program, representative homosexuals from both East and West coasts
testified eloquently to their stubborn refusal to adopt "safer" sexual
practices.

A survey funded by the U.S. Centers for Disease Control found
that among black homosexual and bisexual men, "Although 97% of
the 952 men surveyed claimed knowledge of what constitutes safer
sex and unsafe sex, only 54% 'always or nearly always' practiced
safer sex."[33] The *Los Angeles Times* reported on a 1991 survey of
4,500 homosexual men from 16 U.S. cities. In the survey, 31 percent said they had engaged in unprotected anal intercourse in the
previous two months. The article noted, "The problem isn't lack of
knowledge about what is safe, according to health officials,"[34] A
study of over 600 homosexual men from New York city found that
despite their obvious awareness of the AIDS crisis, 75 percent continued to engage in sex with multiple partners.[35] In another study,
when questioned about how risky their sexual practices were in the
"age of AIDS," 56.5 percent of homosexual men admitted to involvement in the highest risk sexual behaviors during the prior six
months.[36]

Worse yet is that what minimal effect health education campaigns do have on homosexuals is temporary. Multiple studies document that homosexual and bisexual men are relapsing into high-
risk behavior and that a reversal from low-risk to high-risk sexual
activity is on the rise.[37] The United States Public Health Service reports, "Previous studies suggest that among persons who are HIV
seronegative, counseling and testing alone – particularly in clinic
setting – has little or no effect on reducing high-risk behavior."[38]

Essentially, the same conclusion can be drawn from studies on
heterosexuals. In a poll conducted at four universities, only 5 to 8

percent of the students said that they always used condoms during sexual intercourse. "Despite all the courses on sexual behavior and all the 'safe sex' advertising on campus, 66 percent of the students said they never had used a condom. About 25 percent of the women and 53 percent of the men polled said they had had more than 5 sexual partners during one year."[39] The *Journal of American College Health* reports, "The conclusions of research into the knowledge, attitudes, and behaviors of college and university students concerning human immunodeficiency virus (HIV) diseases have acquired a numbing kind of predictability" The studies show that students have, "very good to excellent levels of knowledge," but that "most students neither reasonably assess the risks inherent in their own behavior nor connect such an evaluation to useful strategies to reduce those risks."[40]

On the basis of these abundant studies, it seems logical to conclude that since "safer sex" education cannot achieve sufficient behavioral change among the highest risk group (homosexuals) or among one of the more intelligent groups (college students), it is highly unlikely to be effective with other groups. Not surprisingly, the ineffectiveness of "safer sex" education has also been demonstrated for numerous other population groups, including promiscuous heterosexuals,[41] intravenous drug abusers,[42] teenagers (as we shall see later), and even the heterosexual partners of HIV-infected persons.[43] Finally, and perhaps most importantly, the research on condoms uniformly demonstrates that those who are at the highest risk of contracting HIV are the least likely to use them.[44]

People are "educated" but too few are changing their behavior. As a review article in the *American Journal of Public Health* states, "There is little actual evidence that an individual's knowledge and attitudes toward AIDS significantly shape his or her behavior."[45]

"Safer sex" education clearly is not the answer to the HIV crisis. The answer lies in dealing with the whole truth about this killer and about sexuality. We can disregard reality in the short run, but ultimately, reality will catch up to us. It will come slowly and through a variety of experiences, but eventually it will be evident.

We will discuss much more about the promotion of abstinence from premarital genital sexual activity when we discuss adolescent

sexuality, but it should be mentioned briefly here. Premarital abstinence is rarely given more than token acknowledgment in literature
dealing with "safer sex" even though, for many, it is the most reasonable approach to the HIV epidemic. Encouragement of premarital abstinence should certainly be part of our nation's education efforts. We see full-page "Living with HIV" advertisements in major
newspapers, but see no advertising for the one sure way to virtually
eliminate one's risk of having to "live with HIV." Promotion of abstinence will not bring an end to the HIV crisis. No single measure
has that potential. But it is likely to benefit many who are at risk,
and the scarcity of such encouragement, beyond all but the most orthodox religious communities, is astonishing. For nearly twenty
years, our Public Health Service has been calling for "innovative"
approaches to this epidemic and as each one fails the call goes out
again – all without ever showing even a passing interest in promoting the traditional standard of premarital abstinence.

Relying on education as the sole weapon in the battle of prevention is clearly insufficient at a time when numerous public health
measures could be implemented to help contain the HIV epidemic.
To date, few of these have been activated because existing laws
overemphasize protecting the confidentiality of HIV carriers.

A heterosexual HIV-positive male patient in my care admitted to
having had multiple sexual partners, and displayed little interest in
"safer sex" or abstinence. He failed to show up at his follow-up appointments, and to the best of my knowledge, he is still sexually active and currently infecting unsuspecting female sexual partners.[46]
Nothing can be done to stop him, and nothing can be done to protect
the women in the community from this man. While physicians are
required to report other contagious diseases to the local public health
authorities, in my state any physician who reports a positive HIV
test faces a $10,000 fine and a year in prison.

HIV-infected prostitutes are shown on television openly acknowledging that they do not practice "safer sex." Many well-
informed infected homosexual males maintain "safer sex" practices,
but many do not. What is truly appalling to those of us who have
been watching the statistics on the AIDS crisis is that the Public
Health Service has done so little for nearly two decades, while indi-

viduals who cannot control themselves continue to raise the death toll.

Modern public health measures can run the gamut from serious infringements of civil rights, such as quarantining (as has been done for some types of tuberculosis), to putting up "safer sex" posters. Somewhere lies a balance between the threat of disease to the community and the threat of disclosure and restrictions to infected individuals. In the case of HIV disease, our government has so grievously erred on the side of protecting individual rights (by adopting an extremist, education-only approach) that it has not measurably affected the spread of the virus. Our government has failed to control the HIV epidemic because that has not been its focus. The focus has been on protecting people's feelings and their civil rights. Dr. Stanley Monteith, author of *AIDS, The Unnecessary Epidemic,* writes: "This is the first epidemic in all history where the population is being told that the major problem is not the virus, the major problem is 'discrimination.'"[47]

Although extensive discussion of measures for controlling the HIV epidemic is beyond the scope of this book, the following list of eight possibilities will suggest the range of pragmatic but as yet inadequately developed measures that could be tried.

1) Require confidential reporting of all positive HIV tests to the public health authorities. We cannot begin to manage this epidemic until we know the extent of it. The current restrictions on doctors, hospitals, and blood banks have no scientific basis or precedent. At present, almost half of the states require reporting of positive HIV results – but more than half of the states do not. Information about the prevalence of HIV can be used to target health education/risk reduction and early intervention programs; provide counseling, testing, referral, and partner-notification services; offer testing for further evaluation of HIV infection and screening for other diseases; expand HIV surveillance data collection; and assist legislators and policy makers in targeting resources.[48] As more effective treatments become available, the criminality of the extraordinary measures now taken to preserve confidentiality will become clear to all.[49]

2) Mandate HIV testing of all hospitalized patients, It has been estimated that if all hospitalized U.S. patients 15 to 54 years-old had HJV testing, 110,000 previously unrecognized cases of HIV infection would be identified annually.[50]

3) Mandate HIV testing of all person diagnosed with other STDs.

4) Establish a program of contact tracing to inform those who are unknowingly having sex with an infected spouse or partner. Our Public Health Service continues to delay implementation of such a strategy pending further "evaluation."[51]

5) Establish HIV disease treatment centers.

6) Close all houses of prostitution, sex clubs, and homosexual bathhouses. Statistics on the incidence of HIV among prostitutes have varied widely. As many as thirty-three percent of the female prostitutes are infected in some countries, with those using intravenous drugs being particularly high risk.[52] Studies also document the high rate of HIV infection among male prostitutes and that they continue to engage in high-risk sexual activities.[53]

7) Test all prisoners for HIV and all persons arrested for prostitution, other sex offenses, and drug abuse.

8) Mandate prison sentences for anyone who has previously tested positive for HIV and who is arrested for prostitution or other sex offenses with an obvious potential for transmitting the virus.

In one way or another, the epidemic of HIV disease will come under control. The Public Health Service, because of its obsessive sensitivity toward those infected, has thus far abdicated its leadership role. It has opted for a strategy in which the populace must cure itself. Some would defend their strategy because the most recent statistics show a leveling off of the incidence of AIDS. Of course, any STD epidemic has a saturation point. No disease with specific behavioral risk factors would be expected to kill everyone. But there exists little evidence that Public Health efforts beyond blood supply screening and, possibly, needle exchange programs have made any difference.

As more and more movie stars, sports personalities, and next-door neighbors become infected we are seeing a gradual renewal in popularity of monogamy and abstinence out of desperation. Without leadership from our Public Health Service, society is "educating" itself about the realities of HIV – mostly through some kind of private, personal experience with the disease. Lesbians are a low risk group, yet some do become infected with HIV, as a sex education newsletter records, "An (AIDS) hotline counselor picks up the phone that has begun ringing several minutes before the 9:00 a.m. opening. Before she can even say, 'Good morning,' a woman's voice starts yelling, 'What the hell are you people doing over there? Why didn't anyone tell me? Why isn't anyone talking about this? You're killing women, you know! My girlfriend tested positive a year ago, and now I just did. No one told me! No one, not her doctors, no one I spoke to and now I've got it! How can you sleep at night? Someone should have told me."[54] When a homosexual man was diagnosed with AIDS in our office in 1991, he claimed to have been in a monogamous relationship for 15 years. Following his diagnosis, a public health worker visited his home to explain "safer sex" and condom use to the patient's lover. Overwhelmed by the personal reality of AIDS, the lover threw the visitor out of the house.

These two people have *experienced* the truth about AIDS. As the reality of the situation becomes undeniable for all of us, we will, in turn, be forced to give up the "safer sex" fantasy.

AIDS is a horrible disease, and it is understandable that it generates strong emotions. Regrettably, many people react with anger and hatred. Heterosexual rage is evident in that many AIDS victims are unmercifully ostracized by family, friends, the medical profession, and employers. Fifteen percent of the 7,000 hate crimes against homosexuals each year are considered "AIDS-related"[55] Rage is also evident throughout the homosexual population. The homosexual founder of ACT UP says, "We are an activist organization, and activism is fueled by anger"[56] and, "I think the time for violence has now arrived . . . I'd like to see an AIDS terrorist army . . ."[57] (i.e., to terrorize anyone who disagrees with ACT UP's foolhardy reliance on education about condoms and its protest against FDA restrictions on the release of new drugs).

Such emotions from both sides of the issue are understandable but unhelpful. They thwart reflective dialogue. To effectively combat HIV disease, our society must move beyond anger, fear and hatred to address the epidemic with intelligence, resourcefulness, courage, and compassion.

Our response to the AIDS crisis has been typical of the way we trivialize the risks of other sexually transmitted diseases. Only by understating risks are people "freed" to fulfill their "needs." By downplaying the risks from these diseases, it seems not so unloving to put "lovers" at risk for the sake of satisfying their own selfish desires.

Today, there is a general aversion to criticizing sexual behaviors for fear of appearing repressive. But "safer sex" education is safe only in the sense that those offering it are safe from being admonished for being repressive or judgmental. We are left to battle this disease through skills education (such as how to put on a condom), which allows us to distance ourselves from the realities associated with the disease.

Our government's own statistics reveal its failure to protect both those in the major risk groups (homosexuals and drug abusers) and those in the general population. Citizens must speak out against governmental inactivity. We need more than research, money and education. We need action. The purported "realistic" approach of condom education is anything but realistic. "Sort of" safe sex "sort of" prevents risks for lovers we would "sort of" like to protect. And the crisis continues.

Part III

Sex and Society

Chapter 6

Pornography and
Dehumanizing Influences

The widespread preoccupation with appearances in our society is but part of a more general obsession with sex. Society is fixated – hung up – on sex. As the leader of a popular rap group says, "Today's society is based on sex."[1]

Living in the modern world means constant exposure to various "cores" of pornography or erotica in the form of sexually stimulating entertainment, advertising, and even news stories. The general lack of concern about all of this exposure results from

Misconception #10: Pornography and incessant exposure to sexual innuendo are not necessarily harmful, and possibly negative effects from them can be eliminated through awareness.

Researchers from the Kaiser Family Foundation have found that the sexual content of television programs aired during the "family hour" (8–9 p.m.) has quadrupled during the past 20 years.[2] But entertainment is not the only source of sexual stimulation. Bikinis, for example, are used to sell everything from air mattresses to golf resorts.

Pornography is one of those terms that is much easier to recognize than to define. Because standards and customs undergo changes from time to time and place to place, establishing a universal definition of precisely what constitutes pornography is not easy. When challenged to define pornography, Supreme Court Justice Potter Stewart observed that, although he could not define it, he knew it when he saw it.

According to Webster, our word *pornography* comes from a Greek root for prostitute, and means "depiction of erotic behavior (as in pictures or writing) intended to cause sexual excitement."[3] The main source of its power is that it makes light of and glamorizes casual sex. In the fantasy world of pornography, no one gets pregnant, no one catches a disease, no one shows signs of guilt, fear, remorse, embarrassment, or distrust. No one suffers from the sexual activities of others and, at least the men, are always carefree, unrestrained, and ultimately satisfied.

The priority of lovingly protecting one's partner is of little concern in pornography because no harm seems possible. The participants, therefore, can freely concentrate their efforts on priorities such as pleasure, fun, and excitement. Sex, as presented in pornography, need not concern itself with love, but only with the goals of experiencing pleasure and fulfilling supposed irresistible urges or needs.

Pornographers make no excuses over the fact that theirs is a world of fantasy; yet, because it appears realistic, and is so prevalent, pornography has become a prominent cause of confusion about sex. Misconceptions abound in pornography. It is based on the false assumptions that women enjoy being used sexually, that all women are buxom, that the sexual conduct of consenting adults does not affect others, that casual sex leads to mutually fulfilling experiences, that good sex is that which is the most sensually stimulating, and that the more sexual partners a person has had, the better "lover" he or she is.

Pornography also reinforces the "needs" misconception. Sex is portrayed as an activity that requires no discipline or self-control; attention is concentrated on fulfilling sexual requirements. Men, as portrayed in pornography, never go long without their needs being met, and women rarely say no; if they do, they either don't really mean no, or they get raped anyway.

Hugh Hefner speaks of "needs" to justify the pornography in his *Playboy* magazine. He says, "I think the bottom line of all this is that you *need* beauty and dreams – erotic and other – to make life worthwhile. You *need* those magic, bigger-than-life more-beautiful than life images and ideas to make your daily life worth living." (emphasis added). Only the deeply disillusioned would assert that people require sexual fantasies to make life worth living. It is no surprise that Mr. Hefner describes spending his childhood in a "repressed home – not just sexual repression, but the inability to show love in any kind of physical or emotional way."[4] His distorted views on sex clearly derive in part from an emotionally deprived childhood.

Another example of a rationalization for pornography comes from an attractive rock star who posed for *Playboy* magazine. In a subsequent interview she explained that she exposed herself so that women wouldn't be "so ashamed of their bodies." It seems more likely, however, that her posing would make women feel more ashamed of their bodies, because most women don't have her proportions and distribution. Her comment might be understandable if she were unattractive with, say, a conspicuous weight problem or an unsightly skin condition. If, even under such circumstances, she could appear desirable, then it would reassure women who lack confidence in their own appearance. But being trim and beautiful, her posing reinforces women's insecurities; she is yet another woman who is valued for having what they do not. Pornography reduces the self-esteem of average women by creating heightened expectations about their own appearance.

The increasing acceptance of pornography is part of a more general problem that has escalated during the sexual revolution: the emphasis on people's looks and image over their substance or true inner self. Women in particular are generally expected to expend much time and effort, and go to considerable expense, to make themselves physically attractive and glamorous. Magazine advertisements tell us that, "The most important thing we improve is your self image."[5] A billboard advertisement reads, "Image is Everything."[6]

We have become a society of collagen treatments, hair transplants, tanning salons, and liposuction. We wear artificial hair and have nonprescription contact lenses to change the color of our eyes. We see advertisements for makeovers that can transform any woman into a voluptuous enchantress, or any man into a veritable Samson from pectorals to scalp. We keep looking better and better on the outside, but at incalculable cost to what is on the inside.

Nearly five hundred cosmetic breast surgeries were performed on teenaged American girls in 1994 along with 92 *buttock* implants performed in California alone (at an average cost of $3,171).[7] During a television special on breast enlargement surgery, a young woman described how the surgery had boosted her self-confidence. Unfortunately the confidence gained was in her image, not her substance.

In my own practice, I often encounter patients whose real problems are more "image" than medical. The chart of one recent patient said that he had a "weight problem." But when he came into my office, I noticed that he was a surprisingly athletic, trim appearing young man. His "problem" was with the size of his thighs. He felt they were disproportionately small, and in an effort to increase their bulk through weight lifting, he was ruining his knees. The examination revealed that he had sturdy, muscular thighs typical of an athlete with his build. His request for anabolic steroids was denied, and he was offered a referral for counseling. On another day, a young woman, who disliked the look of her navel, injected it with baby oil causing an unsightly lumpiness. She called my office in a panic, wondering what she should do.

The quest to improve one's appearance need not involve going to such extremes as these. And even though wearing expensive clothing or having a nose job is not necessarily improper in itself it may suggest confusion over priorities and an over-emphasis on "looking good." Many people believe that sexually stimulating forms of entertainment, though not beneficial, cause no harm. Typical comments from this faction echo the sentiment, "It's all in fun, no one is getting hurt." We've encountered this refrain before in defense of sex without love. But it is no more valid here than it was in Chapter

2, and again it indicates an unwillingness to consider obvious ramifications. As long as no obvious physical consequences (blood loss,
loss of consciousness, or death) result from a particular behavior or
form of entertainment, then some people assume that no one is getting hurt. But some of us are not so easily convinced that no one is
getting hurt because we have seen evidence of psychological damage done to both performers and observers of such entertainment

The distress caused by pornography may be subtle: one woman
wrote to advice columnist Abigail Van Buren (Dear Abby) about her
boyfriend's habit of frequenting topless bars. Abby responded,
"Your boyfriend was being honest when he told you he wasn't comparing you with 'those topless girls,' so you have no reason to feel
insecure."[8] Abby was trying to be reassuring, but she couldn't possibly know that her boyfriend wasn't comparing her to them. People
compare everything from parakeets to lasagna recipes. The real
problem here is a preoccupation with genital sexuality. Whether
consciously or not, this fellow will make some kind of comparison
between his girlfriend and "those topless girls" – just as men compare their neckties with those worn by others. Unfortunately, exposure to such forms of entertainment encourages men to dwell on
comparisons, and while such absorption can never benefit a relationship, it can readily create frustration and turmoil. Pornography wea-
kens relationships because most partners can never "measure up" to
the air-brushed fantasy women and men it features.

Those who support pornography argue that it helps men to relieve themselves of sexual tension, in particular through acts of self-
stimulation. But this argument assumes that climaxing, in and of
itself, is a good thing, an assumption which is especially untrue
when men abuse themselves or others to achieve it. Further, pornography does not *relieve* tension but rather *creates* it, causing men to
feel yet *more* needful of relief. When stimulated beyond control, one
crosses the line between perceiving a *desire* and perceiving a *need*.
Self-stimulation is supposedly a benign way to fulfill this "need,"
but even if pornography were truly harmless for the masturbator, his
or her search for ways to relieve pent up sexual tension may lead to
many other behaviors. Various grades of sexual abuse of others can
result from the failure of men to restrain themselves after viewing

pornography.

Bachelor parties now quite routinely provide entertainment in the form of X-rated videos, strippers, and the like. After the party ends, the men leave with fantasies and residual sexual tension as a result of being teased and stimulated. Where they go and how they relieve themselves may mark only the beginning of long, sad sequels. A patient came to my office recently because the week before his wedding, he had contracted herpes on the night of his bachelor party. His fiancé was not amused. Such occurrences are to be expected in the wake of pornographic forms of entertainment, belying the assertion that no one gets hurt.

Not only are we unresponsive to the possible effects of pornography on the viewer, but we rarely give serious consideration to possible consequences for performers. They may be smiling on the outside but no observer can know their innermost thoughts. A popular magazine ran a story about a porn star who decided to quit her occupation while showering following a particular photo session. She felt terribly dirty, and no matter how hard she scrubbed, she was unable to remove the oppressive feeling of filth.

Pornography exemplifies the conflict between the priorities of love and pleasure. People who seek out degrading forms of entertainment often ignore or deny its consequences. An essential function of pornography is to create sex objects – people who become *things* whose role it is to please, entertain, or excite. By focusing on genital, sexual arousal, pornography dehumanizes, depersonalizes, and devalues. It encourages people to view others as objects – sex objects and objects of desire. It offers Sex Kittens, Bunnies, and Pets. This perspective subtly disposes one to less caring and, ultimately, selfish attitudes. There seems no need to be concerned about the person in the photograph or on stage because he or she is performing a function of pleasing others.

By emphasizing the sexiness of others, we lose sight of their character, their humanity, their value as a person, We disregard the constraints of decency which demand that we treat other humans with respect and dignity. Through pornographic forms of entertainment, the person's appearance takes unnatural precedence over qualities such as intelligence, courageousness, sensitivity, wit, kindness, skillfulness, and resourcefulness – all of those human traits. Pornography distracts attention from essentially human traits and focuses it on genital sex. Not that the sexual aspect of relationships is to be avoided or condemned; nor is it wrong to be attractive. It is only that our focus should be the essential core of human relationships, not the peripheral phenomena of genital stimulation. This dehumanization is the worst aspect of pornography. By casting people as fantasy objects, by creating the illusion that they are less than whole persons (like pieces of "meat" to use the slang), pornography creates the illusion that it is permissible to exploit and degrade them.

Soft-core pornography is of a different magnitude from hard-core, but both convey essentially the same message. We are exposed to it in varying grades, and the softer it is, the more prevalent it is, from girlie calendars to cologne advertisements. Television is saturated with endless exposes, teases, and risqué sitcoms and soap operas. Mainstream movies routinely show even the most famous stars nude or "making love" with someone other than their spouses.

Soft-core pornography has achieved a high level of acceptability because of the old idea that it is permissible to tease. Some argue that no one gets hurt unless the porn becomes unarguably obscene. In truth, however, all forms of pornography reinforce the same stereotypes and misconceptions as hard-core porn. Soft-core porn may be somewhat less harmful because the messages are less forceful; yet, because it is so commonplace, its overall effect is great indeed.

Sports Illustrated's annual "swimsuit" issue is a good example of soft-core pornography. This widely circulated issue has a layout of pictures of full-figured women wearing revealing bathing suits. (The caption next to each picture carries data such as the brand name of the swimsuit and the price, and one can just imagine sports fans across the continent eagerly digesting such information.) Not surprisingly, soft-core pornography makes this the single best-selling issue each year and, subsequently, other sports magazines have followed with their own swimsuit issues.

Another example of subtle pornography comes from the pages of *Life* magazine. A photographer, discussing "boudoir" or "glamour" photography states, "Boudoir photography is just another name for taking pictures of women in a revealing way. *Don't get the idea that this is pornographic.* In boudoir photography, it's what you don't show that's important: It's suggestive as opposed to blatant."[9] (emphasis added)

Porn is porn, whether "soft," "hard," or "suggestive." Pornography can be made as inoffensive as necessary to avoid guilt, but all forms promote the same unhealthy attitudes. All forms degrade and dehumanize people and dismiss the serious risks associated with the abuse of sex. Fun, freedom, and pleasure are given preference, while consideration and respect are spurned.

Both pornographers and sex educators commonly refer to the idea of "celebrating sexuality." This should read "celebrating genital sexuality" as the message invariably fails to suggest anything about celebrating holding hands or kissing. "Celebrating sexuality" is like celebrating a basketball team's free throw percentage in that it fails to consider the larger picture. Even if the last place team in a league has an outstanding free throw percentage, they are unlikely to be celebrating. What we should celebrate is not sex but whole and healthy relationships within which sex contributes joy, pleasure, mutuality and, often, babies.

Acceptance of all grades of sexually stimulating forms of entertainment has achieved new heights during the past few years. A local fire department held a bachelor auction to raise money for burn victims. The newspaper article reported "hundreds of women yelling for Orange County firemen who peeled off their yellow slickers like strippers and bumped, thrust and pranced their way down a runway. The shouts created a wall of sound that crested at the sight of bare, oiled, muscular chests." Defending this use of sexual stimulation as a way to raise charity money, a magazine publisher (who was also a contest judge) explained that she was "a little shocked at some of what went on" and "a little embarrassed . . . But apparently the firemen think it's fine. . . . You'll always have critics. . . . If we sold pencils, they'd say we were taking money from the blind."[10]

The chaplain for the firefighters commented that, "The whole purpose is to help the burn victims. It's not Chippendales (a male strip joint). If it was, then we wouldn't be here and the firemen wouldn't be, either." No elaboration was offered to distinguish the firefighters' act from that at Chippendales.

It's interesting that the misconception "no one is getting hurt" was once applied to drug use. Society open-mindedly accepted "doing your own thing" because "no one got hurt" using drugs. Only prudes criticized recreating with drugs. But now we read in the *Los Angeles Times*[11] of a pastor who, during services, "called on anyone in his congregation to stand if they had relatives who were either hooked on drugs or had died because of them, "'Every single person in the church stood up, about 800 of them,' he said. 'It just blew my mind." Like drugs, pornography and other sexually stimulating forms of entertainment do hurt people, even though insensitive people continue to deny the harm they create.

In today's world, we are uniquely inundated with sexual stimulation. Any other type of such over stimulation might be called brainwashing, mind control or indoctrination. We know that "a picture is worth a thousand words" because it can communicate so many things. Surely, constant exposure to degrading attitudes causes some people to become less sensitive to them. As the saying goes, "Dripping water wears the rock."

Hollywood defends its preoccupation with sex by denying its own influence. A media representative states, "We don't influence society – we just represent it." But, as a political correspondent writes, "It is typical of the hypocrisy in Hollywood . . . that on one hand they say their art has no impact on society and on the other they decide to make films that address politically correct concerns such as the environment."[12]

We argue about whether nature or nurture has greater influence in a wide variety of other matters, but curiously disavow the possibility that the environment influences our attitudes about sex. The question is not whether such an effect exists but how to manage it. Our challenge is to achieve an harmonious balance between curbing desensitizing influences while maintaining an openness to new ideas.

Not all people, of course, who are exposed to pornography become child molesters or exhibitionists. But it need not have such a dramatic impact for us to object to it. The job security for women involved in pornography depends on their ability to turn men's thoughts inward and intensify men's self-interests. One flip through a skin magazine or one visit to a strip joint does not a rapist make, but clearly such entertainment degrades and dehumanizes women and caters to men's insensitivities.

Sexual fantasizing may be of benefit in a limited way for the treatment of certain sexual disorders, but it is a very safe generalization to say that for anyone without a diagnosed sexual problem it is of no benefit. One practical guide to the management of sexual fantasizing is the "three second rule": if one concentrates on sexually stimulating material, entertainment, or fantasy for more than three seconds, it is unlikely that that person is doing himself, herself, or anyone else a favor.

Not all nudity is pornographic, but we should acknowledge that due to the effects of nudity, the porn industry grosses eight billion dollars on erotic entertainment a year.[13]

In our contemporary environment, which is so saturated with dehumanizing, image-emphasizing propaganda, we need to consider the reasonable and appropriate responses to it. In the search for ways to maintain healthy, humane approaches to sexuality in this environment we can consider three general recommendations.

1) As individuals, we should make a serious effort to reduce or eliminate our own exposure to pornography and sexually stimulating forms of entertainment and product promotion. This effort includes eliminating such material from our homes, our places of work, and the sites of our recreational activities. It means throwing out some magazines and canceling some subscriptions. It means avoiding those situations in which we might be tempted to break the three-second rule. We should be willing to turn off the television or radio, leave the theater, or leave the party when the entertainment becomes objectionable.

2) We should dress modestly, not spend inordinate resources and time on appearances, and encourage others to do the same. Virtues are those character traits that we admire most, and modesty has been considered a virtue by the great thinkers of all cultures throughout history.

Modesty is a difficult word to define precisely. As with some other virtues, it can be taken to the extreme. It doesn't mean that women must always wear long black skirts and veils. Modesty, most fundamentally, means not dressing or acting in such a way that we call undue attention to our sexual natures.

Perhaps it is easier to think in terms of immodesty than modesty. String bikinis are perhaps the least modest apparel. Sending a boyfriend a boudoir photograph of oneself wearing skimpy underwear is anything but modest. It is obviously immodest to have one's breasts enlarged and then to wear clothes which highlight one's newly acquired fullness. Pornography is the antithesis of modesty, and thus of virtue.

Some people defend suggestive dress, even for children, by saying that it simply shows that one is "comfortable in expressing one's sexuality." But this idea is another example of our obsession with the genital aspects of sex, since wearing suggestive clothing neither enhances nor inhibits non genital sexual activities, e.g., holding hands, hugging, or walking arm in arm.

We should acknowledge not only the obvious effects of nudity, but also the effects of immodest clothing. Because people communicate by the way they dress, the emphasis should be on being clean and attractive, not on being seductive. Women should discard the fantasy that immodest attire has no effect on men. A former female congressional staff member complained to a *USA Today* reporter that a congressman once asked her "not to wear a particular dress again when she leaned over to explain a point." She huffed, "I was really embarrassed. I was talking to him on a professional level and what was he doing? Staring at my cleavage."[14]

3) We should publicly discourage pornography in all its forms. By tolerating insensitive, uncaring attitudes on the part of marketing and promotional sales people, we permit their pornography to affect all of us. We should, instead, work actively to reduce the presence of pornography in our communities and to raise others' awareness of advertisers who exploit pornography to sell their products.

The media consistently defend pornographers. For example, the *Los Angeles Times* urges tolerance of television pornography by edi-

torializing that "the best judges of what youngsters should be allowed to watch or hear (on television) are parents,"[15] without addressing the question of who should be the judge in the parents' absence. Would that it were the case that all across America parents
always directly monitored their children's television time, but this
ideal is unrealistic even in the more protective households. Further,
it ignores the fragmented nature of many families and the widespread parental neglect found in the modern era. As media commen-
tator Howard Rosenberg writes, "Like it or not, the U.S. reality is
that many, many children watch television unsupervised, for a variety of reasons. And TV programmers must address that reality, not
hide behind that idealistic old saw about every set having an off
switch."[16] Since the media have proven repeatedly their inability to
self-regulate, who, in the absence of discerning parents, is left to
protect children from their influences? Until the media demonstrate
the ability to self-regulate, external pressure in the form of picket-
ing, boycotts, or letter writing or billboard campaigns, have proved
to be legal, moral, and sometimes effective means of expressing disapproval of pornography.

For fear of being oppressive, and bearing in mind the difficulty of
defining pornography, we must not interfere with the constitution-
ally guaranteed freedom to produce and distribute material which is
not readily identifiable as pornographic. However, we have no obligation to tolerate, much less facilitate, production or distribution of
material which is overtly so. Pornography should not be accessible
through sidewalk newspaper stands to any child with a few coins in
his pocket.

These recommendations raise the specter of censorship, an essential part of life that has a clear potential for abuse. The debate about
censorship must be ongoing and should not center on whether one is
"for" or "against" it, but rather on its judicious use. Surely no one is
against censoring X-rated commercials from children's television
programming.

The controversy surrounding censorship typifies the conflict between the priorities of freedom and love. Though freedom is rightly
cherished, there should be some intolerance of material that encourages selfish attitudes and the degradation of others. Censors must

strive to balance the personal freedom to produce, distribute, and obtain pornography against the deleterious effects that pornography has on individuals and on the general population. Unfortunately, the general relaxation of sexual mores in the past four decades has fostered an environment which overwhelmingly desensitizes us to sexual degradation. We have grossly erred in favor of the priority of freedom. Ultimately, despite this ongoing power struggle, the best way to reduce the influence of pornography will be for individuals to reduce their own exposure through personal decisions.

Part IV

The Regulation of Fertility

Chapter 7

Artificial Contraception and Sterilization

We will continue our focus on the development of healthy attitudes about sex by considering whether artificial contraceptives and sterilization encourage or discourage such attitudes. As a prescribing clinician, I gradually developed an uneasiness with these methods, but for some time I was unsure why. The reasons became clear as I began to consider seriously what patients were saying. For example, one woman told me of her frustration with her husband who demanded sex everyday. They were using artificial contraception and I wondered how different his attitude might have been if it were not available. Unless he was interested in a very large family, he would most likely learn to temper his daily demands. While this couple's relationship may have had problems from the start, it is logical that contraceptives could have played a part in encouraging his abusive attitudes. If contraceptives were not available, some men would maintain their abusive attitudes, but many would not.

Another woman disclosed her boyfriend's demand for sex. He said that she must not love him if she would not have sex with him. Reassured by the fact that she was on the pill, she consented. Within a few weeks, she was back in the office – with an STD, but without a boyfriend. Again, these two people may have had unhealthy attitudes before they started dating, but clearly contraceptives can reinforce those attitudes.

Such experiences have led me to a conclusion which our society does not discuss, let alone accept. *Our approaches to fertility regulation, whether through contraception, abortion, sterilization, natural methods, or no method, affect our fundamental attitudes about sex.* Sexual intercourse is the behavior through which we procreate, and there is little to match the effect of the responsibility of a new life on a person or a couple. How couples approach these realities profoundly affects attitudes and behaviors. We grossly oversimplify the issue by saying, "Let's not get pregnant, let's use the pill" or "We've had our family, let's get sterilized." A couple's attempts to control their fertility affect not only their risk of pregnancy but also their relationship *in toto*.

Artificial forms of contraception reaffirm the misconception which lies at the heart of the abuse of sex and which is the source of addictive attitudes toward sex: that people have specific, genital, sexual "needs." Contraceptives transfer the responsibility for the consequences of sexual activity from people to technology and reinforce the fallacy that sexual urges cannot be controlled. Supposedly uncontrollable sexual urges become "needs," which can only be met through the use of contraceptives.

Contraceptives are part of a male-oriented sexual revolution. They facilitate an emphasis on "needs" (mostly of males), and intensify the pressure, especially on women, to take risks. Contraception, pornography, and the misconceptions related to STDs all minimize realization of the risks associated with sex. All reinforce the message that genital sexual interactions are without serious consequences. It is more acceptable to use a woman to fulfill one's needs, if the risk of pregnancy is low.

Contraceptives promise to improve our love lives by "freeing" us from the risks of "unwanted" pregnancies and abortions. Yet it is interesting that during an era of increased use and widespread acceptance of these methods, there have been more, not fewer, "unwanted" pregnancies,[1] illegitimate births,[2] and abortions (see graph next page).

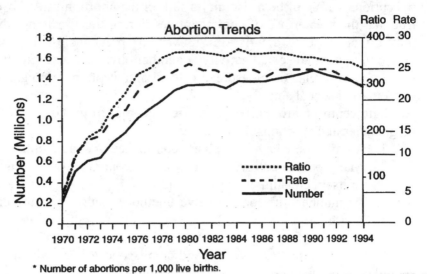

* Number of abortions per 1,000 live births.
† Number of abortions per 1,000 women 15-44 years of age.

FIGURE 3: Number, ratio,* and rate† of legal abortions performed annually — United States, 1970 - 1994. Source: Centers for Disease Control, *Morbidity and Mortality Weekly Report,* 46, no. SS4 (1997): 47, Figure 1.

This increase is the opposite of the expected, and widely presumed, result. Dr. Judith Bury of the Brook Advisory Centres stated in 1981, "There is overwhelming evidence that, contrary to what you might expect, the provision of contraception leads to an increase in the abortion rate."[3] Planned Parenthood researcher Dr. Christopher Tietze notes, "women who have practiced contraception are more likely to have had abortions than those who have not practiced contraception, and women who have had abortions are more likely to have been contraceptors than women without a history of abortion."[4] Sexologist Alfred Kinsey stated at a Planned Parenthood-sponsored conference on abortion, "At the risk of being repetitious, I would remind the group that we have found the highest frequency of induced abortion in the group which, in general, most frequently used contraceptives."[5]

Such results were predicted by some. For example, in 1973, abortionist and past medical director for International Planned Parenthood Federation Dr. Malcolm Potts stated, "As people turn to contraception, there will be a rise, not a fall, in the abortion rate."[6] It is true that the greater use of contraceptives during this era is not the only direct cause of the rise in "unwanted" pregnancies. The increase in premarital sexual activity is another obvious cause, and the two are clearly related: widespread use of contraception led to greater premarital sexual activity.

Contraceptives are unlikely to free people from "unwanted" pregnancies and abortions for three main reasons:

1. Many people have unrealistic confidence in contraceptives.
2. Many people believe that the use of contraceptives, in and of itself, constitutes "responsible sex."
3. A number of contraceptive methods cause nonsurgical abortions.

All three of these reasons are based on misconceptions, which we should consider in detail.

Misconception #11: Contraceptives always work and are, therefore, sufficient for "responsible sex."

This falsehood has been widely accepted even within the medical profession. The "Introduction to the 1987 International Symposium on Contraception published in the *American Journal of Obstetrics and Gynecology* states, "Oral Contraceptives . . . not only offer nearly perfect efficacy but are safer than ever before."[7] Similarly, the American Medical Association's *Family Medical Guide* (1982) states, "It is important to remember that, if you have been taking birth control pills regularly, pregnancy is extremely unlikely."[8] These comments are inconsistent with the widely accepted contraceptive failure rates. The annual failure rates shown on the next page are taken from *Family Planning Perspectives*, a publication of the research arm of Planned Parenthood. These rates are user failure rates, i.e., the actual rates observed in a typical patient population.

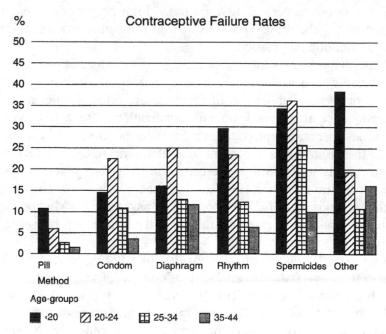

Figure 4: Percentage of women experiencing contraceptive failure the first 12 months of use, by age and method, standardized by race and martial status. Source: The Alan Guttmacher Institute, *Family Planning Perspectives*, 1989, 21:(3)106. Used with permission.

Of note, the above graph was chosen because of its authoritative source and clarity of presentation. It is based on statistical analysis of data from the National Center for Health Statistics by the Alan Guttmacher Institute. It was published in 1989 and, though an updated analysis is not yet available, it remains consistent with recent data from other sources.[9] The main update expected will be the addition of three new contraceptives: the female condom, Norplant, and Depo-Provera. Estimates of user failure rates for the female condom range from approximately 10–26 percent[10] and its efficacy among adolescents has not been evaluated. Both Norplant and Depo-Provera have user failure rates of less than 1 percent; however, enthusiasm for them has been tempered by class action law suites,[11] concerns over noncompliance,[12] high drop out rates (up to 77 percent for Depo-Provera at 12 months),[13] high pregnancy rates after discontinuing the drug,[14] possibly illegal judicial mandates, and coercive promotional practices.[15]

Note that a 10 percent annual failure rate means that one of every ten persons who uses that form of contraception will be pregnant within one year. Publication of these failure rates is especially significant since it comes from an organization with a bias toward downplaying contraceptive failure. Further, the same publication has made the point that a 5 percent annual failure rate for a particular method translates into a 45 percent rate over five years, and a 70 percent failure rate over 10 years.[16] As the graph above shows, few of the methods carry failure rates as low as 5 percent. Methods with higher annual failure rates would naturally have much higher long-term failure rates.

One might wonder why authorities like the American Medical Association overstate the reliability of contraceptives. It is an important but elusive question. The November 1994 issue *of California Academy of Family Physicians* reported the success of a promotional campaign spotlighting the academy's pamphlet *The Women 's Health Quiz*. According to this brochure, which was placed in family physicians' waiting rooms throughout California, all of the commonly prescribed contraceptives had at least a 98 percent success rate (i.e., a two percent failure rate).[17] This, as we have already established, is grossly inaccurate information and contradicted by its own parent organization, the American Academy of Family Physicians, which had (in October of the same year) published the figure of *36 percent* for the failure rate of some of these same contraceptives.[18]

The National Research Council estimates that nearly one half of the unintended pregnancies each year are due to contraceptive failure.[19] Dr. Louise Tyrer, Vice President for Medical Affairs at Planned Parenthood, estimates that two-thirds of unintended pregnancies in the U.S. are due to contraceptive failure[20] and, according to Planned Parenthood, fifty-eight percent of the 1.6 million induced abortions performed annually in the United States are for pregnancies attributed to contraceptive failure.[21]

All forms of contraception have significant annual failure rates, especially when viewed in the long term. (Few people are sexually active for one year and then call it quits.) But, because artificial birth control methods offer the false promise of perfect efficacy, two consequences naturally arise from their use: the sense of security these methods offer leads to greater risk taking, and subsequent pregnancies are more likely to be a surprise or "unwanted."

Not long ago, a young, single woman who was on the pill came in for pregnancy testing and revealed a typical attitude. When asked what she would do if she were pregnant, her response was, "Oh, there is no way I can have a baby right now!" She was overjoyed that her pregnancy test was negative. Contraceptives invite people to take risks. They lead women to become sexually involved with their boyfriends in spite of there being "no way" that they can accept the possible consequences. She had gambled and, for the moment, got away with it, but many others have not.

The Planned Parenthood article on long term failure rates cited on the previous page concludes with a warning:

> First, in actual practice, almost every contraceptive method carries a nontrivial annual risk of accidental pregnancy. Second, this risk mounts to a surprisingly high level of failure in the long term . . . [and finally], couples will experience a substantial amount of unwanted child bearing in the absence of abortion.

> Abortion is needed as a backup for couples who have committed themselves to the idea that they will not for the near future have children and who place an unrealistically high level of confidence in their method of artificial birth control.[22]

People trust technology. When confronted with the above failure rates, a teenager responded, "But *something* has to work!" In her eagerness to accept an easy solution, she ignored the reality that the game of fertility regulation deals with odds, not absolutes. Even if artificial forms of contraception were not falsely touted to have nearly perfect efficacy, they would appear to because they are technological innovations. Because of risks taken with the expectation of unfailing reliability, when these methods fail, couples are often neither receptive to a pregnancy nor prepared to cope with it.

Ordinarily, when people engage in unnecessary activities such as hang gliding, bungee jumping, or race car driving, they are expected to accept responsibility for the potentially serious, harmful consequences of their actions. They accept a high degree of responsibility because they freely choose to engage in these activities. Unfortunately, in the case of sexual activity, some degree of responsibility often is forsworn because of a perceived "need" to be involved in risky behaviors. Couples who use them tend to ask contraceptives (or those who produce them) to assume a share of the responsibility for preventing pregnancy. Instead of assuming full responsibility for their own actions, the couple may claim an out – that they are "victims" of a method failure. Again, such a perspective encourages sexual risk-taking. Couples are led to believe that if a pregnancy occurs, it is not their fault; they were being "responsible."

Misconception #12: All contraceptives work by preventing conception.

Several contraceptive methods may end the life of the developing embryo by inducing a medical (nonsurgical) abortion, i.e., they are abortifacient. The IUD commonly acts by this kind of mechanism, and hormonal methods infrequently do (perhaps one or two cycles per 100).[23] It seems somewhat incongruous to applaud these methods for lowering the (surgical) abortion rate when they do so, in part, by increasing the nonsurgical abortion rate. While some people consider this a minor technicality, others consider it vital. Given this range of concern, it is disturbing that the fact of contraceptive induced abortions is generally withheld from patients and from the public in general, thereby preventing informed choice.

* The Intrauterine Device

Standard medical references consider the major mode of action of the IUD to be the creation of a uterine environment hostile to the developing embryo. The embryo cannot implant into the uterine wall (normally a week or so after conception) and so perishes. Many writers of contraceptive literature strive to conceal this fact by using a form of double speak or evasion. For example, when asked if IUDs work by an abortifacient mechanism, Planned Parenthood's

Louise Tyrer, M.D., responded, "According to the medical definition, conception occurs not at fertilization but at implantation."[24] When scientists refer to polliwogs and gerbils, conception is considered to occur at fertilization. Unique to humans, according to Dr. Tyrer, this event is mysteriously postponed a week. A popular (but not very accurately worded) sex education course states, "IUDs inhibit implantation of the ovum."[25] The ovum, or unfertilized egg, of course, never implants into anything.

- Hormonal Contraceptives

These include oral forms (the birth control pill), injectable forms (Depo-Provera) and implantable forms (the Norplant system). A typical informational insert for a package of oral contraceptives explains that, "combination oral contraceptives act by suppression of gonadotropins. Although the primary mechanism of this action is inhibition of ovulation, other alterations include changes in the cervical mucus . . . and the *endometrium (which reduces the likelihood of implantation)*" (emphasis added). In other words, one way in which these methods work is to inhibit the developing embryo from attaching to the uterine wall, causing it to die. Depo-Provera and Norplant have similar effects.

When birth control pills are used on the "morning after," they work *primarily* by inhibiting implantation. As another example of biased reporting, a *Los Angeles Times* front page report on this regimen remarked once in each of the first two paragraphs that it is effective in "preventing pregnancy," and yet reported on an inside page that what they really do is "prevent a fertilized egg from implanting in the uterus."[26]

Contraceptive Technology, a popular medical reference, in acknowledging that the pill and IUD induce nonsurgical abortions, admits that the "once clear distinction between contraception and abortion is now blurred considerably."[27] It is also interesting that an impressive amount of overlap occurs psychologically as well as medically between contraception and abortion. For example, both diminish the perceived risk of an "unwanted" pregnancy: "Don't worry, you are on the pill." And if that fails: "Don't worry, you can have an abortion." Don't worry, take the risk. Or, as the Supreme

Court of the United States put it in the decision on *Planned Parenthood v. Casey:* "For several decades couples have based their intimate relationships on the availability of abortion should contraceptives fail."[28] When they fail the man commonly pushes the woman
to have an abortion, or the woman may feel she owes it to him to
have one.

   Although contraceptives have not fulfilled their promise of liberating us from the tragedies of "unwanted" pregnancy and abortion,
we cling tenaciously to the dream. C. Everrett Koop, M.D., former
Surgeon General of the United States, has correctly stated that to
solve the problem of abortion, we need to reduce the number of
"unwanted" pregnancies He proposed to do this by increasing the
use of barrier methods of artificial contraception such as the diaphragm or condom.[29] In making this recommendation he displays a
sensitivity to the abortifacient nature of other methods, but he ne-
glects basic issues. Barrier methods offer a false sense of security
and have significant failure rates, They invite risk-taking behavior,
leave couples less prepared to cope with subsequent method failures
and act as a convenient scapegoat on which a couple can blame "unwanted "pregnancies.
   The overwhelming acceptance of contraceptives in recent years
has not reduced the rate of unintended childbearing. The use of contraceptives became legal 30 years ago. After noting that the rate of
unplanned pregnancies since that time has only dropped from 66
percent to 60 percent, Pamela Maraldo president of Planned Parenthood, has admitted that "anyone could argue that this is not overwhelming progress."[30]
   Contraceptives have not achieved significant progress because
they are not directed at the primary source of "unwanted" pregnancies. If we seriously want to reduce the number of "unwanted" pregnancies we must work on a more fundamental level – the willingness to risk an "unwanted" pregnancy. We must contend with the
effect of contraceptives on this willingness and, in particular the association of contraceptives with the priority of freedom and the consequent neglect of love.
   Widespread use of contraceptives has, in effect, facilitated the

systematic erosion of the five characteristics of love from many contemporary relationships.

Respect

Instead of respect for, rather than use of, the other person, use of contraceptives provides a host of ready responses: "I know you're afraid of getting pregnant, but don't worry, I'll use a condom." "I realize you don't want to have sex tonight, but you've been sterilized and I have needs."

Responsibility

We introduced the concept in Chapter 5 that contraception, and we should now add sterilization, are "sort of" being responsible, but not fully. If a "method failure" occurs, the blame is shifted from those directly involved in the procreative act to the surgeon, the device, or the medication. For example, a new patient came to my office to be evaluated for vaginal bleeding. She had undergone a tubal ligation (sterilization procedure) the year before, but on this day, was found to be pregnant. She expressed dismay because following confirmation of a previous pregnancy, while she was on the pill, her husband would not speak to her for three days. With great apprehension, she telephoned her husband from the office and told him that she was pregnant again. His response overcame her with grief and she handed the phone to me. To my surprise, he was concerned more with suing the surgeon whose sterilization surgery had failed than he was with his wife's or baby's immediate safety!

Contraceptives and sterilization encourage people to accept only limited responsibility, and limiting our responsibility means limiting our love. Use of artificial means of birth control is analogous to the driver of a car demanding that the passengers buckle their seatbelts and then driving recklessly.

Discipline

Such methods require essentially no restraint with regard to sexual behavior, and only the minimal discipline of remembering to use them.

Commitment

"I would never marry her and would not consider helping her raise a child, but there's no chance of a shotgun wedding or unintended pregnancy here because she's on the pill." Because people mistakenly trust the effectiveness of contraception, they have sex under circumstances in which they have no intention of marriage or of raising a child. One of my patients was in a stable dating relationship with a "wonderful" man whom she envisioned as her future husband. Their contraceptive failed and when he learned that she was pregnant, he wrote her a check for an abortion and disappeared,

Trust

"I don't really love him, but we can 'make love' anyway because this contraceptive sponge will protect me."

"I'd really rather just snuggle sometimes but it's all so easy and risk free with the I.U.D., so why mention it?"

Artificial contraception can lead to compromises on love and to coercive sex in a variety of ways. Society generally accepts the simplistic assertion that contraceptives and sterilization free people, but denies their unhealthy influences on attitudes. This is another example of conflict between the priorities of freedom and of love.

Surgical sterilization procedures (tubal ligation for women and vasectomy for men) for couples who have "had their family" are also cause for concern because they further the same unhealthy attitudes as contraception: emphasizing needs, minimizing risks and "freeing" people to compromise on love and take advantage of each other. Sexual relationships don't end with the birth of the last child, nor do they ever cease influencing the greater relationship of which they are a part. A great many divorces occur after couples have "had their family," after one of the partners has been sterilized. By encouraging misguided attitudes, sterilization burdens those relationships that have survived the delivery of the last "planned" child.

Two women recently came to my office on different days but with similar complaints. Both were in their forties, had been sterilized years before, and were now divorced. Both had new boyfriends and both were now seeking treatment for sexually transmitted diseases. We can only speculate on the relationship of the sterilization procedure they had undergone to their divorces, or to their having acquiesced to sex with new partners following their divorces. But while sterilization is not necessarily the primary influence leading to such circumstances, in some cases it is surely a *significant* one.

Yet another patient, a forty-year-old married woman with two children, told me that she was having an affair because her husband, who had always been faithful, was boring. She had been sterilized and so she was unconcerned about the possibility of becoming pregnant by her lover and felt free to cavort with him. Though her relationship with her husband may have been deteriorating for many other reasons, her sterility freed her to ignore the problems in her "boring" marriage. Her infertile state could play a prominent role by encouraging her to succumb to fantasies rather than face the reality of having to restore an ailing marital relationship.

Because of these many concerns with the effects of contraceptives, I stopped prescribing them or recommending sterilization procedures in 1989. I was worried that, by prescribing such measures, I was doing patients more harm than good. Contraceptives are enticing because they promise to give people control over an important aspect of their lives, but, as use of contraceptives becomes more widespread, people's sex lives become not less, but more, chaotic. At a time when 90 percent of sexually active couples are now contracepting,[31] our society is experiencing unprecedented numbers of "unwanted" pregnancies, diseases, premarital promiscuity, marital infidelity, and divorce.

Contraceptives foster destructive misconceptions and misplaced priorities; they open a path toward sex without love and lesser compromises on the integrity of relationships. They have not led to higher levels of psychosexual functioning, but rather to greater abuse of what should be a wondrous, cherished aspect of marital relationships. While couples who use contraceptives may love each other deeply, they must struggle against such inherently negative influences as the rampant "needs" misconception, irresponsibility, risk-taking, and selfishness. We may well question how much stronger their relationships would be without having to contend with such pressures.

In spite of my concern about the detrimental effects of artificial contraception on interpersonal relationships, I readily acknowledge that medical technology benefits society in countless ways. The birth control pill is a potent steroid hormone with legitimate medicinal value. It can be used, for example, to treat painful menstruations and uncontrolled menstrual bleeding. The hormones in the pill may legitimately be used to improve the quality of life despite their side effect of relative infertility. The concern here is only with the misuse of products or procedures that technology provides. To distinguish between proper and improper uses of contraceptives is, at times, an unmistakable challenge. And while this challenge has often been met with apathy and closed mindedness it is a challenge that our society, inevitably, must confront.

Chapter 8

Fertility Awareness

When artificial methods of birth control are associated with so many problems, we logically ask whether "natural" methods are a more reasonable option. In this chapter, we will explore how Natural Family Planning, or Fertility Awareness, affects relationships, and what its limitations are. Unfortunately, lack of knowledge, misconceptions, and bad press have caused many people to prejudicially rule out Fertility Awareness. So let us take a careful look at the facts.

During the course of an office visit, the head nurse of a local hospital's labor and delivery department mentioned that she was having infertility problems. When I asked if she had considered using Fertility Awareness to better understand and treat the problem, she summarily dismissed such methods as "garbage." After a brief discussion, she developed a bit more appreciation.

Many people harbor similar feelings about Fertility Awareness. A few years ago I did, too. I wondered why anyone would even consider a form of birth control widely believed to be ineffectual.

In essence, Fertility Awareness means achieving greater awareness of a woman's natural, biological rhythms and using this knowledge to attempt to achieve or avoid pregnancy. Three methods can be used to identify the period of time each month when the woman is fertile (able to conceive) and when she is infertile. All three methods identify about two and a half infertile weeks per month. If a couple wishes to attempt to avoid pregnancy, they should have sex only during these infertile periods (periodic abstinence).

1) Rhythm Method – With this method, it is assumed that a woman is most fertile on a calculated day approximately midway between her last and next expected period. The couple avoids intercourse during the week that spans that day. Use of Rhythm does not involve any particular awareness of one's fertility. Unlike other methods, this method is based on arithmetic calculations and requires no understanding of the signs and symptoms of ovulation. It is included here because it is so widely recognized. This method decreased in popularity because it relied on the woman having *regular* menstrual cycles. It is relatively unreliable, because many women have an occasional long or short menstrual cycle. Though it is no longer taught, it is the method most commonly mentioned by detractors of Fertility Awareness. These people typically opt to disregard the two modern methods which were developed for women with irregular cycles.

2) Ovulation, Billings, or Cervical Mucus Method – With this method, the woman charts her signs of fertility based primarily on the characteristics of her cervical mucus. This mucus emits from the vagina and has discernible characteristics at different times of the month. Each time a woman uses the restroom, she looks for mucus on a piece of tissue and observes certain qualities of the mucus collected. With records of these observations and some training, she can distinguish between fertile and infertile days.

3) Symptothermal Method – This method is similar to the Ovulation Method except that a few additional signs are used to help define the period of fertility. These signs mainly include basal body temperature observations, which are taken and recorded daily upon arising. Characteristically, a woman's temperature will rise approximately one half degree around the day she ovulates. The rise is

then correlated with other signs to determine her period of fertility.

The last two of these methods have been used for decades in a variety of cultures, including the uneducated poor in developing countries. Motivation, not educational level or intelligence, has consistently been found to determine the effectiveness of these methods.

According to the latest estimates from Planned Parenthood, even the outdated Rhythm Method is more effective than the popular diaphragm. The Rhythm Method also compares quite favorably with the condom (see graph, p. 87). Modern Fertility Awareness is even more reliable. As with artificial forms of birth control, estimated failure rates vary. In the largest study, 19,843 predominantly poor women from Calcutta, India were found to have a failure rate of only 0.2 percent.[1]

It is estimated that fewer than one percent of couples using Fertility Awareness methods correctly would become pregnant after one year of use (a method failure rate of less than one percent). The more realistic user failure rate has been reported to be up to twenty-five percent (i.e., of 100 couples using such methods, correctly or not, up to twenty-five women will become pregnant). It is generally agreed that Fertility Awareness requires a high level of motivation, and that couples who use it and who are without serious motivation are likely to get pregnant. While some early, poorly designed studies showed higher failure rates, the more recent studies have generally shown user effectiveness rates from 95 to 98 percent (a two to five percent user failure rate).[2] These rates compare favorably with those of the most popular forms of artificial contraception.[3]

More important than these statistics, however, is the effect of natural methods on relationships. In the same critical ways in which artificial contraception fails to support relationships, natural methods excel. Fertility Awareness is more than just an alternative method of birth control. It is, in concert with positive, nurturing, unitive attitudes toward sexuality, and is perhaps the most important means of discrediting the abusive "needs" misconception. For example, a couple has predicted that they will be infertile tonight, and, throughout the day, they have consciously planned on genital sexual contact, and they have felt "needful." That evening, unexpectedly, the woman discovers fertile mucus; they postpone intercourse to avoid pregnancy. Their need for genital sexual relations is not fulfilled, but they survive by going to bed early, lying close to each other and talking quietly until they fall asleep. They have been reminded once again that strong sexual desires can be contained.

Because Fertility Awareness confronts the most significant misconception about sex, it also has a positive influence on achievement of the goals of sexual interactions. To return to our celestial analogy in Chapter 1, Fertility Awareness encourages couples to think in terms of the more general relationship – represented by the sun, planets, and moons as a unified whole. It challenges the idea that genital sex is central to relationships and leads couples to accept its more natural role at the periphery of the "solar system."

For example, during the question period following a lecture, an engaged couple posed a problem based on their own personal situation. They had planned on using Fertility Awareness, but now the man was concerned that infertile periods might not coincide with their honeymoon and that they might have to abstain from sex throughout it. He was noticeably distressed by this possibility and asked which form of artificial contraceptive should be used as a back-up method in that eventuality. He had become preoccupied with a specific, genital sexual "need," the need to have sexual intercourse during their honeymoon. Regardless of whether the week was delightful in every other way, he would be sincerely disappointed if this particular need were not met. An otherwise cherished and memorable trip would not be sufficient. He *needed* genital, sexual relations or the honeymoon would be spoiled.

Fertility Awareness had the potential for teaching this young man that he had no specific sexual "need," but rather that marriage is for a lifetime with many opportunities for sex. It could have taught him that a marital relationship can exist without genital, sexual relations for periods without being diminished, but only changed. This was an opportunity to learn a lesson about the correct emphasis within a marital relationship – on the heart and soul of the relationship – but he was going to miss the point by turning to artificial contraception. Fertility Awareness had a lesson to teach this couple even as they prepared for marriage!

While artificial methods emphasize the priorities of freedom and pleasure, Fertility Awareness promotes the priority of love. It teaches a balanced approach to relationships, with sex in its proper place. In contrast to the effect of artificial contraception on the five characteristics of love (see Chapter 7), let us consider the effect of natural methods on these characteristics.

Respect

Because Fertility Awareness undermines the "needs" misconception, the spouse is not regarded as a mere sex object who is expected to fulfill needs, to give pleasure, or to satisfy. Mutual consent is the rule in healthy relationships, but is too often not the case when one person is perceived as having a need. To accept willingly the request of one's spouse for occasional abstinence, for whatever reason, shows respect; and Fertility Awareness encourages openness to this.

Responsibility

Natural methods of fertility regulation leave little room for doubt about where responsibility lies for the possible consequences of sexual activity, and couples who use them are less likely to assume that pregnancy is an impossibility than are those who use artificial methods. There are no technological devices to blame if a pregnancy occurs. Therefore, couples are obliged to assume full responsibility instead of being "sort of" responsible as they are with contraceptives. With Fertility Awareness, one doesn't perform the act with the hope of no untoward consequences. Rather, the act is replaced by other kinds of behavior, in order to *eliminate* the risk of such consequences. Fertility Awareness requires partners to accept equal responsibility, while contraception generally places the greater responsibility on the woman. When contraceptives fail, pregnancies are commonly perceived as being "her" fault.

Discipline

Fertility Awareness teaches sexual discipline, and is, therefore, liberating. Those who are disciplined have the freedom to choose to restrain themselves or not. Those who are undisciplined have no choice. By teaching temperance, natural methods encourage an openness to not having one's desires satisfied. People learn to control their instinctive sexual urges, instead of being controlled by them. Fertility Awareness, therefore, can be a key to true sexual freedom. Fertility Awareness is not easy. It may take years before a couple begins to appreciate its positive effects on attitudes, and years beyond that to realize fully its immense potential. Fertility Awareness offers a sound education, though often at a leisurely pace. These methods are not a quick fix, but the more difficult a couple finds them, the more the couple stands to gain by them; and as the couple gains, the easier it becomes to sacrifice for greater goods.

Commitment

Since the possibility of pregnancy is so much more clear without contraceptives, Fertility Awareness promotes awareness of the kind of commitment required for intimate sexual relations. Because natural methods of fertility awareness clarify the risk-taking nature of premarital sex, they are unsuited for "serially monogamous" couples. They are appropriate only for couples willing to commit to a lifetime together.

Natural methods make greater demands on couples than artificial methods, requiring a greater investment in the marital relationship. And this investment itself reminds us of the adage, "You get out of life what you put into it." The best things in life are often not the most easily acquired.

Trust

Because of its positive effect on so many aspects of love, Fertility Awareness fosters trust, perhaps the most important of the five characteristics.

Attempts to Discredit Fertility Awareness

Despite its effectiveness and many benefits, Fertility Awareness is commonly denigrated. A number of unfounded arguments have been advanced in attempts to discredit it, and examination of them will prove enlightening.

Misconception #13: Disadvantages of natural methods of fertility regulation include increased risk of birth defects and required "long" periods of abstinence which cause sexual dysfunction.

Risk of Birth Defects

Planned Parenthood's pamphlet, *Basics of Birth Control* states that, "There appears to be increased risk of birth defects in babies born to women using Fertility Awareness Methods with abstinence, when an aging egg is fertilized."[4] No supporting arguments, data, or references are given to substantiate this statement. In contrast, the same pamphlet discusses the side effects of the pill without mentioning that it is universally known to cause birth defects. The birth control pill has, in fact, been designated Pregnancy Category X by the Food and Drug Administration. Drugs are placed in Categories A, B, C, D, or X, in order of decreasing safety. Drugs in Category X are the most dangerous since they have been conclusively shown to cause birth defects.[5] It is enigmatic as to how Planned Parenthood derived this assertion. Apparently the assumption was that natural methods more often led to fertilization of aging (postovulatory) eggs. Planned Parenthood's own literature refutes this idea however, with the statement that, "Most accidental pregnancies experienced by women using these methods occur during the preovulatory phase of the menstrual cycle"[6] (when the egg is most fresh). Women experience a menstrual period approximately every 28 days. The ovary releases the unfertilized egg, i.e., ovulates, approximately two weeks after the prior menstruation. "Preovulatory" pregnancies occur when a couple has sex prior to ovulation and the sperm remains viable long enough to fertilize the egg when it is ovulated. "Postovulatory" pregnancies occur when the couple has sex after the egg has ovulated but before it has expired.

"Long" Periods of Abstinence[7]

Five to ten day periods of abstinence are typical when attempting to avoid pregnancy. For couples capable of avoiding genital sexual gratification for such periods, natural methods are a realistic option. For couples who live for the next climax, they are not.

Sexual Dysfunction

The criticism that periodic abstinence causes sexual dysfunction is based on the unfounded "use it or lose it" philosophy. In fact, however, a couple does not get "out of shape" as a result of taking periodic breaks, nor does sexual intercourse require keeping skilled techniques finely tuned. Like other pleasurable activities, sex becomes more interesting when it is not so routine. Respites obviate the need to search for ways to spice up a love life.

Far from being a source of psychological problems, periodic abstinence is routinely used by therapists to *treat* sexual dysfunction. By teaching moderation, Fertility Awareness is naturally conducive to a therapeutic balance within relationships.

Misconception #14: Use of Fertility Awareness is restricted to couples with an unusually healthy relationships or to certain religions.

Many people argue that while natural methods may be ideal in healthy relationships, artificial methods are better suited for relationships marred by poor communication, distrust, abuse, or inequality. It is true that natural methods many not be capable of healing seriously dysfunctional relationships. In such cases, the positive influences of Fertility Awareness many not become manifest. Contraceptives appear to be a desperate but perhaps necessary alternative, particularly when women can see no other escape.

The problem with this idea is that artificial methods enable couples to avoid addressing the fundamental problems in their relationships, and so those problems persist. For example, if a man is raping his wife, use of contraceptives actually facilitates continued rape by reducing the fear of having to raise a child as a consequence of the act. Perhaps more importantly, because of their innately detrimental influence, artificial methods have little capacity, in and of themselves, to alleviate underlying tensions, e.g., over the "needs" misconception, which can lead to abuse and cause still more tension.

For example, in a letter to popular psychologist Dr. Joyce Brothers,[8] a woman expressed her fear of contracting AIDS since her husband seemed to be going to prostitutes. The husband refused to talk to her about the situation or to use a condom. Dr. Brothers answered that, "Any partner who respects and loves his spouse should be willing to take precautions." She discussed condoms ("precautions") briefly and then concluded with an admonition to the wife "to be more assertive with your husband and demand that he change," the obvious inference being that he use a condom.

To recommend condoms to this innocent woman is scandalous and requires not only that one ignore the failure rate of condoms but, far more importantly, that one ignore the fundamental problems threatening this couple's relationship. This woman should not have to risk her health or life for her husband's pleasure. Dr. Brothers should have told her to fully protect herself by refusing to have sex with him until truly safe sex was reasonably assured. Use of contraceptives, whether to avoid pregnancy or disease, allows underlying abuse to continue unchallenged. They are an easy but unhealthy way out of unpleasant circumstances

Natural methods are not a cure-all for serious psychosexual dysfunction, but while artificial methods may encourage a facade of normality, they can be expected to stimulate unhealthy processes within already ailing relationships. Instead of offering contraception to desperate women, society should help them evaluate whether or not to remain in their current troubled relationships and should work to develop resources and realistic options for these women. We fail women who are faced with such dilemmas by suggesting that contraceptives are the only reasonable solution.

Above all, it should be understood that natural methods of fertility regulation are available to, and can be used by, any couple who knows the method and is committed to his or her spouse. These methods are restricted to no cultural background or religious affiliation.

With so many advantages and so few *bona fide* disadvantages, it is surprising that Fertility Awareness incurs such widespread ridicule. There are many reasons for this response. One reason is that artificial methods are more easily implemented. Natural methods require patience and an investment in time, both by the couple and the instructor, whereas artificial methods are more in tune with the modern emphasis on convenience. Another reason is that modern medicine uses a disease-oriented approach to health care. Artificial methods treat fertility as a problem, a disease, that must be cured with drugs, devices, or surgery – much in keeping with the approach used for battling cancer or infections. In contrast, natural methods work in unison with the body's natural rhythms and accept fertility as a state of health.

Finally, we should recognize that contraception and sterilization procedures bring immense profits to pharmaceutical companies and others in the health field. Vast sums are spent on research, promotion, and implementation of contraception and sterilization. Advertisements are plentiful in medical journals, and medical offices and clinics are kept well stocked with free contraceptive samples. Physicians have become familiar with the routine of pleasant pharmaceutical company representatives dropping in to deliver lunch for the office staff and to discuss the latest contraception update. One study estimated that, in 1983, $1.7 million was spent advertising these methods in five academic journals alone. That study also estimated that $272 million was earned annually just on prescriptions for the pill written by obstetricians.[9] Beyond private expenditures, our federal government spends an estimated $715 million annually supporting these methods.[10] There are over 7,000 publicly funded family planning clinics in the United States.[11] Medical schools, universities, and high schools, too, help spread the word.

In contrast, natural methods are promoted by a few small nonprofit organizations. Most physicians remain unaware of modern methods of Fertility Awareness since there are no advertisements in medical journals, no fancy patient information brochures, and no free lunches. Natural methods are inexpensive or free, and not monetarily profitable.

For these reasons, artificial methods are here to stay. Because of such successful promotion of artificial means, couples who choose natural means may receive little support from the many health professionals who remain uninformed. As an example of how ingrained the contraceptive mentality is, following the birth of our fourth child, my wife and I were counseled by the *anesthesiologist* to be sure to "protect" ourselves from future pregnancies. He offered this opinion with full knowledge that I was a practicing family physician, as if we weren't clear on where little babies come from!

Although artificial methods currently dominate the field, both information and support for those interested in Fertility Awareness are available. (See "Resource Appendix," for more information.)

It is no coincidence that the widespread use of contraceptives was followed by a sexual revolution based on misconceptions encouraging compromises on love. And although contraceptives have not been the only instigators of mistaken attitudes, they have played a pivotal role in spreading many of these misconceptions. The great irony is that artificial birth control was supposed to offer modern society sexual freedom, but the reality is just the opposite. It is natural methods of fertility regulation that are the key to true sexual freedom, whereas artificial methods bind people to addictive attitudes and an endless pursuit of "needs."

As discussed in Chapter 2, there is a natural link between the unitive and pleasurable aspects of sexuality; sexual interactions imply affection. However, because women can conceive for only about one week each month, there is a natural, temporary disengaging of the *loving* (or unitive) and *life-giving* (procreative) functions of sexual intercourse during the remaining three weeks. In contrast, the natural association between the loving and *pleasuring* aspects is constant for all sexual acts, whether genital or non-genital (those without potential for procreation, e.g. holding hands). Natural methods of fertility regulation work within this construct, but contraception and sterilization do not. Artificial separation of the loving and life-giving aspects of intercourse allows for simultaneous separation of the loving and pleasuring aspects as well (as, for example, in the case of sex with a prostitute). Because artificial methods interfere with the connection between pleasure and unity, they promote compromises on love and encourage sex without love – sex for the sake of pleasure alone. They interfere with the most elementary requirement of healthy sex, a moral context, and therein lies the most "artificial" aspect of their nature. Fertility Awareness methods conform with the natural, intermittent separation between the loving and life-giving aspects of sexual intercourse while maintaining the vital connection between the pleasuring and loving aspects. By preserving this bond, natural methods support the priority of love – a priority easily displaced with the use of artificial methods.

Modern society consistently ignores the vital difference between the way artificial and natural methods of fertility regulation influence relationships. This has not always been the case; contraceptives did not achieve public acceptance until the 1930s. In 1931 during this transition, *The Washington Post* editorialized, "The suggestion that the use of legalized contraceptives would be 'careful and restrained' is preposterous."[12] Some years before, in 1925, Mahatma Gandhi had counseled, "I urge the advocates of artificial methods of birth control to consider the consequences. Any large use of the methods is likely to result in the dissolution of the marriage bond."[13] Natural methods, in contrast, promote cooperation, expose misconceptions and provide support for the goal of unity and the priority of love. Natural methods, thus, are good and reasonable alternatives to contraception and sterilization.

Couples using Fertility Awareness enjoy an extremely low divorce rate (3 percent).[14] One reason for this is that many, if not most, of its users belong to religions that proscribe divorce. It is unknown what the relative contribution of the methods themselves is on these couple's commitment to each other. However, in a society in which, according to *Harpers' Index,* two out of every three future marriages are expected to end in divorce,[15] anything that works to promote genuine intimacy, maturity, and mutual respect deserves appreciation.

Chapter 9

Abortion

Discussions of abortion raise a broad range of complicated controversial issues. We will limit our discussion to our primary concern of the connection between abortion and the development of healthy attitudes about sexual relationships We can gain some in sight here by examining three specific points: 1) what the act of seriously considering an abortion reveals about the attitudes that led to the pregnancy, 2) the effect of an abortion on a couple's attitudes toward each other, 3) the effect the legal status of abortion has on people's attitudes.

Considering an Abortion

Popular wisdom often mistakenly isolates the issue of abortion from its antecedents. Just as so many people ignore the conspicuous psychological ramifications of contraception, so too many ignore the larger picture with abortion.

When a woman or couple is willing to consider having an abortion, the immediate problem they are trying to solve is the "unwanted" pregnancy. Whatever the ultimate resolution – abortion, adoption, single parenthood, having a relative raise the child, a forced wedding, or abandoning a newborn in a trash bin – there will be other problems. When a mother or father, or both, do not want their unborn child, someone must pay a high price. Since this scenario is repeated over and over again, the grief associated with it throughout society is immense.

Just as the problem of abortion should not be isolated from the problem of "unwanted" pregnancies, those "unwanted" pregnancies should not be isolated from the even more fundamental problem of dysfunctional or unhealthy psychosexual relationships. These are, in turn, the root cause of "unwanted" pregnancies, i.e., the problem that abortion is called upon to resolve. Psychosexual dysfunction lies at the heart of the abortion issue. If an abortion is being considered, or is an accepted possibility for handling a future pregnancy, tragic circumstances *already* exist. If a couple is having sex without being *fully* responsible, without *fully* protecting each other from the unnecessary, serious risk of an "unwanted" pregnancy, then something other than love has highest priority in the relationship. When priorities are disordered, it is due to goals being disordered. The primary goal of sex is to bring people closer together, but an "unwanted" pregnancy has the opposite effect – it creates havoc in the relationship. Those who have healthy attitudes about sex, who look for sex to be one positive experience after another, do not put each other at risk for an abortion.

Any woman who has had an abortion, or who has seriously considered one, can be considered a victim of abuse. Her partner has abused her and she has abused herself, because both people have failed to protect the woman from this grave predicament. I do not mean to discount the psychological distress many men suffer during all stages of the abortion decision, but it is a fair generalization that women suffer greater consequences from abortion than men.

Society assumes that abortion prevents a tragedy, without acknowledging that tragic circumstances existed prior to the pregnancy. The tragedy is in the relationship that created the "unwanted" pregnancy, a relationship in which the couple allowed themselves to put each other at risk of an unintended pregnancy. Sadly, abortion often enables people to circumvent this more fundamental issue, and thereby helps preserve dysfunction (as with women who "give up control of their bodies" to their husbands). Once the abortion is done, the "mistake" is put out of mind, and the couple can revert to old ways.

As documented earlier, the number of illegitimate pregnancies has risen dramatically during the sexual revolution. Ultimately, no matter what happens in courtrooms across this nation, the issue of abortion can only be resolved in the bedroom, through individual decisions. If we are to resolve the crisis of 1.6 million abortions annually in the United States,[1] we must look to the source: psychosexual dysfunction. Unhealthy attitudes will remain at the heart of the abortion issue, no matter how much "rescuing" is done, no matter what laws are passed to restrict abortion, no matter what penalties are imposed for breaking those laws. To cure this problem, a new approach toward sexual relationships is required: not accepting, not being passive about, and not promoting the misuse of sex. For example, since 80 percent of those 1.6 million abortions are performed on single women, if just one-half of sexually active unmarried couples valued each other too much, esteemed each other too much, cared about each other too much, to put each other at risk of an "unwanted" pregnancy and chose premarital abstinence, 600,000 fewer abortions would occur each year in the United States.

To have a meaningful effect on the tragedy of abortion, all of us – abortion advocates and opponents alike – must address *attitudes* that put couples at risk for "unwanted" pregnancies: we must expose falsehoods such as the "needs" misconception we must expose disordered priorities and goals.

Effect of Abortion on a Couple's Attitudes Toward Each Other

There is a wide range of reported effects of an abortion on a couple's relationship. Some couples claim that an abortion led to a reduction in stress, including financial burdens, and allowed them freedom in other areas of their lives. Others say it led to, or was associated with, sexual dysfunction, communication problems, isolation, or the termination of the relationship. Studies have shown that from 25 to 70 percent of relationships terminate following an abortion.[2] Unfortunately, however, isolated statistics like these cannot be applied directly to our specific concern. The effect of abortion on the couple's relationship cannot readily be compared to the potential impact of other possible responses to an unintended pregnancy. We must leave this question largely unanswered for lack of available data.

Effects of the Legal Status of Abortion on People's Attitudes

We have discussed the potential adverse effects of artificial contraception on attitudes and have noted the similarities between some of its methods and abortion. Abortion, like contraception, pornography and downplaying STDs, minimizes the risks of sexual activity and encourages risk-taking. Abortion also, therefore, commonly leads to the misuse of sex, from which women, in particular, suffer.

By now, all of this should sound familiar. But there is a paradox: an apparent contradiction. The above logic suggests that the more accessible abortion is, the greater the sexual exploitation of women will be. Yet the popular notion is that abortion should remain legal and available for the *sake* of women. Legal abortion is supposed to liberate women, to give them "choice," and to empower them. So, are women benefited or harmed by legal, easily accessible, inexpensive abortion?

Examination of the conflict in priorities helps to resolve our paradox. Abortion advocates rarely acknowledge the connection between abortion and sexually abusive attitudes. They fail to give due consideration to the priority of love in assessing sexual risk-taking. Instead, they make the priority of freedom ("choice") their flagship.

Although freedom is a valid and important priority, the abortion issue is one example of what can happen when we place any priority higher than love. Legalized abortion, like artificial contraceptives, has placed women at a disadvantage by making it harder for them to choose not to be sexually active with their partners. Abortion advocates argue that this problem is balanced by the freedom that couples, and women in particular, gain from abortion's legal status. The truth is more complicated, however because this freedom involves three often painful and difficult choices:

- Whether or not to have sex.
- Once pregnant, whether or not to abort.
- Once the decision to abort has been made, how to assure a safe abortion.

Whether or Not to Have Sex

Legal abortion offers an escape from the consequences of sex and thereby encourages sexual risk-taking. For example, it encourages premarital sex, an inherently unhealthy activity. Easy access to abortion disarms women who prefer not to engage in premarital sex – women who know that they are the ones most vulnerable to its negative consequences Easy access encourages unhealthy attitudes in struggling relationships and infiltrates healthy relationships with misuse. The thought is, "But, Honey, I have needs (and if you become pregnant you can get rid of it)." Not that this is a premeditated or even conscious stance, but it is a thought that influences decisions.

The number of abortions has doubled since it became generally legal in the early 1970s (see graph Chapter 7). An increasing number of people have been willing to take risks and to put each other at risk. Legalized abortion and greater reliance on contraceptives are contributing causes of this increase. By making abortion legal and available, we create a greater demand for it. And, as with most other consequences of sexual risk-taking, it is women who pay the greater price.

Once Pregnant, Whether or Not to Abort

Our society tends to approach this question simplistically with the thought: "By making abortion legal, a pregnant woman who wishes to can chose to have an abortion." Fair enough. But the reality is far more complex and many women are having choices made for them by self-interested others.

Not long ago, I informed a patient that her pregnancy test was positive. She became tearful because this was an unintended pregnancy but said that she would keep the child and asked that I call her boyfriend in from the waiting room. I left them alone for a few minutes and before they left, the *man* had talked the *woman* into an abortion. He had succeeded in reversing her decision; he had made the *woman's* choice for her. Another time, a pregnant teenager wished to give up her baby for adoption but complained, "My boyfriend and my parents want me to have an abortion. What *choice* do I have?"

Little is reported in the media about what is happening among those struggling with the decision about whether or not to have an abortion. Many women, with or without their significant or not-so-significant other, choose to have an abortion, but many times men make the choice for women or strongly influence that "choice." Easy, legal access to abortion affects this power balance. In a voluntary survey of men who accompanied their partners to abortion clinics, four percent said that they alone, and not their partners, wanted the abortion.[3] The men – not the women – had made the decision. Undoubtedly, the actual percentage of cases in which the men make the decision is much higher, since less sensitive men are less likely to be found escorting their partners to an abortion clinic. Also, of those who do go, many would not volunteer the information that they had forced the abortion. Further, there are certainly many other cases in which the man, although not forcing the abortion, strongly influences the decision.

In an early survey of women who had undergone an abortion, 20 percent responded that they felt "forced" by a man to have the abortion against their will.[4] According to a survey published by Planned Parenthood in 1990, 23 percent of women said that their decision to have an abortion was based partially or solely on the fact that their husband or partner wanted it.[5]

What "choice" is there for women when men tell them, "Take care of it," "You weren't careful enough," or "It's not my problem"? It is naive to think that when a pregnancy occurs, men simply leave the decision up to the woman. Men exert great influence over all other choices couples make regarding their sexuality, such as the method of fertility regulation or how frequently to have intercourse, and the same should be expected of the choice of whether or not to abort.

It should be no surprise that easy access to abortion encourages men to use women and then force them to dispose of the product of that abuse. Abortion frees men of responsibility and commitment. Nor should it be surprising that men who manipulate women into sexual risk-taking would also endorse continuation of legal abortions, which offers a relatively uncomplicated painless escape for the man. Speaking to this issue, many years ago, Alice Paul, the author of the original Equal Rights Amendment, said that "abortion is the ultimate exploitation of womnen."[6]

My patients provide all too painful examples of this kind of exploitation. After being told she was pregnant, one woman initially expressed great excitement about having a baby. She had been unable to conceive for many years and was delighted with the news. A week later, at a follow up appointment, she was distraught. Upon hearing of the pregnancy, her live-in boyfriend suggested that she take a long horseback ride.

Another woman and her boyfriend had one daughter, and during a subsequent pregnancy, the boyfriend argued strenuously for her to have an abortion, She kept the pregnancy, over his bitter objections. Three years later, she came in to the office with a multitude of health concerns, many of which are commonly associated with anxiety. When questioned about the stress in her life, she became hysterical. She said that after intense, protracted, internal debate, she had recently decided to leave her boyfriend. The woman realized that she would never get over her boyfriend's attempt to force her to abort their son. She could never trust him again. It was with great relief that she revealed her secrets and her health concerns subsequently resolved.

Because of the extraordinary emotions involved, the question of whether legal abortion really allows women to choose to abort is difficult to answer. But clearly the amount of pressure others place on women to have abortions is enormous, and the more accessible abortions are, the more likely women are to acquiesce. When an argument ensues, free, legal access to abortion favors the person wishing to abort. Often this is the woman, but often it is the man, the parents, a friend, or health advisor.

How to Assure a Safe Abortion

Whether abortion is legal or not, psychosexual dysfunction will remain, "unwanted" pregnancies will occur, and abortions will continue to be performed. Allowing abortions to be performed legally should logically insure some measure of safety for women undergoing the procedure. Abortion advocates were quick to assert that legalizing abortion led to a marked reduction in deaths and other complications from abortions. The statistics, however, are marked with contradictions and controversy.

An enormous discrepancy exists between official statistics and those used by abortion advocates who contend that, prior to national legalization in 1973, abortion deaths were grossly underreported and that 5,000 to 10,000 deaths occurred per year. Such numbers conjure up images of droves of women dropping dead in back alleys throughout the country. Dr. Bernard Nathanson, who once ran the largest abortion facility in the United States and was the pro-choice cofounder of the National Association for Repeal of Abortion Laws (NARAL) now states, "I confess that I knew the[se] figures were totally false"[7] but he continued to use them. The graph on the next page presents the official statistics. The significant decrease in abortion fatalities occurred between 1940 and the late 1960s. This period was distinguished by advances in medical technology (such as antibiotics and safer abortion methods), not by legal decisions. Since 1973, when abortion became legal on a national level, the number of maternal deaths from it has further decreased from a national total of forty-four in 1973 to five in 1998, whether as a result of legalization or of continued technological advances or a combination. Since the total number of deaths from miscarriages experienced a similar decrease during that same period[8] without any help from the judicial system, it seems likely that the advance of technology, not legalization, was a primary factor in reducing abortion deaths after 1973. This data does not take into account the fact that the abortion rate nearly doubled during this time while the rate of miscarriages remained relatively stable. Therefore, one could surmise that legalizing abortion has led to some reduction in the number of deaths related to the procedure. Every maternal death, whether before or after legalization, is a tragedy, but the enthusiasm for legal abortion as the solution to the problem of abortion-related deaths seems misplaced.

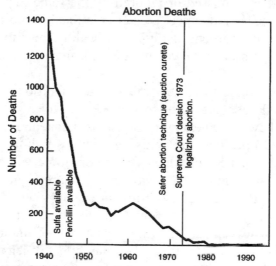

Figure 5. Number of deaths of women due to abortion. Source: National Center for Health Statistics, adapted from *Abortion: Questions and Answers*. Hayes Publishing Co., Cincinnati, Ohio. p.166.

It is also interesting that the reported number of nonfatal complications from abortions contradicts the apparent downward trend of fatal abortion complications. Evidence indicates that there has been a rise in nonfatal complications from abortion following legalization. For example, in 1969 the number of reported nonfatal complications treated in U.S. hospitals was 9,000, but in 1977 the number had increased to 17,000.[9]

These statistical contradictions indicate that the correlation between legalization of abortion and subsequent health problems is a far more complicated issue than people are generally led to believe. Because of these contradictions, the benefits of legalization on the physical health of women is debatable.

Along with the physical consequences of abortion are psychological consequences. If legal abortion creates a demand for itself, and if abortion has a psychological aftermath, then abortion is in itself an argument against continuation of legal status. Strangely, while the psychological impact of miscarriages on women (and

some men) is unquestioned and supported throughout medical literature, the status of mental health consequences for women after an
abortion is either dismissed or ignored by the same medical literature. Clearly one should expect greater emotional turmoil following
a conscious decision to end the life of a healthy fetus than after an
act of nature (a miscarriage); yet the double standard persists.

The ultimate value to society of legalized abortion remains unknown. After decades of experience since the Roe vs. Wade decision, we can draw three general conclusions: Legal abortion encourages misplaced priorities and goals, and invites risk-taking behaviors to the consequences of which women are more vulnerable than
men. Legal abortion gives many women one more choice in coping
with an "unwanted" pregnancy, but also enables men to influence
women's choices and evade responsibility for the child. Legal abortion has had far less impact than the advance of technology on the
number of abortion complications. The sum effect of legalization on
the maternal death rate, the rate of nonfatal complications, and the
psychological impact of a higher abortion rate remain unclear.

Freer access to abortion is at least as much a threat to some wom-
en as it is a hope for others. The promise of legal abortion to free
women by giving them "choice" is, in great part, an illusion. Too
often abortion is used as a tool to exploit, manipulate, and abandon
them.[10]

The abortion issue is complex and multifaceted. Since it is not
the primary focus of this book, we have disregarded many basic
considerations and have focused narrowly on aspects related to
healthy attitudes and to the conflict between the priorities of love
and freedom. These are not the only issues, but they are important
and often overlooked.

Part V

Approaches to Sexuality

Chapter 10

Sexual Addiction

A cocaine addict *needs a* "snort." A cigarette addict *needs* a "drag." An alcoholic *needs* a drink. What about those who *need* to have sex, *need* to climax, or *need* to fulfill a sexual fantasy? Are they sex addicts?

In her book, *When Society Becomes an Addict,* feminist Anne Wilson Schaef labels the prevailing socio-political system within our culture the "Addictive System." She points out that addictive attitudes are becoming deeply ingrained in our culture.[1] Clearly the addictive attitude about sex is based on the most basic and widely accepted misconception of sexuality: the "needs" misconception.

The study of addiction is complicated, with much confusion and uncertainty in the field. People can be addicted to almost anything, including alcohol, drugs, caffeine, cigarettes, food, television, work, money, shopping, romance novels, gambling, exercise, and on and on. Furthermore, addicts commonly have multiple addictions.

Chemical addiction is the state of one who has a "compulsive desire for and use of a habit-forming substance . . . characterized by tolerance (to that substance) and by well-defined physiologic symptoms upon withdrawal."[2] More generally, addictions are unhealthy or dysfunctional behavior patterns that lead to significant harm for the addict and others; smokers develop cancer, alcoholics cause traffic accidents, workaholics become divorced. Addicts commonly lose their jobs, their families, their homes, and their health.

What do addicts gain by knowingly creating such serious risks for themselves and others? Why do addicts reach for a cigarette or a drink? Clearly powerful forces must be at work when one considers the extreme behaviors addicts are driven to and the consequences they suffer. As a group, addicts have not been shown to be lacking in intelligence. Addicts "use," in part, out of habit, and some truly enjoy their "drug of choice." But, when addicts respond to a question about why they "use," their fairly uniform answer, whether explicit or implicit, is "stress." Addicts "use" whatever they use to cope with stress.

Since all of us have stress, it is essential for each of us to learn how to deal with it in positive, functional, growth-producing ways. Although addictions are an attempt to reduce stress, they ultimately – because of the problems they cause – increase stress. Because addicts make irrational, desperate attempts to use, they hurt themselves and others. Addictive behaviors are therefore inherently unloving.

The perfect definition for "addictions" or "addicts" has not been found, but a working definition will be helpful: addictions are habitual behaviors primarily used to reduce, avoid, or escape stress, which entail likely, serious harm to oneself and/or others. They are dysfunctional coping mechanisms.

If stress is the principal cause of addictive behaviors, we must understand what stress is and where it comes from. Stress, when considered in the broad sense, is mental tension – a lack of inner peace or serenity in one's current life. Stress, pressure, or tension comes from a variety of sources including jobs, taxes, bills, spouses, children, illness, and death. Three common, important sources of stress are often overlooked: boredom, loneliness, and sadness or depression.

All of us, at times, deal with stress dysfunctionally to one degree or another. Addicts are unique in that they seriously and habitually fail to deal with some types of stress maturely. It is noteworthy that an addict may excel at coping with one type of stress but need to "use" to cope with other types. A stunt pilot may calmly fly harrowing flight patterns that would terrify most everyone else but compulsively smoke cigarettes to cope with the boredom of a long drive in a car.

Addicts do not have a specific "need" for a fix or a drink. They only feel or perceive such a need. What they do need is what we all need: means for relieving stress that are sustainable and gratifying. With addictions, the problem is not so much controlling the impulse, but managing the stress that incites the impulse.

People cope with stress in many ways, some of which are healthy, and others (such as addictive responses) which are not. An addictive behavior pattern may result from a variety of factors that influence a person's response to stressors. These factors include:

- Current life stress: As cited above, this can include anything from job stress to loneliness.
- Habit: All addictions involve repetitive actions that may become highly ritualized. Habits, however, may be good or bad. Bad ones do not entail the serious consequences generally attributed to addictions and are simpler to break. Bad habits such as sitting with one's elbows on the dinner table can be broken, especially under threat. In contrast, addicts often continue their addiction even in the face of death. As with addictions, habits such as fingernail biting may be associated with stress, but clearly addictions are far more than just bad habits.
- Physiological or chemical addiction: Some addictions, such as alcoholism or Valium dependence, have an element of physical tolerance and/or withdrawal. These elements are obviously not factors for addictions to slot machines, shopping, or sex.
- Environmental conditions: Most important is an abusive or inordinately stressful childhood (e.g., the premature death of a parent), which may predispose one to chronic anxiety, depression, or phobias. Also, because one's environment offers role models, addicts tend to raise addicts.
- Physical illnesses: Problems such as chronic pain or hormonal imbalances may lead to emotional problems.
- Underlying mental disorders: Addicts may suffer from under-

lying anxiety disorders, depression, personality disorders, or psychoses.
- Genetic predisposition: e.g. to a particular mental or physical condition, or a general inability to cope with a particular type of stress.

In an individual, these components combine in unique and unknown ways to produce behavioral responses to various stressors.

One outdated, erroneous theory considers some addictions to be simply genetic diseases. A group of studies from the 70s and 80s appeared to demonstrate a genetic predisposition to alcoholism.[3] These studies, however, are beset with multiple methodological errors and misinterpretations which discredit them. For example, addicts in the parent study population are usually defined through a registry of citizens admitted to inpatient wards for detoxification or incarcerated for alcohol-related offenses. Since experts in the field have long understood that most alcoholics do not meet such criteria, these studies are meaningless. It is a gross oversimplification to consider addictions to be diseases. This concept was promoted to minimize the incapacitating guilt many addicts experience, but too often it was used to abrogate responsibility. Whatever combination of contributing factors is involved, the adult addict is ultimately responsible for his or her behavior.

Once the addict is recognized, the next task is assisting him or her in recovery, regaining control over his or her life. Since the cause of these addictive behaviors is so complex, and each addict is unique, the treatment must be individualized.

Stress management should be a primary issue. Behavior modification can be used to treat the habit associated with addictions and also to address the more fundamental issue of stress. If an addict uses the addiction to reduce stress, quitting is tantamount to surrendering a major support system. It is like pulling a chair out from underneath oneself, a highly unlikely event. The best initial advice for addicts is to focus not on quitting their addictions but on replacing addictive behaviors with more healthy, practical, growth-producing ways of dealing with stress. The list of ways is varied and endless and may include such activities as exercising, eating carrot sticks, playing the banjo, or cleaning out the garage.

More established addictions require a more intensive approach. Treating underlying medical and mental disorders is critical, as is uncovering past and present environmental influences. Treating an addict may involve individual counseling, group therapy sessions, modification of the addict's environment, spiritual direction, or counseling for the people most influential in the addict's life: the so-called codependents. Codependents are the family members, friends, co-workers and significant others who respond to the addiction in a less than ideal manner and may even consciously or unconsciously support it. Sexual codependency will be addressed specifically in Chapter 12, but let us now simply mention that it may play a critical role in the development and maintenance of addictive attitudes. The treatment of addicts is extraordinarily complicated, demanding, and often frustrating work. It is the treatment of the stress of life and more.

Just as we can approach alcohol in healthy or addictive ways, so too can the approach to sex be healthy or addictive. Sexual addiction, or compulsion, is habitual use of sex (within or without marriage) to cope with stress, even in the face of likely serious harm to oneself or to others.

In the movie *Moonstruck,* the protagonist's father has an affair with a younger woman. His wife is aware of his infidelity and explains that the reason why older men have affairs with younger women is that they are afraid of death. As with other addictions, sex can be used to cope with stress. In this case, it was stress associated with the fear of death. In the case of the patient mentioned in the Introduction who had sex with several women in one week in an attempt to cure his depression, it was stress associated with depression. This patient became not only more depressed but also infected with an STD.

Who are sex addicts? Is it the man who feels he must stimulate himself? Is it the man (in Chapter 1) who propositioned the sixteen year-old prostitute? Are all people who acquiesce to the "needs" misconception sex addicts? To better understand sexual addiction, let us examine its relationship to five features that it has in common with other addictive behaviors.

1) Sex addicts use sex to deal with stress.

There is no significant difference between the stress a sex addict feels and the stress a drug addict feels. Sexual tension or sexual stress is not unique, but a generic commodity, and each individual has his or her own responses to various types of stress, depending on the circumstances. Sex addicts "use" some*one* instead of some*thing* (a drug) to deal with stress, or, perhaps more accurately, some*one* (their object of desire) becomes a some*thing* (the drug of choice). Addictive attitudes about sex may derive from general stress as much as from specific sexual tension.

2) Sexual addicts erroneously think that they have a "need" for sex.

U.C.L.A. psychologist Ronald Siegel was widely publicized recently for his theory about what he called "The Fourth Drive." He claimed that all people have four innate drives: hunger, thirst, sex, and the *need* to take drugs. He says that, to get intoxicated "is a basic urge, a need to change feelings, to get release from pain, to entertain ourselves. There would be nothing wrong with this, if the drugs were safe . . . It's like AIDS – we don't treat AIDS by eliminating sex. We make sex safe. The way to handle the drug problem is to make drugs perfectly safe, because we cannot eliminate the Fourth Drive."[4] This supposed *need* to take drugs should be interesting to those who have never used them and have no desire to.

Basic to any addiction is the perception of a need. Such supposed needs are often justified through rationalizations such as the one offered by Professor Siegal. However, as we have noted, arguments supporting the contention that people have specific, genital sexual needs fall as flat as those used to promote the Fourth Drive. When sex is considered a need, it becomes something akin to a god – that to which one turns for sustenance and fulfillment. Yet, sex can no more satisfy true needs than alcohol or drugs.

3) Addictive sexual behaviors create stress.

As we have said in Chapter 1, attitudes based on fulfilling needs interfere with true intimacy and lead to circumstances in which one person takes advantage of another. Sexual behaviors geared toward obsessive self-gratification lead to many kinds of adverse repercussions. To avoid repetition of ideas developed in Chapter 2, we will not review the many consequences of sex without love, premarital sex, and other behaviors that acquiesce to the "needs" misconception and therefore reflect sexually addictive attitudes.

4) Sexually addictive behaviors are inherently selfish and unloving.

One does not "get high" on drugs or alcohol to do someone else a good turn, to help someone else. Rather, one who is inebriated is less capable of kindness and consideration because judgment is impaired. People who are intoxicated tend to drive dangerously, to say things they later regret, and to selfishly attempt to fulfill their "needs." Illicit drug use is associated with divorce, child abuse, crime and much else. Sex based upon perceived "needs" is likewise inherently abusive: using someone to escape or to fulfill a craving.

Professor Siegal, who envisions making drugs and sex "perfectly safe" misses a basic fact. No matter how "safe" drugs are from hepatitis or contaminants, nothing can protect the addict or others from the emotional and social toll of drug use. Drugs by their nature are "unsafe." As the bumper sticker says, "Drug abuse is life abuse." The same can be said about sex based on addictive attitudes. Persons with addictive approaches to sex are grossly insensitive. If there is a need to be fulfilled, or if a person has a need to behave in a particular way, then it makes no difference that someone else is in the way. Like drug addicts and alcoholics, sex addicts may be largely insensitive to the pain they cause in other people's lives.

Promiscuous sex, and sex based on supposed "needs," will never be safe. No matter how "safe" contraceptives and condoms make such activities from "unwanted" pregnancies and sexually transmitted diseases, there is no protection from the many intangible repercussions when one person takes advantage of another.

5) Sexual addicts have codependents.

The classic codependent is the woman who denies that her husband is an alcoholic or drug addict in the face of overwhelming evidence to the contrary. One can consider codependents, or co-addicts, to be addicted to the addict.[5] As the addict responds in an unhealthy way to stress, so also do codependents respond in an unhealthy way to the addict, denying the problem, and thereby making matters worse. Families that respond codependently to the addict are labeled "dysfunctional."

A striking example of sexual codependency appeared in a news item about a sports figure and his new bride. The man had previously divorced his wife, leaving her to raise their two daughters. For four years he intermittently dated a girlfriend, while impregnating a second woman and proposing to a third. Then, while living with the first girlfriend, he called off the wedding to the third. Two weeks later, he proposed to a fourth woman and learned that his third girlfriend was pregnant.[6]

This man's behavior is typical of extreme sex addicts, who appear to exert little control over their sexual urges. Yet his current wife defends his philandering, saying, "Conceiving children is not a sin."[7] Somehow she misses the obvious problem of all those children living in various regions of the country without a full time father. We might wonder how many more children he would have to conceive outside their own marriage before she would consider it a problem. Like alcoholics and drug addicts, many sex addicts are supported in their addiction by codependents.

It is apparent, then, that sexual addiction has much in common with other addictions. We read about notorious cases in newspapers. There is the retired computer programmer with an estimated 3,000 sexual partners in one year. There is the physician who had sex daily with four or five different sexual partners.[8] But sexual addiction occurs far more frequently than in these extreme examples. If a sex addict is anyone who habitually uses sex as a mechanism for coping with stress in the face of serious ramifications, certainly rapists, child molesters, and people who regularly engage prostitutes should be included. Perhaps, too, we should include those who commit "date rape," and those who spend money on a date expecting sexual favors in return.

More important than labeling sex addicts, however, is the identification of those people who are driven by sexually addictive attitudes and therefore on the way to readily identifiable "sexual addiction." Perhaps we should include in this category those who demand sex in a manner that their partners are not comfortable with, as in the cases where women must perform oral or anal sexual acts against their will. Perhaps we should also include those spouses who demand daily sex. A woman patient told me that one day, her despondent husband had pressed her to have sex on three separate occasions. This would seem to be a clear example of a man driven by addictive attitudes. These same sexually addictive attitudes lead some to habitually stimulate themselves over pornography to relieve tension and others to regularly patronize wet tee-shirt or striptease bars.

Sexually addictive attitudes may certainly be considered the underlying drive that leads some couples to risk an "unwanted" pregnancy and surely such attitudes are revealed by those men who run from an unintended pregnancy after it happens, proving that they are unable to accept the consequences of their efforts to fulfill their "needs." Perhaps we should even include those who are unfaithful to their spouses, e.g. the man in *Moonstruck,* or the man who went to Arizona for oral sex.

A popular magazine reported about a famous actor known for his reckless lifestyle.[9] The article reports that he has been involved with "a score of famous beauties . . . The man has also maintained a harem of momentary delights." It goes on to say, "there is an anger in [his] work . . . and a stream of the same negative voltage surges through his private life." The article quotes several of the actor's acquaintances. Says a friend, "Given a choice between [him] and [another actor], women prefer (him) two to one." One actress calls him a "nonstop sex machine." A concerned colleague remarks, "I sense a great sadness in him. Great longing, great pain." And when his girlfriend became pregnant, the article describes him as "not a happy camper," and notes that he continued to see other women. Apparently this "nonstop sex machine" is using sex to cope with his "great pain." He uses women, his "momentary delights," to manage his sadness and loneliness. Is this actor a "superstud" or a sex addict, or are these the same thing? Since addicts often have more than one "drug" of choice, it is no surprise to find that he also smokes cigarettes and abuses cocaine.

While there are those who would question the categorization of some of the above examples as sexual addicts, it is clear that our nation is engulfed in addictive attitudes about sex. A psychiatrist quoted in the *Los Angeles Times* claims that five percent of the general population in one European country are sex addicts.[10] Labeling people as addicts, however, can be more art than science, and thus the exact percentage is debatable. It is clear, however, that the "bachelor party mentality" is widely accepted in this country, especially throughout our male population. Before we as a society can embrace healthy attitudes about sex, before we can improve the increasingly distrustful, resentful and confused atmosphere between the sexes, before we can properly order the goals and priorities related to sex, we must accept the fact that sexually addictive attitudes are widespread, and that the "needs" misconception lies at the heart of them.

Chapter 11

Sexual Orientation
Or Preference

Sexual Continuums

The bumper sticker proclaims "Me So Horny." What are the causes of sexual arousal? Why do some people prefer the opposite sex and some prefer the same sex? Why do some molest children, some have relations with animals, and some expose themselves to strangers? Why are there so many different sexual dispositions and how do they relate to healthy sex? We know that both environmental stimuli, such as pornography, and one's state of mind (loneliness, boredom, anxiety, etc.) influence one's capacity for sexual arousal. But we do not know exactly how these factors interact to create a lustful state.

Sexual orientation is perhaps the most complex subject in the field of sexology. For example, it is well known that men are frequently mistaken for women and vice versa. Female impersonators and unisex clothes often lead to embarrassing double-takes. When I taught sexuality to adolescents, I showed them a particular photograph (frontal view) of a person in unisex clothes. To their frustration, they were unable to identify the person's gender. They did admit, however, that if the person was of the opposite sex, then he or she was reasonably attractive. My wife and I have a running debate about whether one of the actors in a popular television show is male or female. With so much confusion, it should not be surprising that we all have the potential to be aroused by the same sex as well as the opposite sex.

Therefore, it seems reasonable not to segregate people in distinct groups, such as homosexual and heterosexual, but to think of individuals on a continuum of gender orientation. This idea was proposed became popularized nearly 50 years ago[1] and is now generally accepted. The diagram below is a modified version of his proposal:

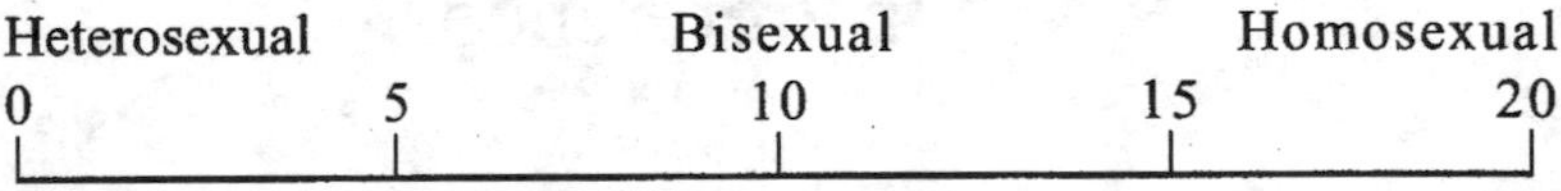

Heterosexual		Bisexual		Homosexual
0	5	10	15	20

Figure 6. Continuum of gender orientation.

Because of the many similarities between the bodies of men and women, it should be expected that no one lies at either extreme (0 or 20), i.e., to be oriented purely toward one sex or the other. Indeed, studies have shown that homosexual fantasies are not uncommon among heterosexual men.[2] While most people are strongly disposed to the heterosexual extreme, there are no pure heterosexuals or pure homosexuals. Even though many heterosexuals lack any memorable homosexual experiences, everyone has some potential (however small) to be aroused by either sex.

Most people are far to the left on this scale. Persons with a predominantly homosexual gender orientation make up a significant minority (perhaps one to three percent[3]) and lie toward the right end of the scale. Relatively few people are considered essentially bisexual (which would include perhaps 8 through 12 on the scale) and others would lie in between bisexuality and either heterosexuality or homosexuality.

We can also examine this continuum with respect to sexual stimulation by children, and again no one fits either extreme. For example, we know that men commonly become aroused while playing innocently with infants and small children. Further, we know that child pornography is a well-established business. Again, because of the great similarity between the bodies of children and adults (on what day does a child physically become an adult?), it is reasonable to assume that all people have some potential for being aroused by children. No one is entirely unable to be aroused by children nor is anyone solely "oriented" toward them.

We may even be aroused by objects that are not explicitly sexual. Some sexuality classes show an unusual video of two hands peeling an orange.[4] It lasts about two minutes and shows nothing more than two hands and an orange, and yet it is an unmistakably sensuous movie. One counselor told me that this film brought back such vivid memories of childhood sexual abuse that she had to leave the room before the video ended. She could not sit through a movie of two hands peeling an orange! Clearly, objects have a potential to arouse. And, again, there is a continuum of predisposition relating to inanimate objects.

The reality is that all people are capable, to varying degrees, of fantasizing about, or responding sexually to, an enormous variety of stimuli. We all have *some* potential, however slight, to be heterosexual, or homosexual, or child molesters, or transvestites, or flashers.

Without getting too carried away with the idea of continuums, we should mention at least one more. There is a continuum of genital versus non-genital orientation. As we mentioned before, women tend to lie toward the non-genital end, to be more non-genitally oriented than men; they tend to crave an embrace more than intercourse. Men tend to be more genitally oriented.

In sum, each person is a unique, evolving individual who can be characterized only within a multidimensional framework, with no person being described adequately by a single term. During adulthood, most changes in sexual orientation are negligible, with little significant change occurring over decades or a life span. Then too, if one is involved in striking behaviors or is exposed to intense environmental stimuli (e.g., pornography), more rapid changes might be expected. To label someone as one specific orientation or another fails to recognize the degree of his or her orientation on many possible continuums. Our society is too rigid in the manner in which it approaches the issue of sexual orientation. Since there are no reasonable alternatives to the terms "heterosexual" and "homosexual," we formally acknowledge their inadequacy but continue to use them for convenience. But in any case, we should be far more concerned about making healthy choices in response to sexual stimuli than about living the "lifestyle" associated with a contrived label with which one "feels comfortable." More important than labels or determining what sorts of things stimulate a person is the question of how best an individual should respond to such stimuli.

Sexual restraint is required from early on in life. Any time a person is attracted to a stranger, some measure of restraint is in order. While we may derive "feelings" from a variety of sexual experiences, acquiescence to most of them would lead to undesirable consequences. Most people have imaginative thoughts, fantasies, and dreams about sex (heterosexual or otherwise), and while these thoughts come naturally, they are not worth becoming preoccupied with.

For example, if a man becomes aroused while entertaining a small child, he has a choice of several options. If he is secure about his own normalcy, he can acknowledge the fact that he has become aroused and can assume that such a reaction is ordinary. In this scenario, he would carry on with the child, allowing the state of arousal to pass, without dwelling on it and without it becoming an issue. This is the healthy option. Alternatively, he can react with abhorrence and guilt and may, from that point on, avoid associating with children for fear of another episode – an unnecessary overreaction. Or, another unhealthy response would be for him to consider this arousal a sign that he has an "orientation" toward children, and that he has a "need" which can only be satisfied by them. This attitude allows for the possibility of making sexual advances toward this child, or others, so as to "explore" his sexuality and learn to "feel more comfortable with who he really is."

Generalizations About Homosexuals

Of all the sexual variations, male homosexuality is the most common, the most studied and the most familiar. Due to lack of space and relative paucity of literature about lesbianism and the other sexual variations, these will not be addressed specifically in this book. Generalization is often useful when discussing these issues, but we stress each individual's unique constitution, and mean to never overlook it.

Until the 1970s, male homosexuality was considered a sexual deviation or perversion. At that time the classification of homosexuality was changed from deviant to normal by political activists in health care professional groups. This decision was not based on new medical or biological knowledge but simply on politics.

Homosexuals have sought to distance themselves from their deviancy by creating the term "gay." This term is meaningless. The excuse for introducing it was that homosexuality supposedly, somehow, denoted more than an orientation and had cultural, social and lifestyle implications; and the term "gay" was meant to reflect this broad view of homosexuality. Thirty years later homosexuals continue to argue about what those implications are, without a clear answer. The only thing "gay" clearly connotes is homosexuality. After 20 years of studying the issue, the only reason I can find that people use the term "gay" is to avoid the term "homosexual." Homosexual leaders argue endlessly among themselves about whether their lifestyle is inherently promiscuous, is inherently associated with anonymous sexual encounters, is only for young men, or is particularly associated with an emphasis on physical appearances, the arts or, more generally, the sensual aspects of life. Because it has no clear definition and because there is no advantage to using it we will decline to use the term "gay" and simply stick with the more credible term "homosexual," however, that is the opposite of what is generally happening in our society.

More and more over the past few decades, homosexuals have increasingly identified themselves as "gay." In today's world there is almost no mention of the word "homosexual" in newspapers, magazines, TV and radio news programs, government publications about homosexuals, school clubs for homosexuals, university programs or activities, private businesses, and even many church-based homosexual ministries. In all of these, people usually use the word "gay" in preference to the word "homosexual." Even medical literature avoids the word "homosexual," and uses the long, rather unmanageable term "men who have sex with men." The widespread use of the term "gay" in preference to the far more appropriate term "homosexual" is evidence of the extraordinary political power of homosexuals in our culture.

Many people today believe that involvement in homosexual behaviors is a healthy adjustment to a predominantly homosexual gender orientation. As a federally financed sex education manual (used to teach teenagers in Dover, New Hampshire) states, "Gay and lesbian adolescents are perfectly *normal* and their sexual attraction to members of the same sex is *healthy*" (emphasis added). In response to the controversy generated by this manual, a program official defended it with the statement, "Our position is consistent with every mainstream medical, psychological, educational and legal group in the country."[5] Though this statement is not true, there is significant support for this position in these fields, in United States government,[6] and within many major religions in our country.[7]

Questions about whether the homosexual behaviors are "normal" and "healthy," whether acquiescence to them maintains the supremacy of love and maintains the correct goal, or is based on falsehoods, and whether homosexual activity is more analogous to addictive sex or healthy sex arouse sharp controversy. Homosexuals commonly exhibit many characteristics associated with unhealthy, addictive sex. While it is an oversimplification to say that all homosexuals are sexual addicts (indeed, some embrace a truly chase approach to sexuality), it is instructive to explore four generalizations under this heading.

1) Many homosexuals participate in extreme forms of behavior.

Genital-anal intercourse is the sex act most often associated with the homosexual activity. It is an accepted norm among essentially all homosexually active men, yet it is unhealthy, it is unnatural, and most people consider it to be offensive.

Anal sex is unhealthy. Aside from sexually transmitted diseases, these acts lead to many other medical conditions including the Gay Bowel Syndrome,[8] hepatitis A,[9] unusual infections of the epididymis,[10] and other disorders of the anus and surrounding muscles such as fissures.[11] Homosexuals who practice anal intercourse are as much as eighty-four times more likely to develop anal cancer than the general population.[12]

Anal sex is unnatural. It obviously is traumatic to the anus, which simply is not made to accommodate the male organ. Not only does the anus have no natural lubrication, but it is clearly the wrong size for genital contact. As evidence of this, consider the difference in size of the speculum and the anoscope. The speculum, which the physician places inside the woman during a gynecologic exam, is roughly the size and shape of the erect male organ. The anoscope, used to examine the anus, is half the diameter of the speculum – more similar in size to an adult forefinger. Any physician who would be foolish enough to attempt to examine a patient's anus with a speculum would quickly realize how unpopular that move would be.

Most people consider anal sex to be offensive. This issue is a matter of opinion and is based primarily on whether or not a person is repulsed by feces. The act of anal sex is analogous to cleaning a soiled bedpan with one's bare hands – direct contact with excrement, or the repository through which it has recently passed – and therefore is reasonably considered offensive. Furthermore, homosexual behaviors often go well beyond anal intercourse. For example, some homosexuals do actually put fingers and hands into each others' anuses ("fisting") and touch each other's anuses with their mouths and tongues ("scat" or "rimming"). No other mammalian species exhibits such "sexual variation." Sporadic examples of homosexual *behaviors* occur throughout the animal kingdom, but *homosexuality* (a fixed, exclusive orientation toward the same sex) has not been observed among higher animals.[13]

The denial associated with these realities is pervasive. People who would naturally cringe when someone passes gas on an elevator dismiss the equivalent reaction of others to stool itself. As with alcoholics who deny that their drinking behavior is a problem, homosexuals and many heterosexuals who accept the homosexual behavior cannot accept the possibility that these acts might be considered offensive. In fact, they say that any sexual behavior a person desires can be normal, and if another finds it repulsive that is because of social conditioning or rigid Puritanism. One can only wonder what sex acts are reasonably considered offensive if genital-anal sex and oral-anal sex are not. The leader of a popular rap group, when asked what he thought was obscene, stated, "When people start cutting heads off of bodies and having sex with corpses, I find that (expletive) obscene. That's in a lot of music. But if you're into it, then that's your thing."[14] It is inevitable that dialogue will deteriorate in this manner, if criticism of any sexual activity is viewed as fear-based intolerance.

Addicts are well known for bizarre behaviors in their desperate efforts to satisfy their needs. Obsession with fulfilling their needs impairs their ability to assess their actions rationally; recall the man who encountered the sixteen year-old prostitute when he had a daughter of the same age. Although physicians perform gloved rectal exams routinely, no sensible person would place an unprotected body part into someone else's anus. Involvement in such strikingly degrading activities requires an intense preoccupation with sexual fantasy. Anal sex is on the level of drinking through one's nose. Given adequate preparation it can be done, but it is hardly nature's way. Anal sex is not normal and healthy – not for homosexuals, heterosexuals or anyone else – nor is there justification for the charge of "homophobia" simply for holding such a reasonable opinion.[15]

2) Most homosexuals are promiscuous.

Promiscuity is a characteristic of the more flagrant heterosexual addicts who fulfill their "needs" compulsively. Homosexuals, too, generally accept promiscuity. Sex researcher Alfred Kinsey considered homosexuality a normal variant. A 1978 study from the Kinsey Institute showed 28 percent of homosexual males having had sexual encounters with one thousand or more partners. In that study, 79 percent of those questioned said that more than half their sex partners were strangers, and only one percent of sexually active men were found to have fewer than five lifetime partners. The authors of the study conceded, "Little credence can be given to the supposition that homosexual men's 'promiscuity' has been overestimated."[16]

In literature on homosexual behavior, monogamous relationships are rarely documented. In his autobiographical book *Straight,* William Aaron wrote, "In the gay life, fidelity is almost impossible. Since part of the compulsion of homosexuality seems to be a need on the part of the homophile to 'absorb' masculinity from his sexual partners, he must be constantly on the lookout for (new partners)."[17] In a study from the Netherlands, 62 percent of those homosexual couples who had stayed together for 6 years were having sex outside the relationship.[18] In another study on long-term male homosexual relationships, two researchers who were homosexuals themselves found that of 156 couples, only seven had maintained sexual fidelity and none had done so for more than five years.[19] Homosexual writers consistently associate homosexuality with promiscuity. *In The Gay Report* we read, "Essential to promiscuous sexuality are two gay male institutions – the one-night stand and the quickie."[20]

A young homosexual man whom I saw in my office for anal problems acknowledged an inability to control his sexual urges. He said that he compulsively stimulated himself and was unable to maintain "safe sex" practices for more than four months at a time because he "needed" these acts to relieve his tension. He added that while anonymous sex was in keeping with the homosexual lifestyle (as he perceived it), monogamy was not. While there is some discussion within the homosexual community about whether theirs is an inherently promiscuous lifestyle, it is clear that the majority of homosexuals are promiscuous.

Unintended pregnancies are generally the most feared risk of sexual interactions. Both homosexual activity and contraceptives sever the association between intimate sex acts and the risk of procreation, thereby "freeing" people to fulfill their needs promiscuously. In this way, both foster the most important misconception about sexuality: that people cannot control their sexual desires. As we indicated before, this is the fallacy which lies at the heart of addictive and abusive attitudes about sex, and which changes the goals of sexual interactions. Promiscuous and anonymous sex are unencumbered by intentions to enrich relationships.

3) Most homosexuals are unable to accept abstinence as a primary
   means of HIV disease prevention.

Addicts are compelled to fulfill their needs and they display an
abnormal lack of concern about the risks associated with "using."
Addicts are incapable of abstinence, even when threatened by conspicuous dangers. The homosexual community's response to HIV
disease has clearly demonstrated the general inability to abstain
from genital sex.

Promotion of abstinence in and of itself will not end the crisis of
HIV disease because our society is plagued with addictive attitudes
about sexuality, and teaching abstinence to addicts is not generally
effective. One would, however, expect that abstinence would be the
first thought of anyone at risk for such a devastating disease as
AIDS. Yet, aside from requests for research money, what we hear
from homosexual leaders is the promotion of condoms and the de-
nouncement of abstinence as an assault on their lifestyle, with surprisingly few voices within the homosexual community willing to
question the well-defined homosexual agenda.

A number of studies cited in Chapter 5 have established that insufficient behavioral change has occurred among mature, well-
educated homosexual men, and the inability of those who do change
to sustain the new mode. The following examples illustrate the typical homosexual community's inability to consider abstinence in the
face of HIV disease.

In 1990, public radio carried a panel discussion of AIDS film
producers. On the issue of disclosure, the question was: should a
man tell his lover that he has tested positive for HIV? Not one person on the entire panel offered an answer! The only comment made
was that, whether or not the man disclosed his status, he should at
least be sure to use a condom. No one objected! No one pointed out
that such a disclosure is a basic responsibility each of us has to a
fellow human being!

Also in 1990, in the middle of a worldwide HIV epidemic spread
by promiscuous sex, *Newsweek* reported on a "pro-sex" campaign
starting among homosexuals – "Just Say Yes" to promiscuity![21] In
1993, the *Los Angeles Times* reported with bewilderment, "For rea-

sons that no one really understands, a generation of young homosexual men . . . seem to have turned away from the fundamentals of
safe sex. They . . . appear to have abandoned caution, acting as if a
decade of sexual education about AIDS had never taken place."[22] In
an article on the "alarming increase in high-risk sexual behavior
among young gay males," another *Times* article quotes an expert:
"The figures (of HIV-positivity) are high, very high, especially if we
consider that these young men have become sexually active in an
era in which massive effort was exerted to increase awareness of
HIV risk behaviors and to promote safer sex."[23] More recently,
newspapers have carried reports of an "explosion" of Circuit parties
of promiscuous sex and drugs involving tens of thousands of homosexual men in their 30s.[24]

The homosexual community's response to HIV disease has been
irrational and, as the statistics now tell, tragic. In their vehement rejection of abstinence, homosexuals have shown how far they will
compromise on the priority of lovingly protecting each other, and as
a result they have brought upon themselves untold amounts of unnecessary anguish. After over a decade of hearing the "safer sex"
message throughout the homosexual population, it remains the highest risk group for newly acquired HIV infection.

Perhaps the only thing more appalling than our government's
lack of response to the HIV crisis is the need for such a response. In
a society with healthy, nonaddictive attitudes toward sex, one would
expect a fatal STD to cause immediate, widespread endorsement of
abstinence, and a dramatic change in behaviors. The great surprise is
that HIV disease did not go away by itself following the early an-
nouncements of how it is transmitted. It seems only sensible that
those at highest risk for it would have promptly adopted the one behavioral change that would have fully protected them from it. The
lack of such a response is further evidence of the addictive attitudes
of our society in general, and of homosexuals in particular.

Whether one teaches abstinence or condom use, if we rely solely
on educational efforts to stop HIV disease, we make the presump-
tion that people care about each other; we presume that educated
people will protect one another. The catch is that addictive attitudes
are rampant in our society; and addicts, because of their obsession

with their own *needs,* typically fail to protect themselves let alone others. Ironically, education about condoms and outercourse (intimate sexual activity without genital-genital contact) actually fosters addictive attitudes about sexuality, the same attitudes which have made such educational efforts ineffective.

4) The homosexual lifestyle rejects the nuclear family.

The standard social unit of all cultures has been based on heterosexual union. The homosexual lifestyle choice directly dissociates one from this basis. Although the nuclear family has been subject to various extensions in the course of history, it has been the obvious natural foundation for human community life. The universal standard has been that children are raised by their biological parents. The common man of past societies has been consistently committed to this standard, and today it remains the "lifestyle" to which the vast majority of people aspire.

Homosexuals obviously cannot establish a traditional family and, like other addicts, they display unreasonable indifference this. Alcoholics, workaholics, and drug addicts, for example, commonly give up their families to maintain their addiction. So too, many a marriage has ended over heterosexual indiscretions of an addictive nature. In rare instances, homosexual make strenuous attempts to mimic the nuclear family (e.g., living with a male partner while attempting to impregnate a lesbian). But these attempts to circumvent nature are simply frustrated forms of the real thing.

A final comment on this issue applies to sexual variations in general. Studies have consistently shown a striking preponderance of males among all forms of sexual addictions: heterosexual addicts, sexually active homosexuals, child molesters, transvestites exhibitionists, transsexuals etc. This is as might be expected, as it directly coincides with the concept that males, especially, have specific genital needs.

In the final analysis, the homosexual behavior is not a normal, healthy adjustment to a predominantly homosexual inclination. Many people arbitrarily sanction some variant behaviors as "alternative lifestyles" while other variations, such as fetishes, are rebuked as abnormal. Due to the inexact nature of the term *addict,* labeling all sexually active homosexuals as sexual addicts is inappropriate. However, one can say that addictive attitudes are the rule among sexually active homosexuals and among persons actively involved in other deviations from the heterosexual standard.

Homosexuals need not come "out of the closet," but the issue of sexual orientation must. For this to happen, we must recognize the inadequacy of terms like "homosexual" and "heterosexual" and redirect our thinking. Each person has a variable and unique potential toward all manner of sexual variations, but relatively few succumb to active involvement like homosexual promiscuity. Terms such as "homosexual" or "transvestite" are artificially restrictive labels applied to individuals who dwell on certain, (e.g., homosexual) thoughts, fantasies, or dreams which others reject. Even men with well established heterosexual identities may experience homosexual dreams and find these dreams, like nightmares or other strange dreams, unrewarding and perhaps disagreeable but within the natural order.

Further, not all sexual deviates fall under familiar labels. In a letter to an advice columnist, a woman described her situation.

> "I think I'm in love with my daughter's boyfriend. I just turned 40, and 'Eric' is 18. He doesn't have the slightest idea that I feel this way and, of course, I'd never tell him. I have wild fantasies about this young boy. . . . I still love my husband, but our lovemaking has become boring and tiresome. I get through it by substituting Eric. . . . As if this isn't bad enough, I'm envious of my daughter. I'm hoping and praying that she marries Eric because it would break my heart if I couldn't see him anymore."[25]

While no particular label fits this woman, she is developing deviant fantasies which may lead to great harm for herself or others. The problem is not that she has had an unusual thought, dream, fantasy, or desire, but that her response to it has gotten out of hand. She may feel content with her "orientation" toward this boy, but to anyone else, it is evident that she has a serious problem.

Homosexual activists claim that they do not have a problem because they "feel comfortable" with themselves. But feeling comfortable with oneself, or being ego-syntonic, is not a valid measure of health. For example, when I confronted a morbidly obese patient about her weight problem, she denied that she had a problem because she "felt comfortable" with herself. In fact, she had two serious problems: her morbid obesity and her denial of her obesity. Or take the case of the woman who has an IUD placed without being told of its clear abortifacient potential. If she considers abortion wrong and is unaware that the IUD within her could induce one, then she might "feel comfortable" with using one, although by her own criteria she should not. A person's comfort level may reflect defense mechanisms or ignorance more than anything else. To accept a standard of "feeling comfortable" with oneself ignores the often unreliable nature of such feelings.

To assign people to a specific orientation may seem a benign simplification, but it changes the fundamental manner in which we approach the issue of sexual orientation. All people are challenged by undesirable stimuli and must decide how best to respond to them. It is said that homosexuals need to "come to terms with their orientation," but the more viable approach is for all of us to learn to respond to sexual stimuli in healthy ways – ways that will lead not to uneasiness and suffering but to contentment and joy for ourselves and those we love. People should not so much "find themselves" in a category with a contrived label, as help themselves by shaping their own future.

Like addicts in general, some heterosexual addicts, homosexuals, pedophiles, etc., will be incapable of simply replacing unhealthy responses to stimuli with healthy ones. Like others suffering from significant mental health problems, these people face great challenges and must be supported in developing an intensive, multifaceted individualized approach to treatment. One does not choose to be a homosexual any more than one chooses to be obsessive-compulsive. Our society must move beyond the issue of tolerance (no homosexual person is "bad") and begin to focus on offering genuine support to those who struggle with their sexual identity.

The presence of a variant sexual tendency should always stimulate a search for underlying sources of stress and insecurity. As in the approach to alcoholism the goal should be not so much to cure the condition, as to treat the underlying problems to which this condition is a response.

As mentioned previously, the treatment of established heterosexual addicts and sexual variants may involve psychological counseling, stress management, and possibly group therapy sessions for the addict, or counseling for the people most influential in the addict's life. It may also involve modifying the person's environment, treating underlying medical and mental disorders, and spiritual direction. In the past, attempts to treat homosexuals often met with failure as a result of grossly misdirected therapy (such as aversion techniques), but an ever-expanding contingent of ex-homosexuals and ex-homosexuals attest to the validity of modern approaches. Due to the anonymous nature of the many self-help programs like Homosexuals Anonymous, statistical verification of their effectiveness is difficult. However, the proliferation of ex-homosexual ministries suggests the magnitude of this population, as does scientific literature.[26] Exodus International, one of the largest of these organizations, claims to receive 500 calls each month and to have 6,000 persons attend its 90 ministries in the U.S.

Although such programs have benefited many patients, as with other addictive disorders, one would expect that even comprehensive treatment plans for motivated patients will not be uniformly successful. Further, some patients who do resolve their underlying developmental deficits may continue to have deviant thoughts. Though such thoughts may linger, the response to them must be consistent. Like the woman who is obsessed with her daughter's boyfriend, they need to recognize that it is unhealthy to act on deviant thoughts. If that woman's daughter marries "Eric," the mother may be burdened with a lifelong obsession. Whether or not she develops a successful treatment plan, she should not act on her fantasy. Analogously, no matter how persistent or consummate their deviant orientation, homosexuals must refrain from intimate homosexual activities, particularly unnatural sex acts. Homosexual acts not only conflict with human nature but sustain an underlying deviant orientation. All people, including homosexuals, must constantly strive to integrate their sexuality into relationships only in healthy, fulfilling ways.

Variant sexual behavior should be treated in the same manner as drunk driving. Both are indicators of an underlying problem which should be addressed. The primary goal of treating the sexually disoriented is to resolve underlying causal factors. Such intervention will commonly induce a shift along the relevant continuum toward normalcy. Nevertheless, while it would be expected that this shift will be conclusive for some, for others it will be minimal. In any case, the goal is not so much to change the person's label as it is to address underlying issues and to discontinue behaviors which sustain deviant orientations,

Of note, the most comprehensive clinical investigation of female homosexuality was undertaken by a self-described "liberal and liberated woman" psychiatrist, Dr. Elaine Siegel, who at the time considered homosexuality and homosexual acts to be normal variants. Dr. Siegel found to her surprise that through exploration of the primary issues in these women's lives, over half of her patients converted to being "fully heterosexual."[28]

There is much discussion today about a possible hereditary origin to homosexuality, an idea which seems to conflict with the above presentation. Many researchers seek to prove that homosexuality is based primarily on a person's genetic make-up. A recent, exhaustive, scholarly analysis of the subject concluded, "Critical review shows the evidence favoring a biologic (genetic) theory to be lacking."[29] The mainstream press is rather uniformly uncritical of the studies that claim to prove a biological basis for homosexuality and ignores scientific documentation to the contrary, such as this analysis. This will be discussed more in the next chapter, but as one example, the fact is often ignored that most twin studies on the subject have been done on twins who were raised together.[30] Obviously, it is most difficult to distinguish between environmental and genetic influences among children who have both in common. The genetic theory also fails to account for the many established homosexuals who subsequently convert to a heterosexual orientation. People's chromosomes do not change in mid-life.

Evolutionary theory offers another reason to question a significant genetic basis for homosexuality since it would predict natural selection against a predominantly homosexual gender orientation. This issue is not raised in an attempt to further either side of the controversy over evolutionary theory. It is raised because my undergraduate training in evolutionary biology as applied to behavior has provided a perspective on the possible origins of homosexuality not often considered. Natural pressures discriminate against behaviors that reduce one's biological fitness (that is, one's ability to produce viable offspring). Selection pressures encourage the survival of the fittest, which is to say that they select adaptations, including behavioral adaptations, directed toward successful reproduction and nurturing. Homosexual behaviors, in the most direct way, abandon that goal; therefore, from a biological standpoint, they are highly undesirable. "Homosexuality," as *Newsweek* puts it, "is hard to explain as a biological adaptation."[31]

It is inconsistent to endorse homosexuality as an acceptable genetic variant while at the same time discrediting transsexuality, voyeurism, pedophilia, transvestitism, and bestiality. The most plausible explanation for the development of any of these variations from the norm is a troubled childhood, not a genetic predisposition.[32]

Whether there is a variable, lesser, genetic component to a predominance of variant sexual yearnings is unknown. In truth, all attitudes and behaviors have some genetic component. Everything from the color shirt one chooses to wear to the manner in which one drives a car are manifestations of both one's "nature" (genes) and "nurture" (environment). As with alcoholism, anxiety disorders, and any other form of mental illness, the existence of a minor genetic component to sexual variations would not be a surprise, but the relationship between such a vague predisposition and environmental factors will likely remain unclear. Perhaps sexual variations are but one possible expression of a genetic proclivity. Moreover, if a significant genetic factor exists, it does not alter the responsibility of each person to cope with aberrant predispositions in healthy ways.

Chapter 12

Sexual Codependency vs. Healthy Responses to Sexual Addiction

Where there are addicts (dependents), there are codependents – people who respond to an addict in unhealthy ways in an effort to avoid "rocking the boat," to remain in the addict's good graces, or to cover up the addiction. Because codependents feel a need for the addict or for the relationship, they accept the stress created by the addict's abnormal behavior.

Codependent individuals are thought to lack self-understanding and self-love. Due to their insecurities and relative inability to nurture and control themselves, they often make excessive attempts to nurture and control others. They have an inordinate desire to feel needed while at the same time feeling particularly needful. Both dependency and codependency are unhealthy and lead to negative experiences.

Two specific problems related to sexual codependency are of particular importance: 1) women's codependent responses to male heterosexual addiction and 2) the generally codependent attitude of our society toward sexual addiction.

1) Women's Codependent Response to Male Heterosexual Addiction.

The natural response of a woman to a man who is under the false impression that he has specific sexual needs should be concern and assertive confrontation. In this way she helps the man recognize his mistaken attitudes and change them. Frequently, however, women reinforce sexually addictive attitudes by responding to them in non-assertive ways. Due to sometimes real and sometimes imagined insecurities, many women tolerate unreasonable demands by men. "Without him [her boyfriend] I can't go on," sings Diana Ross in the Motown classic *Back in Your Arms Again.* A sexually codependent woman cannot live without a man.

At times, sexually codependent responses are readily apparent: for example, women who feign climaxing so that men may gloat over their sexual prowess, or women who "give up control of their bodies" to men, or women who, in their insecurity, take the lead in initiating a premarital sexual relationship.

Another example is the woman who told me that it is "unnatural" for women to abstain from sexual intercourse with their boyfriends. Her comment, no doubt, is music to the ears of irresponsible men. Irrational attitudes such as this are possible only in a world of easily available contraception and abortion. Without contraception, any woman who had sex with every boyfriend would soon develop a complicated reproductive history. The idea that premarital sex is natural leads one to the untenable position that *artificial* contraception allows sex to be more *natural* – that artificial contraception has finally delivered mankind from thousands of years of unnaturalism.

Another patient told me about her mother who maintained that premarital sex was natural because it has been accepted by numerous indigenous cultures. This idea comes primarily from the work of Margaret Mead[1] who depicted the people of Samoa as sexual libertines who accepted all forms of indiscriminate sex without question or reservation. Mead's work, however, has been thoroughly discredited.[2] Anthropological data, in fact, supports just the opposite conclusion: that cultures of all varieties have clearly defined, restrictive customs related to sexual activity. Sex is naturally associated with procreation and the profound implications of this association have not been lost on any known civilization. Civilizations strive for ordered coexistence, and since illegitimacy invariably creates disorder, civilizations disparage illegitimacy.

The "I do's" of the marriage vow have traditionally implied "I do agree to have sex with you" and "I do agree to raise children with you." They are *the* consent for sexual intercourse and procreation. Modern "progressive" societies, while attempting to break free of these implications, have witnessed the strangest sorts of discussions – attempts against all hope to define precisely when premarital sex is "consensual" and exactly what constitutes "date rape." These discussions, which inevitably fall into the realm of the absurd, are irrelevant when the marriage vows are given their due and when sexual intercourse retains its natural status as the "marital act."

Other examples of codependent attitudes are more subtle. One of the most pervasive indications is the preoccupation of so many women with appearance, and the inordinate amount of time, money and effort they spend making themselves into "hot babes" or "lookers." In a letter to a newspaper, one woman voiced her complaint:

> "In the '50s when I was first married, my husband wanted me to dye my hair and wear padded bras. OK, I thought, I am a modern woman, I am not a prude. I'll still be the same person underneath; I won't suddenly turn into a hussy (my notion of people who dyed their hair). And so I did it. And sure enough, I didn't turn into a hussy. But I was still wrong. I didn't remain the same person underneath. I had denied a fundamental part of myself – the very genes I was born with. My accommodations were mild compared to today's embrace of cosmetic surgery. What can be said of the self-esteem of someone who will submit to the risks, discomfort and cost of a surgeon's knife to remove some wrinkles? It is denial pure and simple. An investment in illusion instead of truth."[3]

Women, as a group, and for a variety of reasons, make more effort to be attractive to men than men make to be attractive to women. Women's fashions are conspicuously more sexually suggestive and it is women alone who routinely spend hours "dolling them-selves up." Many women accentuate their sex appeal because they feel that they *need* men. Many insecure women, aware that many men believe they "need" sex, use physical attractiveness to attract men and to keep them happy.

Unusual rationales have been developed to obscure reality. For example, some women claim that they dress for other women. Or, as in the case of the former congressional staff member who was upset over her boss "staring at (her) cleavage," people scorn the notion that women's fashions encourage men to have "one thing on their minds." Many women respond that they simply enjoy getting dressed up and looking their best – a legitimate response on the part of many, but self-deception on the part of many others.

Though it is easy to criticize women who fall into codependent attitudes, it is difficult to dismiss entirely the notion that many women must depend on men. Because of their natural childbearing and breastfeeding roles, many women find themselves in a depend-ent and vulnerable state. They must rely, to some degree, on the magnanimity of their men. Thus, women may be anxious for the security promised by committed men, and become overly dependent or "needful." For these women, however, it is especially important to respond in healthy ways to sexually addictive attitudes so as not to fulfill their codependent potential.

Sadly, women as a group are headed in the wrong direction. Not only are sexually codependent attitudes common among married women, but they are becoming more common among single women and even teenagers. Teenagers are having premarital sex earlier and more frequently than ever before. A teenaged patient explained to me that when she had sex with her boyfriend, all of her many prob-lems disappeared. She made no effort to prevent pregnancy or dis-ease because, after a three-week relationship, they were "in love" and nothing could go wrong. The reality is that this girl was in-volved in a disturbingly abusive, superficial relationship – one that a pregnancy would clearly have ended. This is a typical codependent fantasy, the distorted view that having a man will solve all of a woman's problems.

Sexual addiction and sexual codependency readily sustain each other. For example, a male patient recently asked me what he should do when a woman is the aggressor in initiating sexual relations with him. We discussed what would happen if he declined the invitation. One thing is certain: he would learn more about the woman by doing so. By not responding to her sexual advances, and thereby avoiding an artificially intimate relationship, he would see her in a more realistic context, insecurities and all.

There is no excuse for men who abuse women. But women should not underestimate the pressures men are under today (especially from pornography) which encourage them to develop and maintain addictive attitudes. Men with such attitudes cannot be expected to protect women, and women should not encourage such attitudes by codependent responses.

Sexual codependency may be as common among women as sexual addiction is among men. And as much as men are inundated with messages to "go for it," women are inundated with messages that encourage unhealthy responses to men's mistaken attitudes. Like sexual addict "superstuds," there is a deep-rooted cultural thread of admiration for those who demonstrate overt sexually codependent traits. After divorcing her sixth husband, a movie star who is adored in great part for her glamour and surgically assisted beauty said, "I really am an addictive personality! – I suppose I will, someday, marry once more."[4] She is ready and willing to profess her need for men.

Sexually codependent attitudes among women have become more prevalent during the sexual revolution. As evidence of this consider the fact that more women than ever are doing more extreme things to their bodies to gain the attention of men; for example, plastic surgery and expensive, time-consuming hair treatments. Some women do such things for fun, for cultural appeal, or to look good for themselves, but, certainly, many women's primary motive is sex appeal. As in the case of other types of addictions, addressing the issue of codependency is critical to loosening the grip of sexual addiction on affected men.

2) Codependent Attitudes of Society Toward Sexual Variations.

Tolerance is the politically correct stance in a society that considers freedom its highest priority. However, tolerance of unhealthy behavior may be extremely dangerous. The idea that "anything goes" is less a sign of societal tolerance than it is the denial associated with codependency. A compassionate person does not deny or ignore another person's problem. A compassionate society should not deny that heterosexual addiction and sexual variations are problems.

Because of the priority so many in our society give to unrestricted sex, all forms of sexual expression are considered normal. Yet, acceptance of abnormal as normal is a fundamental characteristic of codependency. The husband of the alcoholic says, "She's just a social drinker"; the wife of the cocaine addict says, "He's just stressed about his job"; the girlfriend of the heterosexual addict says, "He reads so much porn because boys will be boys." None of them accepts the reality that the addict's behavior is abnormal.

The concept of tolerance toward all sexual behaviors rests on the assumption not only that everyone has specific sexual needs, but also that these needs are unique from individual to individual. Therefore, some people accept any kind of behavior toward which a person feels compelled as normal and healthy for that individual.

But such ready acceptance of all forms of sexual expression only sets the stage for conflict between the priorities of freedom and love. The ultimate in love is nirvana. Unlimited freedom is anarchy. For example, if there were no traffic regulations, anarchy would prevail and result in a disastrous increase in traffic accidents. Restrictions are necessary to insure social order.

In addition to situations in which many women have come to accept addictive attitudes among men, there are other areas in which sexually addictive approaches to sex have found acceptance and now threaten our world with suffering:

- Extramarital Affairs – Mary Calderone is the past President of Planned Parenthood and first Executive Director and Founder of SIECUS (Sexuality Information and Education Council of the United States is a most influential organization dedicated to introducing compulsory sex education for school children). Calderone has said, "An extramarital affair that's really solid might have very good results."[5] Naturally, she fails to cite any studies to support such a claim.

• Rape – Sexologist Alfred Kinsey, in his scientifically flawed yet influential *The Male Report,* wrote, "Many small girls reflect the public hysteria over the prospect of 'being touched' by a strange person; and many a child, who has no idea at all of the mechanics of intercourse, interprets affection and simple caressing, from anyone except her own parents as attempts at rape. In consequence, not a few older men serve time in penal institutions for attempting to engage in a sexual act which at their age would not interest most of them . . ."[6] He seemed unconcerned about why these "strange" men were touching small girls in the first place.

• Homosexuals – If the homosexual lifestyle is a serious problem – call it sexual addiction, call it severe psychosexual dysfunction, call it what you will – then the acceptance of it by a large segment of our society as normal and healthy is nothing more than societal codependence. Further, homosexuals have organized into a socio-political entity, the prime objective of which is to legitimize their sexual preferences. The ability of addicts to manipulate is well known, and so it is not surprising that homosexuals have had great success in influencing laws, the media, schools, and public opinion.

   For example, a review of the last five year's coverage of homosexuality in the *Los Angeles Times* demonstrates that despite the lack of consensus among researchers, the *Times* considers it a foregone conclusion that homosexuality is genetically determined. In one front page article,[7] the *Times* reported a study which showed a "strong genetic component" to lesbianism. The article claimed that, "Previous studies of male homosexuals have obtained the same result, but those studies have been highly criticized because the groups examined did not include women." No other reason is given as to why the previous reports were criticized, as if to imply that they were not "highly criticized" for poor study design or other considerations. Another front page article[8] describes how researchers are *"racing* to identify the specific gene from among the 100 or more genes located" (emphasis added) on a part of the X chromosome that one study suggested might cause homosexuality. There is, of course, little to report on the "race" six years later. Another *Times* report[9] of a twin study says, "But the fact that not all of the identical twins are gay, (the researchers) caution, indicates that other factors, such as exposure to hormones or trauma in the womb or some unknown factor in the everyday environment, are necessary for a genetic predisposition to homosexuality to be manifested." The article fails to mention that much of the scientific world considers the unknown factor that is part of the everyday environment" to be a serious breakdown in the parent/child bond. Another article summarizes the research to date as, "The *mounting* evidence of a biological link to homosexuality"[10] (emphasis added), and yet the *Times* failed to cover the comprehensive, scientific review article mentioned earlier which was published the following year and found the evidence not to be "mounting" but rather to be "lacking."

As an example of the influence of homosexual sociopolitical power in another realm, consider the many school programs geared toward promotion and tolerance of homosexual activity (such as Project 10 in the Los Angeles Unified School District). These programs often operate despite intense pressure from parent groups. In New York City, a "multicultural" curriculum was introduced which promoted homosexuality to small children, including a text called "Heather has Two Mommies." The program was removed from schools only after the superintendent was fired for steadfastly acting against the wishes of parents – he suspended an entire neighborhood school board for rejecting the curriculum.[11]

- Pedophilia (sexual attraction to children), Exhibitionism, Fetisheism, Sexual Sadism and Other Sexual Disorders – The latest version of the bible of the American Psychiatric Association, the *Diagnostic and Statistical Manual of Mental Disorders, Fourth Edition (DSM IV),* includes an extraordinary revision of the diagnostic criteria for these disorders.[12] The prior edition, *DSM III Revised* (1987),[13] stated that each disorder was characterized most essentially by two criteria. First, that the person had recurrent sexual urges and fantasies involving aberrant activities and second, that the person acted on these urges or was distressed by them. In the 1994 version, the second criterion was altered in a dramatic way. It is now deemed by the most prestigious mental health organization in the land that it is no longer necessarily a disorder if one acts on such urges but only if such actions cause "distress or impairment in social, occupational, or other important areas of functioning." In other words, a person who molests a child does not have a problem unless he or she feels bad about doing it or it leads to other untoward consequences. The truth, of course, is exactly the opposite: the person who feels bad about molesting a child, exposing himself or herself, or having sex with an inanimate object is far healthier than one who does not.

It is interesting to note that this precisely mirrors the changes that have occurred in this manual with respect to homosexuality. In 1968 *(DSM-II)* homosexuality was listed first among "sexual deviations."[14] In 1980 *(DSMIII)* homosexuality was moved to the end of that section and only considered pathological if it was "a persistent source of distress."[15] In the 1987 version *(DSM III Revised)* homosexuality is nowhere to be found. In nineteen years, without any scientific basis for change, homosexuality went from being the foremost sexual deviation to being a normal variant so unremarkable as to be not worth mentioning. And now many other deviations are being handled in the same manner.

One common justification for tolerance of sexual variations is the existence of such variations in other cultures of the world. This justification ignores the fact that individual societies have practiced everything from cannibalism to infanticide, and rare (and of course short-lived) societies have even prohibited sexual relations *within* marriage. But the fact that oddities exist in some cultures does not justify their acceptance within our own.

Another justification for tolerance of sexual conduct is that "people should be able to do what they want in the privacy of their own homes." This is another example of our societal fixation on sex, the special rules we apply only to sexual matters. If a neighbor is physically abusing his wife, or if his wife is an alcoholic, do we shrug our shoulders and say that it's none of our affair because it's happening inside their home? Such a position demands either apathy ("I don't care what my neighbor does in his own home" may really mean "I don't care about my neighbor") or a double standard ("Homosexual behavior is not acceptable for my children, but is acceptable for my neighbor's children or for my neighbor"). While it is no one's duty to meddle in every affair of one's neighbor, it is surely everyone's responsibility to identify unhealthy behaviors when, by so doing, someone may benefit. This brings to mind the following passage from M. Scott Peck's best-selling *The Road Less Traveled*:

> The truly loving person, valuing the uniqueness and differentness of his or her beloved, will be reluctant indeed to assume, "I am right, you are wrong; I know better than you what is good for you." But the reality of life is such that at times one person does know better than the other what is good for the other, and in actuality is in a position of superior knowledge or wisdom in regard to the matter at hand. Under these circumstances the wiser of the two does in fact have an obligation out of loving concern for the spiritual growth of the other to confront the other with the problem. The loving person, therefore, is frequently in a dilemma, caught between a loving respect for the beloved's own path in life and a responsibility to exercise loving leadership when the beloved appears to need such leadership.[16]

Sexual codependency is an unhealthy response to sexual addiction. At both the individual and societal level, acceptance of sexual codependency denies the existence of the basic problem. The first step toward a healthy response is to recognize sexually addictive attitudes and accept that they are not normal. Then comes the task of helping those most taken by these attitudes to realize that they have a problem. Our society must stop glorifying or even tolerating such attitudes. A common advertising message in our culture is that real men smoke, drink, and have sex with lots of women. No, that is what addicts do. In times past, we tended to ignore the effects of alcohol and drugs but now we are actively campaigning against these addictions. We are a long way from recognizing the prevalence of sexually addictive attitudes and behaviors and their destructive impact, but when we do, we can begin to move against them, too.

We can no longer afford to ignore the prevalence of sexually addictive and codependent attitudes in our society nor the many factors that promote these attitudes. Premarital sex, pornography, immodest fashions, self-stimulation, artificial contraception, sterilization, homosexuality, and abortion have all become widely accepted. As we have pointed out, each of these in its own way reinforces the "needs" misconception, and enables addicts and codependents to continue their dysfunctional, unhealthy approach to sex.

Addictive attitudes are the greater problem but we must also consider how best to help those individuals who are so swept up by these attitudes as to rightfully be labeled sexual addicts. These people are unable to control their desires for pornography, promiscuity, self-stimulation, sex with prostitutes, or sex with unwilling partners, including children. As mentioned before, typically, they face enormous challenges but there are many reasons for hope. First, as with other addictions, the simple admission on the part of the addict that he has a problem puts him way ahead of the game. Second, because of the prevalence of sexual addiction, the addict can take comfort in knowing that many others face the same challenges. Third, there is no limit as to how much any one of us can improve ourselves, how much more we can truly love ourselves by doing the right thing and acting in good character. All addicts should take heart in knowing that they *have* the ability to find more genuine sources of consolation, fulfillment, and psycho-spiritual sustenance than their behavior of choice.

Once an addict has made the first step of admitting his problem to himself he should find a confidant to confess his mistakes to on an ongoing basis – someone to whom he is accountable but who personifies acceptance and forgiveness. Some consider it unlikely if not impossible for any true addict to achieve control without help from others. The first behaviors to control are the most serious or life threatening, such as indiscriminate sexual intercourse. As control is achieved, lesser acts should be addressed. The final hurdles are likely the most common: to remove pornography from one's environment and to restrain completely from self-stimulation. The Resource section lists several programs available to sexual addicts.

It is common for addicts and codependents to "hit rock bottom" – to reach an extraordinary level of desperation – before they are willing to accept that they have a problem and commence recovery. Our society, too, will begin to seriously question its addictive and codependent approaches to sex only when it is desperate enough, when it is close enough to "rock bottom." We may not be there yet. Even with AIDS, herpes, rampant divorce, and increasing rape, child molestation and "unwanted" pregnancies we may not yet be desperate enough. But, like many addicts, our nation may eventually reach a breaking point, and, at that time, an approach that emphasizes love over freedom and "needs" will likely attract a wider audience than ever. As a *Wall Street Journal* article entitled "The Joy of What?" states, "If we have just lived through 25 years of the Sexual Revolution, it looks as if a lot of people might be ready for the Counter Revolution."[17]

Perhaps the counterrevolution will occur when we begin to address prevalent sexually addictive and codependent attitudes, when we begin to accept that there is nothing considerate about denying other people's problems. Without judging people, or being disrespectful, we should feel as free to express concern over others' sexual failings as we are about their drug abuse. Many fine people are addicted to alcohol, food, or cigarettes, or to sex. The question is not who has made the most mistakes, but rather how each individual and married couple can move closer toward Good Sex, the subject of our next chapter.

Chapter 13

Good Sex – The Higher Level

We have given much attention to the bleaker side of sex. Now let us turn our attention to the potential that each of us has for developing healthy attitudes toward sex, and the extraordinary nature of interactions that may result from such attitudes. The philosopher Dietrich von Hildebrand wrote that the love between man and woman is "the deepest source of happiness in human life," and he counsels that "we must understand that the true antithesis to Victorian prudery is a reverent attitude toward sex, seeing in it something great, deep, and mysterious."[1]

How to ensure that sex becomes something great – a part of the celebration of life – is our major objective in this chapter. Sexual experiences that are vested with love enrich and strengthen relationships. They are sex that is free from emotional turmoil, free from fear of "unwanted" pregnancies and diseases, free from enslaving, addictive attitudes and the mindless pursuit of self-gratification. They are, for the most part, one positive experience after another. Good sex is possible without achieving the ultimate climax, or fulfilling one's wildest fantasies. While truly breathtaking physical pleasures are common to good sex, they are not the primary or essential goal. Priorities such as pleasure, procreation, and fun are entirely valid, but with good sex, the *primary* focus is on bringing the couple closer together.

Good sex is without significant frustration. In fact, frustration may act as an indicator of how unhealthy one's attitudes are about sex. Sexual frustration is a common complaint among my patients. While examining men for hernias, I often ask if they have any problems related with the genital area. A surprising number respond, "No, I just don't get enough (sex)." Struggle and frustration burden relationships and often result from emphasizing contrived needs, because some of these needs are invariably left unmet. Among people with realistic expectations and goals, however, frustrations are lessened and pass more easily, without being dwelt upon.

Healthy sex may not be as glamorous and glorious as the fantasies portrayed in pornography. Not surprisingly, the most spectacular thing about it is the depth of the interpersonal interaction underlying it. Because sex is only one aspect of a relationship, its greatest beauty lies in the way it reflects and contributes to the total relationship.

Because sexual intercourse is "the marital act," it is symbolic of the oath made between a man and woman on their wedding day. From this perspective, each act of sexual intercourse is a "renewal of the couple's own marriage covenant, a symbol of their commitment of marital love."[2] It has the potential to be far more than a mutually pleasurable experience, or an attempt to procreate. Each individual act says symbolically "I do!"

While it is easy to write about healthy sex in general terms, my attempts to describe its specifics fill me with a sense of inadequacy. These limitations bring to mind an analogy involving a weekend drive through scenic countryside. As a physician, I feel more comfortable discussing rules of the road and maps than I do attempting to wax poetic about scenery. While I may confidently describe guidelines for achieving good sex, I cannot hope to describe the scenery of each unique relationship,

It is obvious that one has achieved good sex when the goal of enriching a relationship is maintained, and all lesser goals are achieved. But there are some reasonable (if lesser) limits for good sex. Healthy sex can exist as long as the primary goal is achieved, regardless of whether or not all of its lesser goals are achieved. For example, sex on a higher level may mean that if one person prefers not to have sexual interactions of a particular nature, then the partner respects this preference. If, for instance, a couple is engaged in sexual intercourse and the wife wishes to stop before her husband climaxes, the experience can still be good sex if the couple continues in the spirit of mutuality. Even if the woman prefers not to have further genital, sexual contact for the rest of the night, or the rest of the week, or even for a few months, the couple would not necessarily experience dysfunctional sex or an inherently frustrating situation. If the couple has a healthy underlying relationship, with each person secure in the knowledge that both are doing the best for that relationship, then their sex is good.

This example can be misunderstood because similar incidents occur among couples with serious psychosexual dysfunction. Suspension of genital sexual contact may indicate a significant problem, but rejection of the possibility of periods of abstinence is a certain sign that a problem exists. If they are to be functional, any couple's decisions must derive from open communication, a shared sense of commitment, and emotional intimacy.

In this scenario, the couple has not achieved all possible goals, but has maintained the priority of love. Their sex is on a higher level, though not consonant with the standards of today's world which are based on immediate satisfaction and fulfilling genital "needs." With healthy sex, periods characterized by less genital sexual activity than that desired by one or both of the partners need not effect the essential intimacy between the two people. Such a relationship is not headed for discord, nor should the couple feel less in love with each other, or less compatible. If a mature couple is unable to share one aspect of the relationship, for health or other reasons, they emphasize other aspects in its place. A lack of genital, sexual activity changes, but does not diminish, a married couple's relationship.

While sexual intimacy is not to be discouraged among married couples, we sometimes seem to forget how much more there is to romance. That point is richly illustrated by a pamphlet entitled *101 Ways to Make Love Without Doin' It.*[3] Among others, we find the

following possibilities:
- Tell the other person that you love him or her.
- Hold hands.
- Go for a long bike ride.
- Sit together in the park.
- Snuggle up together.
- Play a game of frisbee.
- Give compliments.
- Cook a meal together.
- Plan and go on a road trip together.
- Go hiking.
- Throw a party.
- Wash each other's cars.
- Listen to hurts.
- Do a work project together.
- Use eye contact to share a private thought.
- Go for a moonlight walk.
- Go to a concert.
- Play music together.
- Go horseback riding.
- Make each other gifts.
- Share lifetime goals with each other.
- Have your picture taken together.

All married couples, whatever their circumstances, can enjoy a full and varied relationship. Sexual restraint may be in order (including periods of genital abstinence), but no couple needs to refrain from holding hands, hugging, lying next to each other, or kissing.

In the same way, the unmarried may also maintain fully integrated relationships. Single people with healthy attitudes do not undress each other or engage in genital sexual activity. But with an understanding of the holistic nature of their sexuality, they can realize their own potential for intimacy in the many less intense ways married people do.

When we talk about "good sex," we distinguish it rather carefully from "ideal" or "perfect" sex. Good sex is not the highest but the higher level, the one most of us can more or less realistically achieve. Perhaps it is easier to understand this higher level of psychosexual functioning by seeing it in relation to others. Optimally, three levels would exist: perfect sex, healthy sex, and unhealthy sex. Unfortunately, due to the prevalence of severe dysfunction such a division is inadequate. We therefore offer the following seven levels.

Level 1: Perfect Sex – The ideal toward which we strive but never achieve.
- Attitudes: always perfect.
- Sexual activity within marriage is all perfectly in balance with, and supportive of, the greater relationship; all sexual activity before marriage stops short of arousal.
- No frustrations associated with sex.

Level 2: The Higher Level – Healthy, functional, basic, normal sex.
- Attitudes: occasional or minor mistakes, with a consistent desire to improve one's attitudes.
- Minimal sexual fantasizing.
- Sexual activity within marriage is usually supportive of the relationship. Sex is routinely enjoyable and reaffirming, and sometimes extraordinarily so. Sexual intercourse takes place only with one's spouse. Sexual activity before marriage leading to arousal is rare and avoided.
- Frustrations associated with sex are relatively uncommon, and usually transient and mild.
- Dress: always modest.

Level 3: Significant sexual problems.
- Attitudes: acceptance of some unhealthy attitudes and misconceptions.
- Moderate sexual fantasizing.
- Sexual activity within marriage is sometimes a significant obstacle to intimacy or leads to serious conflict; sexual activity

before marriage which leads to arousal (perhaps including some undressing or heavy petting) is common but without intercourse; infrequent self-stimulation.
- Frustrations associated with sex are occasionally serious and difficult to control.
- Dress: at times dress in tight-fitting clothes or clothes meant to accentuate one's figure or physique.

Level 4: Serious sexual problems
- Attitudes: more serious submission to "needs" and other misconceptions. Frequent or prolonged sexual fantasizing.
- Sexual Interactions: some insistence on sex in a position or with a frequency that one's spouse disapproves of; sexual intercourse before marriage with one or a few sexual partners; general openness to pornography and self-stimulation, oral sex to climax.
- Frustrations associated with sex are frequent and often uncontrolled.
- Dress: frequent immodest attire.

Level 5: Very serious sexual problems – "sexual addicts" as defined in Chapter 10.
- Attitudes: markedly unhealthy, with full commitment to "needs" and other misconceptions.
- Sexual interactions: sexual intercourse before marriage with many partners; extramarital sex; compulsive self-stimulation; habitual exposure to pornography or erotic entertainment; infrequent payment for sex (including money spent on a date in expectation of sexual favors); men openly reject their responsibility for an unintended pregnancy; occasional use of force for sex in a position or with a frequency one's partner clearly disapproves of; anal sex, whether engaged in by heterosexuals or homosexuals; active involvement in sexually deviant behavior including homosexuality, transvestitism, voyeurism, and any of the others except transsexuality.
- Frustrations associated with sex are very frequent and poorly controlled.

- Dress: typical attire is clearly aimed at being sexually provocative.

Level 6: Severe sexual problems: "Sexual addicts" as defined by society.
- Attitudes: essential disregard for those who satisfy the person's sexual desires.
- Sexual interactions: frequent sexual intercourse whether married or not with whomever is available; pay for sex regularly; frequent use of force for sex in a position or with a frequency one's partner clearly disapproves of; date rape; transsexuality.

Level 7: Most severe sexual problems: Encompassing the most extreme, degrading, violent or life-threatening sexual practices.
- Attitudes: most unhealthy
- Sexual interactions: prostitution; rape; genital sexual activity with a known HIV-positive person (with or without a condom); sadomasochism; child molestation; incest.

These seven levels may seem arbitrary and rigid, but they serve to illustrate some important principles. Both individuals and couples, whether married or unmarried, can identify their current – but by no means permanent – status with reference to these seven levels. The idea then is to move toward Level 2 and remain there.

Psychosexual development is an ongoing process, the goal of which is to make steady, overall progress up the scale. Depending on the individual or couple, Level 2 may take years, decades or a lifetime to achieve. Setbacks will occur and each person or couple will face unique difficulties. More important than achieving Level 2 is the depth of the commitment made to working steadily toward it.

Intimate sexual exploration and discovery are part of the wonder and joy of relationships developed over the course of a marriage. There is great variety in sexual positions and techniques and, as noted, only the most extreme of these necessarily relegates a couple to the lower levels. Of note, oral sex to climax presents the same problem as contraception and anal sex, and other homosexual acts. It disrupts the natural connection between procreation and pleasure and thereby encourages disordered priorities and acceptance of the "needs" misconception. It is also, justifiably, considered demeaning and offensive by many. However, due to the range of less intense oral-genital acts the inherent unhealthy nature of all oral sexual acts is less certain. Similar reasoning applies to mutual manual manipulation.

Those who identify with the lower levels have all the more reason to consider the feelings and circumstances associated with their failures to abstain from premarital sex, purchasing pornography, self-stimulation, sex with prostitutes and other acts not compatible with Level 2. These persons will benefit from an aggressive rehabilitation program as discussed in Chapters 10 and 11.

Though sexually active homosexuals generally operate, by definition, on Level 5, homosexuals may achieve higher levels, including Level 2. This progress is possible through active participation in a program of healing and by maintaining a dignified, fulfilling lifestyle, which necessarily excludes intimate homosexual activity.

Hopefully, these seven levels clarify what this book is all about. It is not about sexual repression. It is not about passing judgment on people or condemning those who make mistakes in their sexual relationships; we all make mistakes. It is an invitation to travel a different road from the one getting so much of the traffic today – to consider the ways in which the richest sexual experiences may be achieved.

This book is also about healing, about binding the wounds that have developed between the sexes, about building bridges to reduce hostility felt by both men and women toward the opposite sex. It is about discarding degrading, abusive attitudes toward sex and adopting positive, life-affirming ones. It is about admitting our mistakes, forgiving ourselves and others, making amends, and moving forward. Some people, no doubt, will refuse to accept these ideas. For various reasons, they will not accept the existence of a higher level of sexual living, or they will not believe that they can achieve the higher level. This book is for those who will challenge themselves on both counts. Level 2 exists and it is available to everyone.

Level 2 is the true "Joy of Sex" – sex as a consistently positive experience. Men and women who live on Level 2 reject addictive and codependent attitudes based on perceived "needs," and maintain the goal of strengthening relationships. They accept a naturally balanced, holistic approach, in which sex is not something separate from the rest of the relationship, something to be turned on by being sexy. Rather, sex becomes an integral part of our lives, whether it is expressed through a simple touch, holding hands, or sexual intercourse.

Good sex can only occur when the mind, not the hormones, is in control. Hormones are altogether insensitive; when they reign, people get hurt. We human beings have strong sex drives, but we are not hormone-driven robots.

We can be misled into thinking that activities on Levels 3, 4 and 5 constitute good sex. These levels, which are now typical fare on TV, in movies, and in magazines, are easy to achieve. The most they require is a condom or other contraceptive, and an available partner. Good sex, on the contrary, is not so easy to achieve. But good sex does exist, it is available to everyone, and it is worth the effort.

Part VI

Sexual Morality

Chapter 14

The Moral Revolution

We have discussed misconceptions, priorities, and objectives in an attempt to distinguish between healthy and unhealthy sex. In many cases, the positions presented thus far in *Sexual Wisdom* would appear to be self-evident yet there has been no overwhelming movement among members of the general public to accept these positions and translate the logical conclusions from them into action. One explanation for this general lack of acceptance is that too little honest, thoughtful dialogue is occurring between the opposing factions on issues related to sex. To facilitate such discussions, we have attempted to bridge the gap between these groups by emphasizing common ground, e.g., that love is the highest priority. Communication between those with conflicting viewpoints is critical if society is to approach contemporary problems with true sophistication. The greatest barrier to fruitful discussion about sex is the issue of sexual morality – the subject of the next two chapters.

Sexual morality, like all other areas of morality, has its foundation in love. The sexual revolution has created such havoc because it is based on misconceptions that promote compromise on the natural priority of love. Love is the essential standard against which we judge behavior and where the sexual revolution has compromised on love, it has failed. Compromise is also evident in areas beyond the sexual realm, and is at the heart of the greater moral revolution our society has been experiencing.

Substantial changes have occurred in our attitudes toward morality in the past thirty years. In the 1970s, *Mad* magazine published a cover cartoon which consisted of two frames. The first showed a flock of white sheep with one black sheep in their midst, and was entitled "Morality Then." The second frame was of another flock of sheep, this time all black, with a solitary white sheep in their midst, and the frame was entitled "Morality Now."

Morality is a word surrounded by many misunderstandings and misconceptions; we will begin by considering the most basic one.

Misconception #15: All morality is subjective and, therefore, relative. Morality means something different to each person.

According to a sex education text popular back in the late 1970s, "what is moral in one society or for one individual is not moral for others. Morality is individual; it is what you think it is."[1] But if morality is anything an individual conceives it to be, then it is really nothing at all, and there could be no moral standards, only individual standards or opinions.

As discussed in Chapter 1, natural law teaches that moral behavior is that behavior which is good or loving. The Golden Rule – "Treat others as you would have them treat you" – is a universally accepted guide for defining loving or moral behavior. From the world's religions we get various phrasings – the Christians, "In everything do to others as you would have them do to you" (Mt 7:12); from Judaism, "What is harmful to you, do not to your fellow man" (Talmud, Shabbat, 3id.); from Islam, "No one of you is a believer until he desires for his brother that which he desires for himself" (Sunnah); from Confucianism, "If there is one maxim which ought to be acted upon throughout one's life, surely it is the maxim of loving kindness. Do not do unto others what you would not have them do unto you" (The Analects, 15, 23).[2] The Golden Rule asks us simply to approach all situations from the perspective of another – to be ever empathetic. It asks us to consider the vulnerabilities of others and to deal with them justly. Morality is simply the behavioral corollary of loving attitudes. For example, dumping nuclear waste next to a residential neighborhood is immoral. Reckless driving is immoral. Both are immoral because they violate the common good and therefore are unloving. Another sex education course states in its study guide, "The choice of a premarital sexual standard is a personal moral choice, and no amount of facts or trends can 'prove' scientifically that one ought to choose a personal standard."[3] But moral choices must be based on empirical evidence or "facts." Dumping nuclear waste near a residential neighborhood is certainly a situation crowded with facts. Premarital sex puts people at risk for a host of very real – factual – consequences. Clearly, facts are an indispensable part of the equation used to determine whether or not a behavior is moral.

Morality is not "anything one thinks it is." It is an essential concern of daily life. Immoral behaviors are routinely discouraged through the mechanisms of social reproach for minor matters and of man made laws for serious ones. Acts which society considers to be seriously immoral acts are made illegal, including everything from cheating on income tax returns to bank robbery and murder. Those who believe that morality varies from person to person say, "Don't impose your morality on others," yet this is exactly what we do through societal standards and laws. Society has a duty to ensure that, through social pressure and laws, those who engage in grossly immoral behaviors are justly punished.

Our legal system reflects the prevalent moral norms recognized by society. Citizens have an obligation to work to amend laws to reflect their convictions about seriously immoral behaviors. For example, if it were legal to murder newborns, as at least one Nobel prize winner has proposed,[4] people would have a duty to work to change the law to make such activities illegal.

At this stage in our discussion three other significant points need clarification:

1) *Subjective* and *Objective* Morality

Objective morality is the morality of an action irrespective of the doer's perception. Subjective morality is the perceived morality of an action as understood by the doer of the action. Objectively immoral behavior is not necessarily culpable or punishable. If a person faces a situation in which he or she cannot decide on the moral action, consultation of an authority is an obvious move. If that authority encourages the person to act immorally, and the person does so, he or she should not necessarily face punishment. The act was objectively immoral, but if the person could not have reasonably known that it was immoral (subjective immorality), then punishment is inappropriate.

In spite of the perception that "everyone is doing it," a couple engaged in premarital sex is compromising on the priority of love. It is incongruous to say that one performs premarital sex to demonstrate one's love because of the many serious, foreseeable, unnecessary risks associated with it (see Chapter 2). Premarital sex is an objectively immoral act, whether or not a couple so involved realizes it.

Objective morality is not based on perceptions, but on wisdom, i.e., on the most profound understanding of objective reality. Immoral acts are often based on misconceptions or falsehoods. For example, the premise that white people are superior to other races is false, as is the premise that premarital sex is an expression of love. The more informed one is about morally relevant facts, the closer one's subjective view approaches objective truth.

2) Judging a *Person* vs. Judging a Person's *Attitudes* or *Behaviors*

We have already touched on the general concern throughout society over being judgmental. We mentioned that one cannot judge other people, but that behaviors with moral implications are judged routinely. This distinction is critical. To judge a person as bad, condemned, or "a jerk," if you will, is to suggest that that person is inferior to those who are not "bad" or is in some essential way less than he or she should be. This inference is the source of extraordinary inhumanity throughout history. One cannot know whether one would be a better person than someone else, should one have been given the other person's particular set of natural attributes and life experiences.

A friend uses the maxim "Love the sinner, hate the sin" to demonstrate the confusion on this subject among both conservatives and liberals. He says that many conservatives are so hateful of sin they forget about loving (and not judging) the sinner. On the other hand, many liberals try so hard to love the sinner (and not being judgmental) that they forget about hating or judging sin.

As an example of the difference between judging persons and judging actions, consider how when children hit each other; supervising adults routinely judge this behavior as wrong. On the other hand, it may be detrimental to judge behaviors for which there are no moral implications, no right or wrong; for example, it will likely create much unnecessary stress if a teacher insists that a left-handed child write with his or her right hand. But to say that one cannot have an opinion about the morality of another's sexual activity is to say that sexual acts do not have moral relevance, which is false. Sexual behaviors may be freely judged because they do have great moral relevance.

Sexual morality does exist. It is not anything one thinks it is, rather, it is sexual behavior based on love. One person's morality may indeed be superior to another's because one person may act more loving than another. We should confront those who engage in date-rape or those who purchase pornography, who do not appreciate the immorality of their behavior. As we discourage lying and acts of bigotry, so too, we should discourage immoral sexual behavior.

3) Distinguishing between Morality and Religion

Another distinction we should make here is between morality and religion, two terms we often hear and read carelessly used, as if they stand for the same thing. They do not; they are not interchangeable. Since moral behavior is that which is the most loving toward oneself and others, it should not only be considered in a religious context. Religion adds a supernatural dimension which often reinforces rational thought on morality and may even provide the basis for reasonable action. But while agnostics and atheists might reject the religious component of immorality, they can fully appreciate the appeal to reason. These people may be just as moral as religious people, and, in fact, frequently are.

While a religious perspective is not required to discuss morality, it may enrich and even dominate such discussions. The management of addictions offers an example of the manner in which the religious dimension of morality augments the others. We have mentioned that addictions are inherently immoral behaviors. One of the most successful treatment programs for alcoholism is Alcoholics Anonymous. This program is based on "Twelve Steps" toward recovery. Six of these twelve steps refer to a "higher power," defined as one's concept of God or an equivalent. There is little doubt that the supernatural component of this program has contributed to its uncommon success. Other successful programs have also emphasized the supernatural dimension of addiction rehabilitation.[5] Such programs might be successful without this added dimension, but they are apparently more effective with it.

Another problematic area in the relationship between morality and religion is the question of whether it is acceptable to *influence* or *impose* one's ideas on another. While our laws impose standards of behavior, the vast majority of people take the reasonable stance that it is wrong to impose a government or individual's religion on others. Still, each person has a duty to encourage others to be more moral, more thoughtful, and more kind, whether through the force of law or more subtly. As David Reardon writes in *Aborted Women: Silent No More:*

> Politicians who support pro-abortion laws saying, 'Personally I don't believe abortion is right, but I refuse to impose my moral views on others,' are at best cowards who are unwilling to stand by their own moral convictions, or at worst, nothing more than hypocrites. When these same politicians vote to build defense systems, they are imposing their values on pacifists. When they vote to tax the rich for the sake of the poor, they are imposing their morality on those wealthy persons who don't care about the poor. Writing moral choices into the law is what their jobs are all about.[6]

Essentially the same point is made with dramatic force in a scene between Sir Thomas More and Cardinal Wolsey in Robert Bolt's play *A Man for All Seasons*. More has been resisting Wolsey's pressure that he publicly support Henry VIII's divorce and remarriage as a means of providing an heir for the throne of England. Near the end of the scene, Wolsey presses hard:

> Wolsey: Now explain how you as a chancellor of England can obstruct those measures for the sake of your own, private conscience?
>
> More: Well – I believe, when statesmen forsake their own private conscience for the sake of their public duties they lead their country by a short route to chaos.[7]

Although we are all obligated to encourage others to be more moral, no one has the right to impose his or her religious beliefs on others. Our United States Constitution specifically protects religious freedom. One may attempt to influence others to accept a belief, but may not force. Religious enthusiasts have every right to knock on one's door, but one is under no obligation to open it.

Part of the confusion over morality and religion results from the political doctrine of separation of church and state. This doctrine was originally meant to declare that no particular religious belief would be forced upon the populace.[8] In modern times, it has erroneously come to mean that one's religious beliefs should not affect the functioning of government. The reality is that politicians should be expected to apply moral principles of their faith to the conduct of their office.

Morality and religion are not one and the same. But the confusion between them often paralyzes efforts to encourage people to be moral, for fear of "imposing religion" on them. A man wrote with bitterness to a newspaper: "That's what religion is all about, folks – forcing others to live life your way."[9] Such comments reflect a paranoia about religious influence which is prevalent in the United States today, and which is one of the greatest barriers to authentic discussion about sexual morality.

Chapter 15

Morality: "Old" and "New"

Reliance on love as the basis for moral choices enables us to refute yet another falsehood:

Misconception #16: *The Old Morality is insufficient for dealing with contemporary ethical dilemmas. For these, a New Morality is necessary.*

Late twentieth century scientific discoveries and revolutionary technologies have made reality of things conceived of only in the realm of science fiction just a few short decades ago. When Aldous Huxley wrote his dystopian *Brave New World* in 1932, genetic engineering in the Central London Hatchery and test-tube babies were the fantasies of his imagination.[1] Now, however; *in vitro* fertilization, selection of sex of child, early pregnancy testing for birth defects, the morning-after contraceptive pill, etc. are commonplace, which confront us with real-life moral and ethical dilemmas. Response to these hard choices has been dramatic and varied. Dr. Ira Reiss, a professor of sociology, offers one solution when he explains that his "careful study of our sexual customs, over the last few decades, has convinced me that our major problem is our society's inability to build *a new sexual ethic,* which can serve as a guide for the much wider range of sexual choices that we are called upon to make today"[2] (emphasis added).

This idea of a new sexual ethic or New Morality has gained considerable attention, and its advocates justify it with the doctrine of Situational Ethics (or Moral Relativism). According to leading humanist Albert Ellis, "There probably cannot ever be any absolutely correct or proper rules of morality, since people and conditions change over the years and what is 'right' today may be 'wrong' tomorrow. Sane ethics are relativistic and situational."[3] In other words, according to advocates of a "New" Morality, all principles or rules of ethics can – and do – change, depending on the situation.

But if moral standards or rules are based on love, they cannot change any more than love can change. Moral standards or rules are guidelines for doing good or being loving. Those principles that always reflect genuine love are infallible. Those that less effectively direct one to the precept "to do good" may be very reliable but have exceptions. For example, the rule that it is wrong to steal is a very reliable rule, but it is not without exception. Suppose one is being held hostage on an island, so one steals the keys to a get-away boat. Clearly this act of "stealing" is well within the limits of moral behavior, but realistically, not many of us will ever be held hostage. Thus the general rule against stealing is a good one because it has so few exceptions.

Many rules are simplifications and have *possible* exceptions. When we say that it is wrong to steal, we mean that, for all practical purposes, it is always wrong to steal. Even the rule against killing unborn children has exceptions on which there is general agreement, e.g., for tubal pregnancies. A tubal pregnancy represents a potentially fatal risk to the mother with no chance of survival for the embryo. To save the mother's life, it is warranted to surgically remove the embryo. Often the embryo has died prior to the procedure but if not, and it is killed by the procedure, all parties agree that the procedure remains morally licit. But it is clearly a violation and abuse of the rule when people have abortions because the child is the "wrong" sex. According to a study of 10,000 abortions performed in India, 97 percent of the fetuses were female.[4]

Obviously, one immediate problem is to determine what rules are without exception and what does and does not constitute a reasonable exception to those rules that have exceptions. For some issues, it is nearly impossible to work out effective guidelines. For example, disputes between biological parents and surrogate mothers may be enormously complex. On the other hand, some rules are unchangeable – rules that prohibit behaviors so intrinsically unloving to oneself or others that they can never be justified. For example, self-stimulation is immoral, because it is inherently degrading and egocentric. It is not respectful of the human person, but rather reinforces unhealthy attitudes, which affect the way individuals perceive themselves and others. For similar reasons, other sex acts are also inherently immoral: prostitution, incest, premarital and extramarital sex, marital rape, homosexual acts, bestiality, and child molestation. The fact that these acts are commonly engaged in is beside the point. Lying is common, too, but that doesn't make it right. The morality of a particular act is not determined by its popularity.

A number of problems result from emphasizing a "situational" basis for ethics. One problem is that, because of the emphasis on the limitations of some moral standards, there is a tendency to assume that all standards are limited and have many exceptions. People excuse themselves from following any rule of morality by claiming that their circumstances are the precise ones covered by the exceptions. For example, more people engage in sexual intercourse before marriage than do not. Yet, the rule that premarital sex is wrong is so reliable that it would appear, not only from a practical but even a theoretical standpoint, to be absolute. Vast segments of our society have become preoccupied with the rare, sometimes unimaginably rare, exceptions to the rules. People earnestly discuss the most remote possible exceptions while ignoring the familiar, everyday situation.

Another important problem with situational ethics is that it is used primarily to justify sexual behaviors, which actually tend to be some of the least "situational" in nature. As Peter Kreeft, of Boston College, illustrates, "The 'new morality' is quite traditional in condemning injustice, genocide, racism, slavery, oppression, prejudice, cruelty, lying, stealing, etc. Nearly all the newness of 'the new morality' is in sex-related areas: divorce, premarital promiscuity, abortion, homosexuality, and contraception."[5]

While the principle of situational ethics strikes many people as unreasonable when applied to other areas of immorality, it is routinely used to justify breaking behavioral codes related to sex. This is another example of the widespread preoccupation with sex in our society and the consequent special, often misguided, treatment afforded to it. Sexual ethics should be expected to be among the least situational. Moral absolutes are especially suited to areas that involve pleasure, since pleasurable activities, such as sex, offer such a strong enticement to contrive excuses for breaking the rules. Not only has it become generally acceptable to defy sexual mores, but violating codes of sexual behavior is justified without any basis in love and virtue. With situational ethics, people lose sight of the standard of doing good upon which the rules are based and replace it with other priorities such as pleasure or freedom.

Pleasure

Situational ethics justifies exceptions to essentially all sexual standards by ascribing a moral value to pleasure. For example, according to a treatise on sexual ethics printed in *The Humanist* magazine, "Physical pleasure is a moral value." And the article concludes with the declaration that, "In order to realize our potential for joyful sexual expression we need to adopt the doctrine that actualizing pleasures is among the *highest* moral goods"[6] (emphasis added).

On the contrary, logic counters that seeking pleasure is anything but "the highest" standard upon which to base the morality of a behavior. While we should enjoy life's pleasures, it is clear that pleasure-seeking, as much as any other motive, readily leads to conflicts with willing the good of another.

It is necessary to distinguish here between "good" in the general sense and "moral good." The sun rose this morning, which was good; it would be very bad if it had not risen. But there is nothing moral about the sun rising. To enjoy the pleasures that life offers is good when done within the moral context of "doing good," but the fact that one is enjoying oneself or feeling good does not imply moral correctness. Pleasure is an important priority, but it is an unreliable guide to morality.

Freedom

Part of the reason why the New Morality has become so popular is that the Old Morality often interferes with freedom and is therefore perceived as repressive. As stated previously, freedom is an important priority, but it is not the most important priority. On the contrary, freedom must always be exercised with reasonable consideration for others. There is a tangible and important difference between legitimate exercise of one's own freedom and abuse of freedom at a cost to someone else. We should be free to vote for, lobby for, or publicly promote issues in which we believe. We should be free to influence the determination of what the speed limits will be, but we should not be free to drive at any speed we like. Just laws or traditions place the fewest restrictions on one person's freedom while preserving the rights of others. The freedom to experience pleasure or express oneself should not come at the expense of others.

Because situational ethics so readily accommodates disordered priorities, it encourages rationalizations that excuse people from being the most genuinely loving of others and allows people to compromise on virtue, particularly in the area of sexual morality. The five characteristics of love that we examined in Chapters 7 and 8 provide effective illustrations of the compromises and rationalizations we so often find in the domain of situational ethics. Instead of respect, we hear, "I love you, and I know that what I'm asking you to do is degrading, but I need to fulfill my fantasy." Instead of responsibility, we hear, "I love you, but if you get pregnant it's your fault so you'll have deal with it." This response is the opposite that is given by someone who is being fully responsible for one's actions, e.g., being fully open to pregnancy, planned or not. Openness to the consequences of one's actions means that every act of sexual intercourse welcomes – or at least is open to welcoming – the potential child into this world and accepts the potential responsibility of nurturing, educating and being emotionally available to that child for the rest of one's life.

Instead of commitment, we hear, "I love you. We'll commit to sleeping and living together, but if you get pregnant, don't come looking for me." Commitment so frequently falls victim to desires for both pleasure and freedom that it is worth examining some examples of common responses. A patient complained to me about her struggle with her boyfriend of nine years. While she and their two children suffered from insecurity, he continued to be "afraid" to commit to marriage. In a pro-choice newspaper editorial, a social psychologist wrote, "The relationship between motherhood and abortion is like the relationship between marriage and divorce. . . . people must have a way out of their most important commitments."[7] But if there is a way out, then *there is no commitment.* Loving commitment means *not even looking* for a way out. The most complete commitment of all is expressed through the marriage vows, when spouses commit to each other "until death do us part." Aside from those who make religious vows, few people are willing to pledge themselves to anything "until death," because that is one serious commitment!

Instead of discipline, we hear, "I love you, but I need to have sex with you now, even if you don't want to." Premarital sex is an undisciplined acquiescence to passion. Though rationalizations are used to excuse it, it involves anything but discipline or self-sacrifice. Instead of trust, we hear, "I love my boyfriend, but I have herpes and don't want to tell him. I'll just suggest we use a condom 'for contraception' instead of telling him the truth."

While many moral standards have been and always will be situational, some standards are objective and have no exceptions. In meeting modern challenges, what we need is not a New Morality but an unwavering insistence on authentic love as the standard of all morality. There can be honest debate about what constitutes the most genuinely loving approach in a given situation, but no amount of debate can change the fact that love is the primary guide to morality. The key is to not get so caught up following rules as to forget the *reason* for the rules. They are guides to our truest nature, to that which is good and leads to the greatest personal fulfillment. Natural law teaches that all people are intrinsically drawn to goodness – that each of us has a call from within to love. St. Augustine (354-430AD), drawing from the New Testament (Romans, 2:15), wrote that this law is "written in the hearts of men, which iniquity itself effaces not."[8] The influence of these ancient teachings is readily recognized throughout the modern world, Consider the following reaffirmation in the popular book *Random Acts of Kindness:*

> In giving freely, purely, for no reason and every reason, you move into another person's emotional landscape – not because you must, not because you have no choice, but because in your heart, that majestically superhuman organ, the castle of your love, you have felt the spiritual necessity of acting out your love. For in choosing to love not only those whom you have committed yourself to loving, but also those whose names, faces, and true circumstances you will never really know, you will be moved palpably, inescapably into understanding that loving and being loved is the one true human vocation.[9]

Fulfilling this vocation on a day-to-day basis is the struggle of a lifetime, "the greatest study"[10] as Plato put it, for there are situations each of us encounter in which the underlying principles involved are far from obvious. Under such circumstances, the mature person educates himself or herself, studies and reflects with an open mind, for only through discernment can one appreciate genuine love. The best of life and the best of sex come to those who embrace the often arduous process of informing and then following one's conscience.

The challenge to humanity is to continually clarify our understanding of love and morality and not to rationalize them away. The New Morality, by exploiting the situational nature of some moral guidelines, provides a "loop hole" – a means for excusing ourselves from obeying all moral guidelines. It is the heart of a movement to remove love from a position of primacy and to replace it with any number of alternatives, especially physical pleasure and freedom.

It is alarming that this promotion of pleasure and freedom through situational ethics is almost ubiquitous – in the media, the medical establishment, religions, and the art world. In the words of best-selling author Gore Vidal, "What is wrong with other-sex even if you're married? What is wrong with same-sex even if you're married? One would *rather not be* the occasion of someone else's pain but we all are sometimes and that's part of being alive; it goes with the turf . . . . The Italians have sex right. They just do it."[11] (emphasis added) In other words, he believes it is inevitable that people will sexually abuse one another. Not true if one is committed to a less popular but more fulfilling lifestyle.

Traditional morality derives from the universal law to which all persons are bound by their nature. The New Morality rejects natural law and insists that all laws are subjective and culturally determined. Allan Bloom defends the age-old concept of natural law when he writes:

> Men cannot remain content with what is given them by their culture if they are to be fully human. This is what Plato meant to show by the image of the cave in *The Republic* and by representing us as prisoners in it. A culture is a cave. He did not suggest going around to other cultures as a solution to the limitations of the cave. Nature should be the standard by which we judge our own lives and the lives of peoples.[12]

During a public-sponsored talk-radio show, the vitriolic host was instructing listeners about the moral equivalence of all cultures and why we should accept any behaviors that originate from local customs. An African-American woman called the station to ask the host's opinion about clitoridectomies – a culturally-dictated, mutilating surgical procedure performed in some areas of Africa on infant girls. The host answered that she would not fault any procedure that was accepted as a cultural norm. The caller pressed the issue, and was no doubt working up to an example such as what if a culture accepts the rape of women by their husbands, when the host bellowed accusingly to the caller, "You're backing me into a corner." The caller was so startled by the host's admission of defeat that she hurriedly responded with a timid "No, I'm not." But despite her stage fright she was, in fact, successfully establishing the host's erroneous logic. To be in touch with one's culture is a valid priority, but it is more important to be true to one's own nature. Our common humanity is timeless and runs deeper than transient cultural dictates.

Natural law is everywhere under attack from the "New Moralists." A *Newsweek* article describes a bisexual university professor who is determined that his 2-month-old will have no gender barriers. The article states that, "When people ask if the child – who has both ears pierced – is a boy or a girl, (the father) responds: 'Ask the baby.'"[13] The professor is so distressed over potential cultural influences that he has lost touch with his humanness He has forgotten that individuals have a given nature, that males and females are fundamentally different: hormonally, anatomically, emotionally, etc. Each person is a composite of both nature and nurture, but with his own child, he has chosen to ignore half of this two-part equation. The denial of nature itself is part of the fallout of situational ethics. The belief that no one can know objective morality rests on the more basic philosophical position that no one can know objective truth about anything, even a child's gender.

The attack on natural law is part of a cultural revolution geared at overturning the natural or "Old" morality. In the resulting confusion, major misconceptions about morality have flourished. These are that morality is subjective, relative, and subject to revision, along with the confusion over the difference between imposing morality and imposing religion. These misconceptions have prevented our society from responding effectively and responsibly to the disastrous moral decline in the United States in recent decades. Studies of personal morality have consistently shown that the "Me Generation" of the 1970s produced a "Decade of Greed" in the 1980s. One study reported on the contrast between what classroom teachers identified as the greatest threats to the education process in 1940 and today. The concerns from 1940 were talking out of turn, chewing gum, making noise, running in the halls, getting out of line, wearing improper clothing, and not putting paper in the wastebasket. The concerns today are drug abuse, alcohol abuse, pregnancy, suicide, rape, robbery and assault.[14]

No matter how many misconceptions our society has accepted, or how ready people have been to change the goals of sex, society would have rejected these mistaken ideas if it had maintained love as the highest priority. But these particular misconceptions about morality have fostered substitution of the lesser priorities of pleasure and freedom for love. Consequently, society has failed to resist and defend itself against the moral revolution.

Now, with belief in these falsehoods so widespread, one cannot present a moral judgment about the actions of others without being accused of imposing morality on them or being "judgmental," or offer concerned moral guidance without being rebuked for trying to force one's religion on others. General acceptance of these misconceptions has prevented us from dealing with the critical sexual problems which affect our society today. Testifying to the seriousness of this situation, the *Wall Street Journal* editorialized "The United States has problems with drugs, high school sex, AIDS, and rape. None of these will go away until people in positions of responsibility come forward and explain, in frankly moral terms, that some of the things people do nowadays are wrong."[15]

Along with the failure of our society in general, some religious communities also fail to address these misconceptions in responsible ways. They condemn people, instead of actions and attitudes, and focus exclusively on religious issues, which are unacceptable to many people. Their insistence on discussing issues of sexual morality within a religious context often prevents mutually respectful, productive discourse.

On the other hand, discussions on morality are often terminated over groundless, contrived fears of religious imposition, especially by liberals. Liberals often assume that conservatives have a hidden agenda of imposing Christianity on them, while some conservatives assume that liberals are working to impose atheism on them. At times, either of these fears may be well-founded. More often, however, these assumptions are based on a misunderstanding of, and discomfort with, issues of sexual immorality, the most important in the field of sexology.

The Importance of Trust

Of the five characteristics of love put in jeopardy by situational ethics, trust is both the most basic and the most vulnerable, and so deserves special consideration. Trust is comparable to the legs of a table. Just as the tabletop rests on legs for support, so too a relationship between two people depends on trust for its foundation. When a breech of trust occurs, it is as if the legs supporting that relationship are cut shorter. Sometimes the legs are cut to different lengths, making the relationship particularly wobbly and awkward. Imagine a couple trying to sit at a table whose legs have been shortened, or the table rocking unexpectedly because of the uneven length of the legs. As the legs of the table are cut even shorter, or more distrust enters the relationship, the couple has more and more trouble using the table and so the two suffer. Finally, when the legs are completely gone and the relationship is devoid of trust, the couple is left with only a table-top lying flat on the floor and no relationship at all.

Many rationalizations have developed which allow for compromises in the area of trust. For example, counselors commonly recommend that adolescents be dishonest with each other about their use of contraception. Many physicians counsel adolescent girls not to tell their boyfriends that they use oral contraceptives (the pill). They justify such dishonesty on various grounds, including that it might lead to greater use of condoms. Jean Emans, M.D., Associate Chief of the Adolescent Clinic at Harvard Medical School defends this approach: "Whether a girl feels that she can tell her boyfriend that she uses oral contraceptives depends on their *established pattern of communication,* her own self-esteem and assertiveness, her perceived risk of sexually transmitted diseases and their prior experience with condoms"[16] (emphasis added).

But Dr. Emans misses the point. By narrowly concentrating on the issue of sexually transmitted disease prevention, she overlooks the destructive influence of lying ("their established pattern of communication") on the broader relationship, that which exists beyond the sexual sphere. She ignores the fact that if a girl cannot tell her boyfriend that she's using contraception, something is intrinsically wrong with the relationship.

We can also consider the dilemma following one of the most extreme breeches of trust that can occur in a relationship, i.e., whether or not to tell one's spouse about an extramarital affair. The advice most commonly heard is that confession of an extramarital affair to one's spouse is unnecessary. This recommendation, though given throughout the mental health field by clinicians with even the most orthodox religious affiliations,[17] should be challenged. Infidelity wounds a relationship to such a degree that it must be addressed openly to initiate healing. The historical fact of the affair can never be changed or undone, and it directly damages the relationship. Whether or not one confesses, the marital relationship has been affected forever; withholding a confession not only allows the past to hover over the relationship, but also leads to suspicion and further diminishes communication. The best key to resolving such problems is communication, but without candor, communication is critically restrained. Open discussion is vital if the couple is to resolve the most significant problems between them, in particular those that led to the affair itself.

The difference between admitting to an affair and not admitting to it is like the difference between suffering through an earthquake, and experiencing the earthquake plus the never-ending series of aftershocks. The affair is like an earthquake hitting the relationship, but without disclosure, the tension created by the original indiscretion is never relieved. If the objection to confessing is that people cannot handle the truth, the next question is how can they handle endless "aftershocks"?

My patients often provide classic examples of these "aftershocks." One man requested sleeping pills to cure his insomnia of one month's duration. After some questioning, he admitted to having had an affair the previous month. Treating his insomnia meant either taking sleeping pills indefinitely, or dealing with the real issues and having an honest discussion with his wife. And then there was the young woman who requested an HIV blood test. Preliminary questioning revealed no risk factors for HIV infection, but only an irrational fear of it. She had been tested repeatedly, and at unusually brief intervals, through several medical offices. After some discussion, the full scenario became clear. She had been married for a number of years. Recently, she and her husband had separated briefly and then reunited. During their separation she had sex once with another man who had no known risk factors for HIV infection. The woman was so distraught over having been unfaithful that she became obsessed with the fear of infecting her husband with HIV. She agreed to discuss everything with her husband, and her phobia resolved following their discussion.

No city that has been struck by a devastating earthquake can ever be the city it originally was, but it can be rebuilt into a beautiful, wonderful place. It can even be made *better* – more organized and charming than it ever was before the calamity. Discussion of serious breeches of trust is essential if a relationship is ever to stand on firm ground again. It should comfort both parties to realize that if one can tell one's spouse about an affair, one can tell him or her just about anything. That knowledge alone may go a long way toward retrieving the lost trust, once the emotions die down. While complete honesty about an affair is advisable in an overwhelming number of cases, there can, of course, be exceptions (e.g., when one's spouse suffers from a serious mental illness such as manic-depressive disorder or schizophrenia), when the most compassionate course of action may be less clear.

It is interesting that the rationalizations used to avoid honesty are often based on misconceptions. For example, much of the dishonesty in sexual relationships is based on the idea that men "need" sex and women "need" men. Some women allow themselves to be sexually exploited by rationalizing that they are being loving and giving when they perform their wifely (or "girlfriendly") duties for a needful man. In truth, they often perform with the more selfish goal of clinging to the security of a man. Honesty requires being true to oneself as well as one's partner and never degrading oneself by performing sex "acts," but rather always interacting with mutual respect.

In summary, trust is the foundation of relationships, like the legs of the table. Singer Billy Joel declares that today "honesty is such a lonely word," and he's right. We rationalize. We make excuses. We impose limits. Telling the truth can be difficult and humbling, and may disrupt relationships – at least for a time. Ultimately, however, keeping our relationships healthy can demand the courage to be assertive and tell the lonely truth. Trust must be the basis if relationships are to grow and gain in emotional intimacy – the environment that surrounds healthy sex.

Part VII

Teaching Sexuality to Children

Chapter 16

Adolescent Sexuality
and Sex Education

After addressing the major topics related to sex and developing some general principles, we can now apply these principles to the sex education of children. Since parents of adolescents and older children face the most urgent problems, we will begin by considering the best means of educating this group.

We should focus attention on two specific questions: first, how parents can encourage adolescents to appreciate healthy, Level 2 psychosexual functioning in a world in which they are constantly exposed to Levels 4, 5, and worse, and second, how parents can ensure that their children become aware that a fulfilling sex life *is* possible and that *each child* can achieve it.

The Question of Premarital Sex

Premarital sex is the most important question in adolescent sexuality. Engaging in premarital sex is the most fundamental mistake that adolescents can make because it leads to so many unhealthy attitudes and so much unhappiness. Premarital sex introduces teens to the idea of sexual risk-taking. It reaffirms the misconception that boys "need" relief from uncontrollable sexual impulses and initiates, in insecure girls, the idea of "giving up control of their bodies" for the security of a boyfriend. Moreover, premarital sex disrupts a fundamental process of adolescence and young adulthood, i.e., developing the ability to distinguish between infatuation and friendship. No one is born with this ability, but developing it is crucial before one makes a commitment to a life-long mate. While infatuation plays an integral role in early dating relationships, it inevitably wears thin; those couples who marry without a strong, underlying friendship are likely, sooner or later, to experience serious discord. Actor Mickey Rooney, who has lived through his share of troubled romances, speaks to this issue when he recommends that people should fall "in like" with each other, rather than "in love." Premarital intercourse serves to intensify infatuation to a potentially harmful level. After having sex, the illusion that "he or she looks so good, I must be in love" becomes reinforced with "it felt so good, I must be in love."

More teenagers now engage in premarital sex than ever. The greatest proportional rise in sexual activity among teens occurred in the most recent years studied (1986 to 1988).[1] Citing shocking statistics is often a good way to move people into action, but adult response to this magnitude of precocious teenage sexual activity has not been uniform. The range of responses derive from three distinctly different adult attitudes:

1) Teenagers having sex is *not* a problem.
2) Teenagers having sex *is* a problem, *but* they are going to do it anyway.
3) Teenagers having sex *is* a problem.

1) Teenagers having sex is not a problem. There is nothing wrong with it.

This is the approach taken by many "experts," particularly those who advocate sex education classes in schools. Their primary concern is preventing the immediately harmful physical consequences of pregnancy and disease; they are relatively unconcerned about the moral or long range effects that premarital sex has on the individuals directly involved. "We are not going to be an organization promoting celibacy or chastity," stated Faye Wattleton, who was president of Planned Parenthood from 1978-1992. "We've got to be more concerned about preventing teen pregnancies than we are about stopping sexual relationships."[2]

Sociologist Phillips Cutright expressed essentially the same philosophy when he contended in an article in Planned Parenthood's journal, *Family Planning Perspectives,* that "the supposed ill effects of premarital sex . . . have never been documented, so long as premarital sex did not lead to an illicit pregnancy that was carried to term. It is the control of these unwanted pregnancies – not the control of premarital sex – that is the problem."[3] And when the California Family Planning Council asked a panel of experts on adolescent sexuality which of three possibilities they would rank as the most serious problem in teen sexuality, their unanimous choice was not teens being involved in premarital sexual activity, not teens becoming pregnant – but *teens giving birth.*[4]

The Sexuality Information and Education Council of the United States, (SIECUS), along with Planned Parenthood, is one of the most influential organizations in the field of sex education today. In an article entitled "Helping Adolescents Learn about Sexuality," one member of the board of directors announced that, "adolescence is a time for exploration, and having multiple partners may broaden one's understanding of sexuality . . . In a sexual relationship, love and commitment may be preferable, but they are by no means essential . . . The first myth [about romance] is that sex without love is empty, unsatisfactory, and even immoral."[5]

Since these "experts" believe that teenagers having premarital sexual intercourse is not a problem, it is not surprising that they spend most of their energy promoting contraception, including condoms, for the prevention of pregnancy and disease. Nor is it surprising that they do not promote abstinence, but present it as only one of many possible alternatives, if they mention it at all.

2) Premarital sex is wrong, and therefore, it is a problem, but they are going to do it anyway.

Or, as some parents express this idea, "I wouldn't encourage my child to use contraceptives but, if he/she is sexually active, I hope he or she gets 'protection' from somewhere."

There are few areas in which so many people disagree with the "experts" as in the approach to premarital sex among teenagers. This second approach is, by far; the most popular among parents who do, as a rule, consider it to be a problem if their teenagers are having sex before marriage. Although this approach is ostensibly a "compromise," on the practical level, it is revealed in exactly the same actions as the first: Teenagers must be provided information about contraception, including condoms, because they will be "doing it anyway," and the promotion of abstinence is essentially ignored because it is "unrealistic."

Because most experts, parents, and educators endorse one of these first two attitudes, our society's strategy for managing the problems associated with adolescent sexuality is essentially promotion of contraceptives. Other factors are undoubtedly involved, but it is clear that, while relying primarily on promotion of contraceptives during the past few decades, we have witnessed significant increases in pregnancy rates,[6] abortion rates, and rates of sexually transmitted diseases among teenagers.[7] (see Figure 7 on the next page)

The approach adopted by our society has failed because, as we shall see, it misses the crux of the issue. We have been unable to reduce the "symptom" problems associated with adolescent sexuality because we have ignored the underlying cause of those problems.

3) Premarital sex is a problem.

Premarital sex is inherently wrong and is always an abuse of the gift of sexuality. This attitude allows for no compromise on the assertion that unmarried teens having sex is a problem. Teen pregnancy is indeed a problem, but it is only one consequence of the more fundamental problem that premarital sex is an inherent compromise on the priority of love. Using contraceptives to engage "safely" in premarital sex is a contradiction in terms, and is being only partially responsible.

Promotion of contraception is widely accepted as the only reasonable response to the problems of teenage pregnancy and sexually transmitted diseases, because contraception is regarded as lesser than the other evils. This message has been promoted by three major

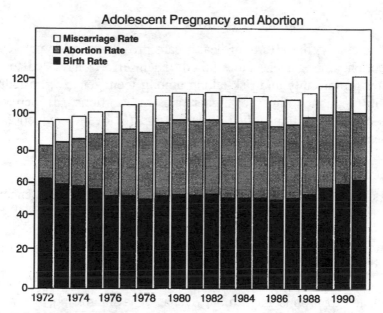

Figure 7. Adolescent Pregnancy Rate and Outcomes, 1972–1991. Source: National Center for Health Statistics and the Alan Guttmacher Institute.

channels of education in the country: (1) by health care providers in private and public medical offices, family planning clinics, and school-based clinics, (2) by sex education classes from kindergarten through twelfth grade, and in college courses in human sexuality, and (3) through physician education, at both basic and postgraduate levels. Throughout contemporary American society, promotion of contraceptives is aggressive. In contrast, the promotion of abstinence has been widely opposed and mostly relegated to patchy efforts by religious activists, because so many people have been afraid of being called unrealistic or appearing judgmental toward teens who do not choose the abstinence option.

Failure of Health Care Providers

Predictably, the efforts of health care providers to promote contraception among teens have failed. Their efforts have led to (a) greater promiscuity and risk-taking among teenagers, (b) no reduction in pregnancy rates, (c) higher rates of abortions, (d) increased rates of sexually transmitted diseases, and (e) overall reduction of self-esteem.

(a) Greater promiscuity and risk taking among teenagers.

As with adults (see Chapter 7), the use of contraception encourages risk taking by minimizing the consequences of premarital sex. The less risky a pleasurable behavior is perceived to be, the more likely teens are to engage in it. The safer bungee cord jumping appears to be, the more popular it will become.

Numerous studies support the assertion that contraception promotion leads to promiscuity among teens.[8] It is interesting that while this idea is accepted by two of the original developers of the pill,[9] by most parents and adolescents,[10] and by practicing clinicians,[11] many "experts" resolutely deny this relationship – a relationship that, by logic alone, should be self-evident.

(b) No reduction in pregnancy rates among teenagers.

According to Planned Parenthood's 1981 report on Teenage Pregnancy: the Problem That Hasn't Gone Away, "We know that many teenagers are making great efforts to prevent pregnancy, that more of them are using contraceptives and using them earlier and more consistently than ever before. Many are doing so successfully, yet pregnancy rates among U.S. teenagers are increasing and teenage birthrates, though declining, are still among the highest in the world. The decline in births is largely contingent on continued access to legal abortions."[12]

Two types of studies (national surveys and evaluations of school-based and other clinics) have been done to determine the effect of contraception promotion on teenage pregnancy rates. The most definitive national survey was done by researchers from Johns Hopkins, who reported, through Planned Parenthood, that in spite of "evidence of increased and more consistent contraceptive use, there was a rise between 1976 and 1979 in the proportion of premarital pregnancies occurring among those who reported that they had always used a contraceptive method,"[13]

The effect of the promotion of contraception through school-based clinics has also been measured.[14] After 15 years experience with such clinics, Planned Parenthood reported that, "there is no conclusive evidence showing that school-based clinic utilization lowers [teenage] pregnancy rates."[15] Sociologist Phillips Cutright also admits that we have found "no evidence that the [family planning] programs reduced white illegitimacy, because areas with weak programs, or no programs at all, experience smaller increases or larger declines [in pregnancy] than are found in areas with strong contraceptive programs."[16]

Professor Kingsley Davis, a member of the board of sponsors of Zero Population Growth, provides a realistic appraisal of the current situation when he writes:

The current belief that illegitimacy will be reduced if teenage girls are given an effective contraceptive is an extension of the same reasoning that created the problem in the first place. It reflects the unwillingness to face the problems of social control and social discipline, while trusting some technological device to extricate society from its difficulties. The irony is that the illegitimacy rise occurred precisely while contraception was becoming more rather than less widespread and respectable.[17]

Promotion of contraceptives to reduce adolescents' risk of becoming pregnant has been studied for decades, now, and the growing consensus among those knowledgeable in the field is that this campaign has failed. The explanation for this failure is complex, but it is most likely related primarily to the increased promiscuity among contracepting teens and the fact that they are the least reliable contraceptors.

(c) Higher rates of abortions among teenagers.

From 1972 to 1985 the rate of abortions among teenagers more than doubled.[18] The previously cited researchers at Johns Hopkins found that, "those young women having an abortion are seen to be almost twice as likely to have been contracepting at the time pregnancy occurred."[19]

This result has also been shown through school-based clinic studies.[20] Proponents of these clinics have reported with great enthusiasm that studies have shown a reduction in fertility (birth) rates following clinic utilization. But the fact that these studies have consistently failed to show a proportional reduction in pregnancy rates is usually inexplicably ignored. The difference between these two rates is the increase in the abortion rate. The reason why the birth rate drops is not that fewer teenagers become pregnant, but that more of them abort their pregnancies, not exactly a mark of progress.

At a lecture on teenage pregnancy given at a local medical center, a pediatrician presented data from a study on a school-based clinic which clearly showed the same results. She cheerfully noted the effectiveness of the clinic in reducing the birth rate among the school population, yet failed to mention that her own statistics showed a clear, concomitant increase in both pregnancy and abortion rates. The speaker offered no explanation when asked about this omission during the question and answer period.

(d) Increased rates of sexually transmitted diseases.

During the last twenty years, sexually transmitted diseases have struck our adolescent population unmercifully. To claim that all, or even most, of this rise is a consequence of contraception promotion is simplistic. Many other factors encourage risk-taking behavior, including widespread pornography, increased acceptance of premarital sex, and legal, publicly funded abortions. To the best of my knowledge, the relationship between promotion of contraception and sexually transmitted diseases has not actually been studied, but common sense can validate the cause and effect relationship. With increased promiscuity associated with contraceptive use, and a direct relationship between promiscuity and the risk of acquiring an infection, it is reasonable to conclude that contraception promotion is, in part, responsible for the current epidemic of STDs among teenagers.

In addressing the reality of this epidemic of STDs among teenagers, it might at first seem logical to turn to condoms, but we would do well to wonder how effective they can be. It is unrealistic to expect teens to use condoms with maximum effectiveness for several reasons. The contraceptive failure rate of condoms among adolescents is reported to be up to 33% [21] and, presumably, condoms are even less effective at preventing infections than they are at preventing pregnancies. Furthermore, adolescents tend to view themselves as invulnerable and have a long history of disregarding warnings. A student survey showed that, despite the AIDS crisis, 42 percent of sexually active high schoolers would continue to have sex even if condoms were not available. According to the publisher of that survey, "These alarming findings confirm our worst fears – high school students see themselves as invincible. . . . Unfortunately, it seems the message of the danger of AIDS will spread only with the number of young people who succumb to it."[22]

A literature survey on adolescent response to STDs reveals abundant evidence that apathy, in the face of the imminent danger, is widespread, and not explainable by ignorance. A study of homosexual and bisexual male adolescents found that the "subjects demonstrated accurate knowledge and beliefs about HIV; but 63 percent were found to be at 'extreme risk' for prior HIV exposure."[23] According to a study reported recently in Sweden, "Though there is a widespread knowledge both of STD and pregnancy protection, and though condoms are easily available, young people have problems practicing the method. This is also reflected in their frequent experience of pregnancies and STDs."[24] Similarly, a study from California found that, "although most adolescents knew that condoms prevent sexually transmitted diseases, an increasing belief in the preventive effects of condoms was not associated with an increased motivation to use themm."[25]

Not surprisingly, condoms are as unpopular among teens as they are among adults.[26] To emphasize the difficulty of achieving maximum effectiveness with condoms, let me repeat that they must be used properly (there are at least seven steps involved)[27] and they must be used every time, but only a relatively small percentage of teens are so motivated.[28] Moreover; just as with adults, a plethora of studies show that the teenagers at highest risk are the least likely to use condoms regularly.[29] As contraception advocate Jean Emans, M.D., from Harvard's Adolescent Clinic, sums it up, "Unfortunately, the record of condom use to date is quite poor among our vulnerable adolescent population."[30]

(e) Overall reduction in self-esteem among youth.

The relationship between contraception and self-esteem, self-valuing, or self-respect is an important and complex issue. The following is a list of reasons why adolescents say they have premarital sex, based on scientific literature and my own discussions with teenagers:

- Loneliness: they are looking for love, attention, warmth, affection.
- Desire to be popular; to prove their self-worth; to prove that they "are somebody" or that they are attractive.
- So that a partner will "love" him or her more.
- Peer pressure: "Everybody's doing it"; belief that something is wrong with them if they don't.
- Infatuation: a "crush" or sexual tension, mistaken for love.
- To prove their "love."
- Curiosity.
- It feels good.
- To avoid hurting a partner's feelings when the partner wants to have sex, even if one does not.
- Desire to be more of a man or woman, i.e., desire to feel grown up.
- To establish their sexual identity; to prove they're not homosexual.
- To get back at their parents or to make someone jealous.
- Didn't plan on going "all the way" (often associated with drugs or alcohol).
- Boredom

Nearly all of these motives are based on insecurity and selfishness, and they show that adolescent premarital sexual relationships are generally not motivated by any sense of caring and consideration, but by a willingness to use others. As one teen says, "Sex isn't about love anymore, there's such peer pressure to do it."[31] When I ask sexually active girls what would happen if they said "no" to premarital sex with their current boyfriends, most predict that such a stance would end the relationship. It is disheartening how aware they are of the self-serving nature of their sexual relationships. Many boys, too, are aware that they are using girls, or, in some cases, are being used themselves. As one teen explained, quite matter-of-factly, "A lot of guys say they won't waste more than three weeks with a girl – if she won't have sex, they drop her."[32]

Adolescent health literature consistently supports a strong association between teens involved in early or promiscuous sexual relations and low self-esteem or insufficient self-love. The lower a student's self-esteem, the greater the risk of becoming involved in the many activities so often found in association with it: premarital sex (including prostitution and homosexual behavior), drugs, alcohol, academic decline, truancy, crime, depression, and suicide.[33] It is not surprising that such adolescents are willing to use each other sexually. Such a willingness derives from the outspoken despair expressed today, exemplified by comments such as, "Life sucks and then you die." As Bob Seeger sings about "awkward teenage blues" in the song *Night Moves,* "I used her, she used me, and neither of us cared." All indicators of disillusionment and low self-esteem among teenagers are on the rise. For example, the suicide rate for ages 15-19 tripled from 1960 to 1980.[34]

When low self-esteem leads to premarital sex, it often initiates a vicious cycle: teenagers knowing that they are involved in exploitative relationships, that they have gotten themselves or someone else pregnant or contracted a disease, that they have had an abortion, or advised a girlfriend to have one. In this way, teen premarital sexual activity leads to more problems, more guilt, more fear, more embarrassment, more distrust, more depression and, hence, even greater loss of self-esteem. Involvement in sexual risk-taking compounds a poor self-image. By encouraging sexual risk-taking, the use of contraceptives accelerates this cycle. By minimizing the risks associated with genital sexual activity, contraceptives invite teens to exploit each other.

The simplistic application of technology (contraception) to the complex psychosocial problems of adolescents has brought anything but success. Even if the strategy of giving adolescents the pill to reduce their risk of pregnancy and the condom to reduce their risk of diseases were successful, there are no technological marvels capable of protecting their self-esteem. Contraceptives cannot protect them from using each other and of being used – from accepting lower levels of psychosexual functioning. As one abstinence campaign puts it, "Condoms don't protect the heart."[35]

Failure of school sex education courses

The late Alan Guttmacher, past president of Planned Parenthood, promised in 1979 that, "the only avenue in which Planned Parenthood has to win the battle is sex education."[36] He should be delighted to know that seventy-five percent of adolescents in the United States now receive classroom sexuality instruction,[37] and that the federal government provides fifty dollars to promote contraception among teenagers for every one dollar it allots for promotion of abstinence.[38] The great majority of sex education courses (so-called "comprehensive sex education") emphasize the same approach as health care providers: they promote contraception to reduce pregnancy rates, and condoms for disease avoidance and "safer sex." Unfortunately, however; formal school instruction has not been shown to be any more successful in its endeavors than are health care providers. Let's take a look at the effect of school-based sex education on the same five areas just discussed: promiscuity, pregnancy rates, abortion rates, STD rates and self-esteem.

Reports of research on the relationship between contraceptive-based sex education and promiscuity are conflicting, so we will not evaluate them here. It may be significant and illustrative, however, that at least three reports from sex education's main proponents support the claim that sex education does, in fact, encourage promiscuity.[39]

Comprehensive reviews of contraceptive-based sex education have consistently revealed that it does not lower pregnancy rates among teens.[40] According to Planned Parenthood, "While studies have documented the disappointing effects of sex education, very little research has been done to help us understand why sex education does not have the desired effects and how it might be strengthened. It seems to have been sufficient for the field to conclude that sex education as currently offered is ineffective in preventing teenage pregnancies."[41]

The effect of contraceptive-based sex education on the abortion rate has not, to my knowledge, been studied.

While much sex education in schools is directed specifically at STD prevention, it does not significantly reduce the risk of diseases among teens. The bulk of the data demonstrates that even specific education about HIV disease has not led to regular condom use by teens any more than it has by adults.[42] For example, a typical study of the effect of condom education on sexually active adolescents revealed that, "although perceptions that condoms prevent sexually transmitted diseases (STDs) and the value and importance placed on avoiding STDs remained high, these were neither reflected in increased intentions to use condoms nor in increased use." The authors of this study described their results as "disquieting."[43]

A few studies have shown some positive effect of specific HIV education, but the effect was always "modest" (e.g., the use of condoms increasing from 33.4% to 34.4%), and none of these studies addressed the critical question of whether at-risk adolescents were the ones affected.[44]

A splashy full-page ad in the *Los Angeles Times* by The Family Connection, A Partnership for Responsible Parenting was entitled "How California Can Fight Teen Pregnancy."[45] The ad, sponsored in part by the California branch of The American College of Obstetricians and Gynecologists, claimed that the first two answers to the teen pregnancy problem are expanded access to contraceptives and comprehensive sexuality education. It stated, "Numerous studies have shown that helping young people avoid pregnancy (through these two interventions) does not increase the rate of teen sexual activity – only that it reduces rates of unwanted teen pregnancy and exposure to sexually transmitted diseases such as AIDS." As the reader may guess at this point, no references for the "numerous studies" were given. Despite such unsubstantiated claims, we have seen no evidence of significant, positive effect of 25 years of contraceptive-based sex education.

Reviewing the content of some of the texts used may help to explain why these programs have been so ineffective. The anatomical and physiological information provided in the courses is not the problem. The problem is in the inappropriateness of some of the material to a particular grade level, the slanted messages sent by some of the casual statements, and the half-truths or actual misinformation communicated in print. Many organizations have documented the problematic material dispensed through sex education courses (see Resource appendix), but a few examples here will illustrate the problem.

The SIECUS pamphlet, *How to Talk to Your Children About AIDS* makes the recommendation that nine year-olds "need to know what is meant by sexual intercourse, homosexuality and oral and anal sex."[46] SIECUS guidelines for sexuality education recommends that five year olds be taught that, "Masturbation should be done in a private place," that nine year olds be taught that, "Homosexual love relationship can be as fulfilling as heterosexual relationships," and that fifteen year olds should be taught that erotic images "help people understand sexuality."[47] Dr. Patricia Schiller, Founder of the American Association of Sex Educators, Counselors and Therapists, (AASECT), calls the text *Learning About Sex: The Contemporary Guide for Young Adults,* by Gary F. Kelly, "a must for all young people." The book includes, among others, the statement that, "Sadomasochism may be very acceptable and safe for sexual partners who know each other's needs and have established agreements for what they want from each other."[48]

Even in schools run by religious organizations, we find material that is clearly not conducive to lowering statistics for pregnancy, abortion or STDs. At a local Catholic elementary school, a "Slang Word Exercise" is used to "desensitize" children; groups of students are invited to "brainstorm and come up with as many synonyms as possible to the words [penis, vagina, and intercourse] in three or four minutes. Baby words, street language, slang or formal language are all acceptable."[49] One disenchanted teacher explained why sex educators would want to "desensitize" children with four statements in sequence: "Teenage pregnancy is a problem. Birth control is the solution. Shame is the barrier to applying the solution. Therefore, [we must] eliminate shame."[50]

A popular adolescent sex education teacher's manual advises that, "it is not necessary to enjoy or 'be into' anal, oral, auto, homo, or group sexuality in order to fit in. . . . Nevertheless, having fixed powerful emotions of revulsion or disgust in response to behavior which is enjoyable to others, may mean *you have a sexual disorder or a psychological problem*"[51] (emphasis added). Ann Landers publishes a pamphlet for teenagers which is used in Christian camps across the United States. In it she says that the birth control pill "is almost 100% effective" and that the condom "is approximately 98% effective."[52] According to any knowledgeable source, these statistics are grossly inaccurate, especially as applied to teenagers.

In the human sexuality class offered at the local university, the students are asked to discuss their favorite position for engaging in sexual intercourse. A video resource guide for family planning clinics and colleges offers a video of a couple having sex entitled "Rich & Judy." In the description of the film, we read that "she has a visible orgasm," and that the film is "recommended to introduce and portray heterosexual intercourse within a very loving relationship."[53] The description does not, however, explain how a visible orgasm proves that the relationship is "very loving." While not all contraceptive-based sex education programs have examples as dramatic as these, many do.

The lack of effectiveness of existing programs has prompted a variety of responses from their proponents, e.g., that they might be more successful if begun at an earlier age. A medical journal report entitled "The Urgent Need for Sex Education" states, "These findings [that sex education is having no influence on behavior] indicate that sex education beginning only during adolescence is too late."[54] If programs were proven to have positive effects, one might expect greater benefits to occur with more of the same. But there is no logic in assuming that ineffectual programs will be successful if taught from an earlier age. Other responses have included the desperate suggestion to encourage anal intercourse as a "contraceptive," accompanied, of course, with careful reminders to use condoms, in deference to the threat of HIV.[55] In frustration, a few forward-looking sex educators have even begun to change their strategy to a more abstinence-oriented approach[56] ("delaying sex") and emphasizing the enhancement of self-esteem and other more essential issues.

Education and training of physicians

Medical literature is rife with articles on adolescent sexuality, which uniformly emphasize the use of contraceptives, including condoms, for adolescents now or soon to become sexually active. For example, the American Academy of Pediatrics policy statement on adolescent sexuality[57] includes two inaccurate and, therefore, dangerous statements: (1) the birth control pill "has been widely and successfully used with teenagers for many years," and (2) the perception that "providing contraception will encourage sexual promiscuity" has not "been substantiated." The evidence previously cited in this chapter establishes that both are false. The same approach is officially embraced by all of the major medical societies including the American Medical Association, the American Academy of Family Physicians, and The American College of Obstetricians and Gynecologists.

Those who advise physicians offer only the briefest reference to abstinence, and when they do, they often include a catch. For example, *Adolescent Medicine: State of the Art Reviews,* developed with the cooperation of the American Academy of Pediatrics, presents an Outline for Guided Decision Making in Sexual Activity for physicians. The author, a medical professor from the University of California at Irvine, discusses the options of abstinence and sex with contraceptives. To implement the option of abstinence, she writes that the "patient and dating partner need to make [a] commitment to abstinence and develop alternatives to satisfy sexual drives such as mutual masturbation."[58] She does not mention the option of abstinence without masturbation; the choice is either contraception with intercourse or outercourse.

With surprising uniformity, health care providers, sex education courses, and post-graduate physician education all emphasize a contraceptive-based approach to adolescent premarital sexual activity, despite the fact that the best data available demonstrates the failure of this approach. This lack of evidence to support using the contraceptive approach has, in fact, been my biggest surprise since becoming involved in teaching sexuality. Almost as surprising is the fact that some of the strongest advocates of contraceptive-based sex education also provide evidence which discredits their own approach.

Presumably, at some time in the future, medical science will devise a contraceptive that will effectively reduce the risk to teenagers of pregnancy and STDs. Unfortunately, this scientific breakthrough will be counterproductive with respect to the fundamental problem associated with adolescent sexuality: lack of virtue and willingness to use others and be used. Those with a sincere interest in the welfare of adolescents must address this dilemma.

Abstinence-only Sex Education Programs

The alternative, abstinence only courses are relative newcomers on the scene; their approach is that premarital sex is wrong and therefore is to be freely discouraged. Ironically, Planned Parenthood has reported on a sex education program for eighth graders in Atlanta, Georgia, which had initially emphasized contraception and was found to have no effect on future sexual behavior; participating students were neither more likely to refrain from sexual intercourse nor more likely to use contraceptives if they became sexually involved. When the course was replaced with an abstinence-only program, however, "students who had not participated in the program were as much as five times more likely to have begun having sex than were those who had had the program."[59] Planned Parenthood has also reported a study in which resistance skills education (i.e., how to say "No") reduced the number of partners and frequency of sexual intercourse among teenage males.[60]

The *Community of Caring* program, in which "promotion of abstinence . . . is a cornerstone," and an interdisciplinary approach is used to stress specific values, takes credit for having lowered the pregnancy rate among participating high schoolers. In one school, the pregnancy rate among ninth graders fell from twelve to three over a six year period after initiating the program.[61] The *Teen STAR* program, which emphasizes fertility awareness and appreciation, has reported significant improvement in attitudes and behaviors and low pregnancy rates among participating students.[62] The *Best Friends* program reports a 22 percent rate of sexual activity among its 9-12 graders compared to a 73 percent rate among non-participants, and a pregnancy rate of one percent among participating girls compared to a 26 percent pregnancy rate among nonparticipants.[63] *Teen Choice,* a one hour, abstinence only presentation, has used pre- and post-program questionnaires to document the positive effect on students' opinions.[64] *Teen-Aid,* another abstinence-only program reports a ten percent reduction in the rate of "transition" from virginity to sexually experienced among program participants.[65] *Living Smart,* a course for seventh and eighth graders, demonstrated that abstinence education results in more positive attitudes toward abstinence and reduced levels of sexual activity.[66] Other reports, however; have demonstrated minimal or no effect of abstinence only programs.[67]

Along with many abstinence-only programs, the most recent literature demonstrates that programs which include a similar multifaceted approach – the clear promotion of behavioral norms like premarital abstinence, resistance and communication skills, family unity – but also include information about contraceptives for those who remain sexually active, produce some positive results including reduced pregnancy rates.[68] These programs demonstrate an effectiveness not found in programs lacking abstinence education and resistance training but, because of the all-inclusive approach of these programs, it remains unclear what contribution each component made. Studies are needed that compare otherwise equivalent programs with and without the contraception component to determine if its inclusion makes any positive contribution. Given the current body of literature, it is most reasonable to assume that the inclusion of contraceptive information, if anything, hinders the success of programs by confusing the message and validating risk-taking behaviors. Programs that emphasize contraceptives primarily are no longer being studied since all agree that they are ineffective.

The available data supports the view that abstinence-only sex education is somewhat effective in improving attitudes and behaviors among teenagers, while contraceptive-based health care and sex education are not. This result is not surprising considering the mixed messages that contraceptive-based programs send, i.e., that premarital sex may be wrong, but we'll give you means for engaging in it without consequences. Mixed messages confuse all of us, but they are especially confusing to young people who are searching for answers. For example, one boy told his mother that his elementary school sex education course taught him that premarital sex is acceptable for boys but not for girls.

But mixed messages do worse than confuse. Ultimately, the message is that teens, like addicts, have needs that they can't control, and so they are going to "do it" anyway. Internationally renowned psychiatrist James Masterson from Cornell University Medical Center, writes that "self control [is] the only basis for self esteem,"[69] and yet we are systematically teaching our nation's children that they have no control over their sex drives. The message is that adolescents cannot be fully loving, they cannot help but abuse themselves and others through sex, so they should be taught how to "sort of" love through the use of contraceptives and outercourse.

Alan Keyes writes, "If we encourage our children to believe they can't control their sexual desires, what of their greed, their anger; their prejudice, and their hate? What condoms will we distribute to protect them from the consequences of those?"[70] It was predictable that the movement to promote contraception among teens would fail, because of the fundamental reluctance to confront basic moral issues. In an effort to be nonjudgmental, this approach avoids principles and relies on sex trivia, such as how to put on a condom, naming sex organs, or explaining positions for sexual intercourse. In *Challenging Children to Chastity,* author Vernon Sattler poses some telling questions when he asks: "How has the knowledge of graafian follicles or the epididymis ever affected the ordinary day to day living of two people who enter into a loving marriage? How has statistical knowledge of the frequency of illicit orgasm helped devoted couples?"[71]

Sex educators and health care providers who promote contraceptives, condoms and "safer sex" are becoming more frustrated with the increasing exposure of the ineffective, if not counterproductive, nature of their well-intentioned efforts. Many are now beginning to advocate abstinence and virtue, but the mixed message persists.

The alternative approach, which considers abstinence the only viable option, is the unpopular; and supposedly "unrealistic" approach in spite of supportive evidence from research. The SIECUS executive director goes beyond calling these programs unrealistic when she brands them "fear based."[72] It is difficult not to respond by charging her with insensitivity to the grim consequences of teenaged premarital sexual activity – what she and her colleagues refer to as "discovering their sexuality."

Besides being considered unrealistic, the other primary criticism of abstinence-only programs is that they promote a rigid value system. Those who attempt to censure these programs rely on our final misconception:

Misconception #17: Sex education should be "values free."

This misconception ignores the fact that sexuality, of its nature, is a value-laden topic. Each curriculum must commit to some method of deciding what value should be given to conflicting priorities. Contraceptive-based programs teach a value system in which the priorities of freedom and pleasure may be equal to, or greater than, love. Students, therefore, may reasonably choose behaviors based on any preferred priority. Abstinence-only educators decry this devaluation of love and demand that it be maintained in its natural position of primacy.

The question is not whether values should be taught, but which values should be taught. With "value-free" sex education, it is the values of situational ethics that allow the situation to determine which priority will take precedence. "Value-free" education is not actually free of values, but only free of the essential constraints prescribed by natural law.

We have concentrated on one question with regard to adolescent sexual activity: whether to promote abstinence or contraception.

Premarital abstinence is a critical issue, but "just saying no" is not enough. Many courses recognize that premarital abstinence is the only truly reasonable alternative, but most also contain much substantive material on self-esteem enhancement, how to "say no," how to cope with peer pressure, and dating strategies. It is clear why an approach that concentrates on more significant issues succeeds, while courses taught at the "Band-Aid" level of contraception, STD prevention, and outercourse fail.

Still, we may well question whether or not abstinence-only courses are ultimately the best solution. Theoretically, at least, they should be a valuable means of encouraging a realistic, holistic approach to sex and discouraging early development of sexually addictive and codependent attitudes among teenagers. But we may also wonder how a few hours of class time can make a lasting impression on children who live in a world (and many, even in homes) with very contrary attitudes.

Several problems are inherent in all forms of sex education, even abstinence-only programs, leading some people to wonder if schools should be teaching sex education at all. Acceptable programs must have solved the problems of (1) being reality-based; (2) not harming some children in an attempt to help others; and (3) not encouraging undue emphasis on the sexual aspect of relationships. The rating of current abstinence-only courses on these points is not uniformly high.

1) While we freely criticized contraceptive-based courses for miscuing students about the primary realities of sex, many abstinence-only courses also include errors. Further, while a particular curriculum may appear acceptable, individual instructors can bring their own biases to the presentation of material. Even with a reliable teacher's guide, an instructor may lack the skills and background necessary to teach a balanced, undistorted, moral approach to sex.

2) Sex education courses should not prematurely expose less experienced students to adult concerns in attempts to benefit those students who have been abused or come from otherwise very challenging circumstances. Even most abstinence programs fail to protect

"inexperienced" children from issues for which they may not be prepared. Children vary greatly in their readiness to discuss intensely intimate issues. Parents or a child's primary caregiver are best qualified to sense their own child's level of maturity and ability to assimilate particular information and concepts. Unfortunately, most programs focus on the more troubled cohort of students instead of the less worldly – one student's innocence is sacrificed for another's possible gain. No one knows how much damage may be done through intimate and detailed group discussions involving school-aged children of diverse backgrounds. Children are already inundated with premature exposures to sex outside school. They do not need further exposure through structured school programs. Sex education should not add to the desensitization pressures which children face. Nor should it be the occasion for emotions such as anger or embarrassment. Questions about intimate, personal issues, which might create discomfort, should be left for parents or primary caregivers to cover at age-appropriate times. Any classroom sex education curriculum should have as a primary goal to preserve the most innocent student from scandal.

3) By their existence, sex education courses over-emphasize the importance of genital sex, i.e., sex is so important that we need an entire course devoted to it. More constructively, we should provide role models and education on whole relationships, and about morality and love, rather than sex. Much of what is taught in abstinence-only courses should be taught elsewhere, for example, biological aspects of sex in science classes.

Family-based Sex Education

Although abstinence-only courses have achieved documented success in some areas, because of these inherent problems, many of us have reservations about using even them for sex education. Group discussions that encourage moral sexual behavior may have positive effects on adolescents, but they could have significant negative effects if the circumstances surrounding the discussion fall too short of the ideal.

It is unreasonable to expect a few hours of sex education to have a persistent, significant effect on children who are growing up in an environment that unrelentingly contradicts what is being taught in the course. The impact of the family is far more important than any classroom sex education. Studies have consistently related premature sexual experimentation and promiscuity with a lack of family stability, nurturing, and supervision. A study of 10,000 high school sophomores, conducted by the U.S. Department of Education, found that parents who had a close relationship with their teenage daughters, and supervised their school work and activities, were able to reduce by 42 percent the likelihood that their daughters would become pregnant.[73] Conversely, a distant or absent father is one of the strongest predictors of health-risk behaviors among adolescents. A Washington State University sociologist found that, among young black females, those "who had a biological father living in the home were 42 percent less likely to make their sexual debut" before age 16.[74]

In spite of classroom sex education of whatever nature, the problems of teenage sexual exploitation, unintended pregnancies, and sexually transmitted diseases will remain rampant until our society unites in serious commitment to renew the family. The home is the site in which to concentrate efforts aimed at promoting sexual health among children.

For high-risk teenagers who come from unsupportive, fragmented households, there may be few realistic answers. There is no panacea or magic pill to cure their complex problems. Contraceptive-based education does not benefit those who are most likely to "do it anyway," and even the best abstinence programs may be of limited value to some of these young people. Only through a myriad of school and community based programs aimed at family disunity, chemical dependency (for both parents and students), and related social ills, can these adolescents find hope.

Sexual Wisdom was written primarily to assist parents in fulfilling their duty as primary sex educators of their children. It grew out of a realization that school-based courses alone cannot be expected to overcome the challenge to today's youth. To effectively respond to the crisis teens face today, parents must become more informed and courageous to discuss sexuality with their children at age-appropriate levels. Children cannot be expected to develop lasting, healthy attitudes without support from home, no matter how strong school programs are.

In the next chapter, we shall discuss specific efforts that can be made within the home to sex-educate children. As for school programs, the optimum situation would be one in which a course on morality and virtue is taught by qualified instructors, with sexual morality being covered as one part of that series. Short of this goal, the primary objective should be eliminating all sex education courses based on the principle of "they're going to do it anyway" rationale, and thoroughly scrutinizing all abstinence-only courses as well.

If courses are not removed, *parents should familiarize themselves with those classes attended by their children.* They should review the course teacher's manual, should question their children about classroom presentations and activities and should even sit in on classes themselves if at all feasible. Since teachers and courses vary widely, parents should monitor each course themselves. Class attendance is effective because sex educators are less likely to make controversial statements when parents are present. While many teachers and administrators have good intentions, parents should assume that no schools or programs are "safe." Some of the examples were taken from religious settings to make this point. Even religious and private school abstinence-only courses should be carefully monitored.

Courses can be evaluated based on the compromises they make on priorities and goals, and how much they acquiesce to falsehoods. Courses should emphasize the advantages of a fully moral approach to sex, and healthy ways to build emotional intimacy with members of the opposite sex. Many of these issues have been discussed in this book, and further information can be found in the *National Guidelines for Sexuality and Character Education* by the Medical Institute for Sexual Health, (see Resource Appendix).

After evaluation of local courses, parents should express their concerns candidly and directly to their local school boards and administrators. Families are losing the political battle over sex education on most fronts. Parents must become politically involved on the local, state and federal levels if schools are to have the most helpful, least harmful effect on students' psychosexual development.

Chapter 17

Parents as Sex Educators

Note: For the sake of simplicity, this chapter generally assumes an audience of two-parent families; there is no intent to ignore or diminish the value of single parents and others who serve as primary caretakers.

Most parents' hope for their children's sexual relationships goes far beyond avoiding diseases and "unwanted" pregnancies, even beyond falling in love (which may precede falling out of love by a surprisingly short time span). Most parents hope that each of their children will find a cherished, lifelong companion. Since they realize that they cannot nurture and protect their children indefinitely, parents or parental figures expect that, eventually, these functions will be taken over by their children's spouses.

Parents hope that their children's marriages will be constantly improving, growing stronger and more committed, flourishing in intimacy and trust; not, as is becoming so common today, temporary arrangements officially terminated by divorce and sustained only in lingering arguments over visitation rights for their children or battles over child support. Few things disrupt people's lives so profoundly as marital dysfunction and divorce, but with the widespread marital failure in today's world, the goal of a healthy marriage may now seem naive. That goal is possible only for couples who are willing to take their relationship very seriously. While attitudes about sex are not the only influence on the success of marital relationships, they are clearly important. Respect inside the bedroom begets respect outside of it.

Parents have tremendous influence on their children's attitudes about sex and therefore can contribute directly to the success of their children's marriages. Parents exert influence by serving as role models, by helping their children to develop healthy self-esteem or self respect, and by serving as sex educators.

Parents as Role Models

Perhaps the most important example parents offer their children is their own treatment of each other. Children tend to define "normal" behavior based on observation of their parents. Therefore, a critical task of parenthood is to model a healthy marital relationship. Children who witness the natural affection of a respectful, mutually supportive spousal relationship will tend to imitate that model.

To offer positive role models for their children, parents must do their homework. They must reflect on and educate themselves about sexuality. The better they understand their priorities and goals, the better they can readily, consistently, reject misconceptions.

Parents who desire that their children travel the high road must travel that road themselves. For parents to maintain not only a team spirit but a healthy romance throughout a lifelong marriage is a most challenging but rewarding task. It is one of the greatest gifts parents can give to their children. Each parent must be willing to contribute more than his or her fair share to the relationship. Children, once married, are less likely to sustain the joy of their own honeymoon if their parents failed to do so. To regulate their fertility, parents should take advantage of the natural nurturing effects of Fertility Awareness. And as important as it is to monitor their children's television time, parents should choose their own entertainment carefully.

Parents as Developers of Their Children's Self-Esteem

Parental involvement is a critical factor in maintaining children's self-esteem. A child's sense of worth is reaffirmed by a nurturing, affectionate parental figure, while self-esteem problems are common among children who are abandoned (emotionally or physically) by their parents. We have become accustomed to hearing about parents, especially men, who abandon their children through premarital sex or divorce. We do not hear so much about married couples who "abandon" their offspring to day care, pre-school, television, or peer groups, but they exist – in substantial and ever-increasing numbers.

Day care is essential for some families, but for many others is essentially parental neglect – the most subtle form of child abuse. Hard luck cases are common since single parents often have little choice and many married couples struggle to support their families. At the other extreme, however, we find parents who drop off their children at day care centers because they are bored doing day-to-day parenting activities. One working mother, on temporary disability for a back injury, requested that she be released to return to work because of the stress of staying home with her own children. "My kids need to go back to day care and I need to go back to work," she stated matter-of-factly.

Many parents of day care children make great sacrifices, financial and otherwise, to maintain their roles as primary caretakers. Such sacrifices are well worthwhile. Children who perceive that their parents value them will value themselves. Parents reassure their children by demonstrating enthusiasm for the daily tasks of parenthood. Some parents rationalize that spending "quality time" with children is sufficient, but wiser parents appreciate the unique benefits of both quantity and quality time.[1] Quality time, for example, is often the means insuring that they are on hand to seize the "teachable moment."

Situations in which both parents work outside the home are complex, and each situation is unique. These observations are not meant to add to the burden of parents already plagued with guilt over unavoidable absences from their children; they are meant to raise the level of awareness of those who might more carefully consider their choices. The point is that child neglect and (just as significant) perceived neglect from the child's standpoint should be a serious concern of all families with two working parents. That point is made emphatically in a letter from a full-time mother to the editor of a newspaper:

Only in the world of academia, not in the real world, do you hear attitudes such as that of U.S.C. [University of Southern California] professor Lois Banner: The "movement . . . to sanctify motherhood . . . could be unfortunate. We're seeing it everywhere, every day – reports of women preferring motherhood to work, preferring to stay home with their children rather than going out to an office."

Motherhood is work, and having been in the business world for 10 years and a full-time mother for seven, I'd take the ease of an eight-hour day, a full lunch hour, coffee breaks and all the social occasions and adult conversation that go along with working outside the home.

So, why have I chosen to stay at home? Because women can't "have it all," as we are led by you to believe. Since no one can be two places at one time, something has to suffer. If you let your job suffer, you lose it. Therefore it is necessary not to let your job suffer. The ones who suffer are the children, the ones who can't fire you for being insufficient.[2]

Despite my concern over the apparent lack of careful consideration many adults give to their use of day care, families with single parents and those with two working parents often do require extra support and sensitivity from the rest of us because of the additional challenges they face. And by support, I mean moral, political, and social, not merely psychological.

In their efforts to foster healthy self-esteem for their children, parents must keep common sense and the principle of moderation in mind. Many "progressive" efforts to build self-esteem begin with the notion that if children are told often enough that they are good, they will start to believe it. (This technique works best with small children, less with older ones.) This is what is known as the "feel good" approach as opposed to the "do good" approach to building self-esteem. One critic of the "feel good" approach puts it, "I don't disagree that self-esteem is important, but you don't help children by giving them a 'You're Special' certificate for doing nothing at all. . . . (That) leads not to self-esteem but narcissism."[3]

Much of anyone's praiseworthiness or true sense of self-worth

comes from the morality of one's behavior. An idea that is somewhat foreign to modern educator parlance is that one of the great
boosts to an adolescent's self-esteem comes simply from the satisfaction of doing good and helping others. "It is in giving that we
receive," and part of what we receive is self-esteem. Adolescents,
particularly those already troubled by low self-esteem, should be
encouraged to be of service to others, because doing so boosts one's
self-image and perception of the world. When I ask teenagers how it
makes them feel to do charity work, they state the obvious: it makes
them feel good about themselves.

To increase our children's self-esteem we should encourage them
to succeed. We should encourage our children to be the best baseball
player; dancer; mathematician, or magician they can be. But, more
important, we need to encourage our children to excel at being kind,
courteous, and caring. One of the great boosts to a child's self-
esteem is the knowledge that they are great at giving of themselves.
Happily, all of us have that potential.

Parents as Sex Educators

Publishers Note:

Since the initial publication of *Sexual Wisdom*, Dr. Wetzel
has created a comprehensive course on sexuality: *Sexual Wisdom for Catholic Adolescents*. This course was written for parents to give one-on-one to their older teenagers, or it may be
self-taught. It is the same course he has given to his own children. This is only available as a free download from our website at www.sexualwisdom.com but will soon be available for
purchase in book form.

Example, supervision, and moral education are crucial, but they are not enough if parents want their children to develop healthy attitudes about sex. As they have in every other generation, many children today believe that "it's a different world now," and what was good for their parents isn't necessarily good for them. Further, children are sex-educated by society from early childhood, with messages full of inconsistencies and falsehoods. Therefore, parents must actively engage their children in discussions about sex and challenge what their children are being taught by the media, the clothing industry, Madison Avenue, our legal system, sex education courses, etc.

Due to natural modesty, parents typically face the prospect of discussing sex with their children with some sense of embarrassment. Maintaining a sense of modesty both for themselves and for their children is prerequisite to any discussion about sex, but discussions must occur. Parents may also feel uncomfortable discussing sex with their children because (a) they have made mistakes about their own sexuality, and (b) they feel that they don't know enough about sex so they had better leave it to the "experts."

We have all made mistakes when it comes to sex, but parents must not let discomfort over their own mistakes keep them from discussing sex with their children. Rather they should take the opportunity to pass on to their children the lessons they have learned from experience. If parents do not teach their children about sex, society's influences will go unchallenged, and their children will also make mistakes, will feel ashamed, and the cycle will continue.

While children today know more about sex trivia than any generation before them, they generally know less than prior generations about the core issues of sexuality. Today's youth are conversant about fashions, sexual slang words, and various sexual positions as displayed in popular movies, but they are surprisingly unaware of how to incorporate their sexuality into their relationships. Sex education courses reinforce this emphasis on trivia. They dwell on minutia, from premature ejaculation to the use of contraceptive foam, and preach the danger of ignorance on these matters. Educators rationalize their approach by citing teenagers' misconceptions, such as the belief that kissing can cause pregnancy, or that one cannot become pregnant when sex is infrequent.[4] Such examples are extreme.

The vast majority of students are well aware that kissing doesn't lead to pregnancy, and even the most sexually ignorant student understands that risks escalate when the clothes come off.

Sex education courses are ineffective because they are filled with error and dwell on trivia instead of fundamental moral principles. Parents who understand the need to emphasize these principles can also feel confident because they possess a greater understanding than their children of what is important.

No matter what uneasiness parents may have about discussing sex, all responsible parents must accept this challenge. In years gone by, it may have been enough to leave the sex education of children to society, but not today. It is unreasonable to expect children who are exposed to so many negative forces to develop truly healthy attitudes without specific instruction from authority figures. Parents who do not discuss sex with their children are negligent. They have failed in a fundamental duty – a duty that *Sexual Wisdom* was written to help them fulfill. Toward this end, I offer seven general recommendations for making it easier for parents to fulfill that duty.

• Treat sex education as a process.

Both parents (if there are two) should make a conscientious effort to discuss issues related to sex with children of both sexes. Educating children about sex is not a one-time "birds and the bees" lecture, but an ongoing process for which all primary caretakers are responsible.

• Be honest.

Teens today are afraid. They know that there may be much to fear in their sexual future. Most of them want to protect themselves, but they feel confused and are searching for honest answers to questions about what to do on dates, how to interact with the opposite sex, what kind of people to date, and the value of virginity. In spite of all they have heard from their peers and the rest of the world, they are confused about contraception, the risk of pregnancy and how it can affect their future, the risks of diseases and how they can affect life and death.

Children respect straightforwardness and honesty from those

willing to help them answer these questions. As much as they may appear to resent parental interference, they will listen to what their parents say if they are convinced of two things: first, that their parents truly have their best interests in mind, and second, that their parents are qualified – that they are generally reasonable, and sufficiently intelligent and knowledgeable. It is easy to hide behind unconvincing rhetoric when discussing sex, especially when one is taking an unpopular position. The best preparation parents can make for such discussions is by studying the issues so they can speak knowledgeably, thoughtfully and understandingly about sex. When I taught a seven-hour abstinence-only course (supposedly the least popular approach) to the most troubled teens, I was often asked by them at the end of the course to return again so they could learn more. Teenagers usually are very interested in sex, and often are eager to discuss it with a parent or other authoritative figure who is honest and responsive.

• Ask challenging questions and work through realistic answers.

Teenagers who are in a rebellious mode, as many are, can be adept at avoiding straight answers, with a shrug of the shoulders or an offside glance. Parents can get them to think by asking basic, open-ended questions with logical follow-up questions, but above all by listening – to the answers – and to the sometimes unspoken questions. To discuss sex or any other topic most effectively, parents may need to cultivate their own communication skills, which include both self-expression and listening. For example, when conversations get bogged down, it may help for the parent to attempt to more plainly rephrase a teenager's question or statement.

• Avoid pronouncements.

Pronouncements and condemnations, like any tyrannical and authoritarian parental attitudes, have never been popular among adolescents, and they are not likely to win many converts among today's independent younger generation. An example from a context outside the normal family situation illustrates this principle. I remember watching a late night talk show with two guests, the founder and a "priestess" of a bizarre religion. Those who donated money to this "church" were allowed to have sex with the priestess. Obviously the church was a cover for prostitution, and the talk show host was appalled when his guests revealed that the priestess had had sex with 2,000 men in the last five years. Both guests were interested in discussing their "vocations," but the host began shouting that she was a prostitute and he was a pimp and refused to discuss any issue with them. After several minutes of name-calling by the host, the guests walked off the stage in disgust, without having been allowed to express their views.

The host's evaluation of the "church" and its staff was valid enough, but he could have handled the situation more constructively. The host missed an opportunity to expose distorted, confused attitudes about sex because he condemned and pronounced instead of discussing the issues. He could have asked serious questions and followed through on them, leading the audience, and perhaps even the two guests, to do some serious thinking.

He could have asked the priestess if she had any children and, if so, what kind of support she received from their father(s); how she would feel if she gave a disease to a client and he gave it to his wife; whether she knew if this chain reaction had ever happened; whether she would inform prior clients if she tests positive for a disease; whether she had any chemical addictions or had ever attempted suicide; whether she had ever been physically or emotionally abused, raped or molested; whether she carried a weapon; or whether she had ever had to defend herself from a client?

By launching into a self-righteous tirade, the host lost an opportunity to demystify prostitution; by making pronouncements, and preventing discussion, the host left the fantasy intact. The prostitute came across as open-minded and unscathed by her "liberated" lifestyle, while the host loomed as a closed-minded, unsophisticated prude. He lost his chance to show what is wrong with prostitution.

Religious pronouncements ("Because God said not to!") can also be conversation-stoppers. Depending on one's background, such comments may or may not be appropriate, but often they are more effective near the end of a discussion, to add another kind of emphasis to a convincing argument, rather than at the beginning when dialogue has yet to be established. Children raised in religious households who have respect for biblical or other religious writings will often take to heart clear teachings of their faith. However, relying on religious pronouncements alone to teach sexuality may undermine parental influence by revealing to children their parent's inability to dialogue on serious issues. As the saying goes, "Rules without relationships lead to rebellion." A hurried pronouncement, a paternalistic lecture, or a flippant put-down ("You're too young to understand") are not adequate responses to a child's challenging question. Parents must have the courage to say, "I don't know, but let's find out" – always keeping the lines of communication open.

• Be a loving guide, not "just a friend."

Parents must be good listeners, but that is only one part of their job. They must also offer loving guidance. Children have many friends, but only one or two primary caretakers who can show their interest and love by giving mature advice based on years of life experience.

The almost universal recommendation today is that parents should not voice *opinions* on the moral correctness of a behavior, they should only discuss *options*. Parents, counselors, physicians, and other authority figures who hear warnings about the dangers of being "judgmental" should not forget the distinction between *authoritative* opinion and *authoritarian* pronouncements. Opinion expressed without respect for the listener can easily be interpreted as an authoritarian pronouncement and can end communication. No person should be judged by another person, but the *wisdom* of certain choices should be judged.[5]

Parental silence, when reason should be heard, is irresponsible or simplistic or both. For example, in response to the parents of a 15-year-old girl who had complained that they did not care for her new boyfriend, Dr. Joyce Brothers wrote, "Parents who oppose a child's friendship may well make it more intense. It might be better to say nothing."[6] That kind of defeatist withdrawal terminates communication as abruptly as does an imperial edict. While there are many remarks that might be better left unsaid or conversations postponed in such a situation, any issue that creates tension within a family deserves to be openly addressed at the earliest opportunity.

Parents should regularly offer opinions on all areas of immorality, without singularly excluding sexual morality. Parents communicate to children their own convictions about lying, cheating and stealing, and should be as willing to offer opinions about sex. Psychologist William Coulson makes the point that it is more dangerous to be in the presence of someone in authority who refuses to judge than to risk rejection from teenagers by demonstrating concerned opinion. Opinions should be expressed in a controlled manner, and responses to assertions should be elicited ("What do you think about my idea?"), but parents should not "say nothing."

• Protect children from saturation with sexually-oriented stimulation.

Children invariably are exposed to much of the selfishness, foolishness and apathy of this world. As we discussed in Chapter 6, our society is saturated with the base side of sex. Parents have a duty to shield children from being inundated with such influences and to expose them to positive ones.

• Provide children with appropriate instruction in basic biology.

It is an age-old parental duty to ensure that each child has a basic grasp of the biological facts of life before they leave the nest. Menstruation should not come as a surprise to an adolescent girl, nor body odor to a boy. All children should be clear on the basic principle underlying the sex act before they move out of the home, and for some the explanation should come much sooner.

There are a number of resources available that cover these issues including our own course: *Sexual Wisdom for Catholic Adolescents*, a free download from our website sexualwisdom.com, soon to be in book form. See the Resource section for other recommendations.

Opportunities for Discussion of Sex

Parents need not worry about creating opportunities. Unfortunately, there are far too many. While preparing for one of my adolescent classes, I bought an issue of *Cosmopolitan* to decide on what issues to raise. Beginning with the cover photo, the magazine included at least thirty items which could be used to initiate a discussion about healthy vs. unhealthy sex. Opportunities for talking about sex abound on television and radio programs, on billboards, at movies, in advertisements of all sorts, on shopping trips, and at sports events. One wily TV producer defended a show in which teenagers were portrayed having premarital sex, as an "opportunity for children and parents to watch together so that they might be able to discuss a little more candidly the concept and consequences of intercourse before teens are confronted with the choice."[7] The truth is that there are so many opportunities for parents to discuss sex that the greater problem is finding ways to shelter children from the barrage of televised immorality.

Specific Topics for Discussion

Ben Franklin, who has given us a lot of good, practical advice, once wrote, "Teach thy children discipline, and then what thou wilt." That is a good lead into this section because discipline is one of the aforementioned five characteristics of love, but I would go beyond Mr. Franklin to advise parents to also teach their children respect, responsibility, commitment, and trustworthiness. Parents fail in the most profound way if they fail to teach their children to esteem or value others – to respect, to empathize, and to treat all humans with dignity.

All of the issues raised in this book are open for discussion with children at age-appropriate levels. Parents must develop a relationship with their children which is conducive to ongoing, open discussion of intimate issues. Generally, children should be told the least amount of sex trivia and the greatest amount about the necessary connection between sex and love. When the subject matter becomes uncomfortable, and the parent is unsure if the child is ready for more specifics, it is better to offer fewer details and return to the subject later than to offer information that is too graphic for the child's level of maturity. If a child seems disappointed by the lack of specifics offered, the parent should make a point of returning to the subject at the next opportunity.

Good sex education can start with the Golden Rule. Parents should teach children how to apply it in their relationships with the opposite sex. They should also discuss what I call the "Silver Rule":

Behave as you would have others behave, i.e., when a child is unsure how to act in a certain situation, the child should consider how he or she would expect or want someone he or she respects to act. If a teenager is at a party or movie where pornography is being shown, he or she should consider how parents or other respected family members would act and follow that example.

Parents should teach children the holistic approach to sexuality, i.e., that sex has a role *within* a relationship, not *instead* of a relationship. They should encourage the gradual development and pacing of relationships with the opposite sex, instead of full-throttle crushes. When I was in high school, I assumed that those of my friends who were sexually active knew a lot more about sex than those who were not. Now I realize that I had it backwards. The sexually active students knew more about sex trivia, but the virgins knew more about holistic sex. Parents should alert their children to the great ignorance among their peer group of the core issues of sex, in particular among those who are sexually active. Parents should explain which issues are trivial and which have substance.

Most of the people a person dates will eventually marry someone else. Parents should advise their children to treat the people they date as they would want someone else to treat their own future spouses. Parents should discuss the discipline required to love someone enough to refrain from inappropriate behavior. Parents should teach their children to say "no" by the way they act and dress, and by the situations they allow or don't allow themselves to get into – use of alcohol and other drugs, arousing forms of entertainment, the wrong peer group, secluded dates, etc. Parents should teach their children how to say "no" to premarital sex with assertiveness (friendly assertiveness or otherwise). Two generally recommended techniques are the "Broken Record" (repeatedly saying "no" until the propositioner gives up) and the "Sandwich" (saying "no" between two pleasant or complimentary comments). Parents should discuss how pornography and immodest dress degrade and dehumanize people, especially women, and lead to unhealthy attitudes and situations.

The inherently risky and unloving nature of premarital sex should be emphasized, along with the fact that the term "safe premarital sex" is a misnomer. Parents should discuss how easily sex can be misused, and how disastrous this can be. They should emphasize morality and the virtues, and how, in the modern world, couples are pressured to have a "limited" approach to love – to only "sort of" love. The teen years are stressful, and parents must encourage teens to deal with their stress in mature, positive ways, rather than with irresponsible escapism of promiscuous sexual activity. As abstinence educator Coleen Mast puts it, teach children to keep their clothes on, buttoned, zipped, and snapped until they get married.

In short, parents should communicate with their children; they should talk, talk, talk with their children, and listen, listen, listen to them – enthusiastically, respectfully, honestly, and as knowledgeably as possible. Also, if an exchange does not go well, parents should always keep in mind that no discussion should be final. If the lines of communication are kept open, there will always be opportunities for parents to clarify a position after further reflection or study.

Parental Response to Sexually Active Teenagers

Many parents are facing this challenging dilemma today. I have worked through it in many settings, and can commiserate with parents faced with it. They wonder if they should give up the abstinence approach and concede that "they're doing it anyway;" or they wonder if they should refer the child to a physician for contraception, or hope that someone else does. This crisis situation calls for a dramatic response, but the options are limited. *There are no simple solutions,* least of all the Orwellian approach of simply handing the child a pill. The following suggestions may help parents to develop an aggressive plan for coping with this situation.

1) Both parents should seek to involve themselves more with the child – to become more prominent in the child's life by emphasizing both quality and quantity time. Parents should consciously strive to offer emotional support and affection, to develop intimacy; then they will have a better chance to affect a desirable resolution in spite of the resistance some children put up.

While parents should never accept premarital sex as a valid option, they must always make it clear that they love and accept their child. Most parents will concede that they have made mistakes, some serious, with regard to sex. So we should stress that the goal for the child is not to be perfect but to improve, to strive continuously for the ideal and to move consistently up the psychosexual scale toward Level 2 and beyond, no matter how poorly the child is functioning at any given time.

2) Parents must carefully consider current and past stressors in the child's life and search for sources of the child's insecurities. Parents should consider family counseling by a secular or religious counselor. Significant underlying family issues are often involved when a teenager is making exceedingly poor choices.

3) Both parents should discuss abstinence and related issues with their child in an atmosphere of honesty, intimacy, and love. They should bring up related issues often, for example, by clipping out newspaper articles worth discussing.

4) Parents should discuss issues of trust, in particular how the parents' trust in the child's good judgment has been shaken and will need to be recultivated. The child should clearly sense the parents' current disappointment as well as their sense of hope for the child's future.

5) Parents should restrict and monitor the child's activities. Because of the crisis in trust, parents should insist on a greater level of supervision, for example, restricting or monitoring phone calls and letters, restricting dating activities, and chaperoning high-risk activities. To balance these restrictions, parents can help the teen develop alternative low-risk activities and friendships. Parents might also consider instituting, with the teen's awareness, a random search policy which includes the child's room, book bag, and locker. Random searches are analogous to random urine drug screens when drug abuse is a question. Both checks reflect the parents' lack of faith in an adolescent's judgment, but seek to ultimately reestablish it. The adolescent should be actively involved in formulating this plan.

Above all, the rules must be clearly explained – in writing – and consequences for breaking them fully understood by all ahead of time.

6) With discretion, parents may discuss their concerns with the child's teachers, employer, etc., and develop allies. These people can help monitor and influence the child's activities at school and elsewhere. Unfortunately, parents must be prepared to find resistance to the abstinence approach among well-intentioned teachers, counselors, school nurses, administrators, psychologists, and even some religious leaders.

7) Parents should have the child screened and treated for sexually transmitted diseases as thoroughly as possible. The child should be vaccinated against hepatitis B and girls should have a Pap smear.

Parents should request the physician not to mention contraceptives, including condoms, to their child. Because physicians are generally misled on these issues, they may consider an abstinence approach unrealistic and may challenge the parents. Parents should be resolute on the issue and, to ensure that the physician does not make such recommendations, the same-sex parent should remain in the consultation room with the child during the exam. Teenagers have a legal right to ask parents to leave the room, but physicians cannot force parents to leave unless the child so desires. Pro-life organizations and local Fertility Awareness educators may be helpful in locating physicians who unequivocally support premarital abstinence.

8) To stimulate discussion, parents may wish to show their child an abortion video. These may be obtained from the local pro-life center. Unfortunately, the tone of most of these videos is biased. To reduce the effect of this bias, parents may want to preview the film and present just the abortion scenes, and those with the audio off. Children are less likely to dismiss harsh realities if bias is minimized. Abortion advocates also make films on abortion. These films have the opposite bias and, because they do not show pictures of the fetus following the procedure, the adolescent's attention is diverted

from the central reality of the abortion: the fact that a human fetus or embryo is destroyed.

There is no guarantee that any of these measures will work, but they are the best alternatives. Teenagers who become sexually active before marriage demonstrate poor psychosexual development and, despite any form of intervention, are at high risk for becoming pregnant, contracting diseases, and developing deeply ingrained, unhealthy attitudes about sex. While a rare child can turn around his or her situation without parental intervention, parents cannot assume that their child will be this exception. They should respond as aggressively as they would to any other situation that is critical to their child's health and well-being.

Parental Response to an Announcement of Homosexuality
Again, while parents must always love and accept their child, they should consider homosexual activity to be a sign of a crisis and should search for sources of stress and insecurity in the child's life. Most of the suggestions about premarital sex can also apply to homosexuality. With homosexuality, parents should discuss what the child means by saying that he or she is "homosexual." As discussed in Chapter 11, each developing child is unique and the general label of "homosexual" fits none well.

Children who are concerned about their sexual orientation often feel afraid, isolated, and insecure, especially when discussing their confusion with their parents. Parents should provide their children with ample opportunity to describe their feelings, and then offer composed, thoughtful responses. Two common concerns should be specifically addressed. First, many children feel that they "have always been different." Parents may respond to this by describing their own feelings of insecurity and self-consciousness while growing up. Second, children may relate experiences of becoming aroused in what they perceive to be unusual circumstances. Children should be reassured that, because of the varied potential in all of us, no circumstances should be considered too unusual. Again, depending on the situation, parents may want to relate their own experiences.

Many teenagers experiment with homosexual behaviors and later adopt a clearly heterosexual orientation. For others, however, homosexual fantasies become strongly ingrained. Parents should not expect a child to divest himself or herself of all homosexual thoughts, and should be prepared for the possibility that the child may never consider himself or herself to be predominantly heterosexual. As discussed in Chapter 11, the goal for such individuals is to address underlying psychological issues and to restrain themselves from behaviors which sustain unhealthy attitudes.

It may require some investigating for parents to find a counselor who considers homosexuality to be abnormal and who is familiar with the contemporary literature on the subject (see the Resources Appendix of this book), but the search is worth the effort. Such a person offers great hope for redirecting the adolescent's maturation process, especially when the child is in the early stages of development of the homosexual condition.

Parental Response to Masturbation

While self-stimulation does not cause insanity or hair loss as was once thought, it does introduce unhealthy attitudes. Masturbation is perhaps the most obvious example of an act that separates the pleasuring and loving aspects of sex. Therefore, as with the use of contraceptives, oral sex, and homosexual acts, masturbation reinforces the "needs" misconception and encourages a misguided emphasis. Because the act is done in isolation, the goal of enriching a relationship is lost. We previously alluded to how it compromises self-respect and encourages self-indulgence and narcissism. As one author has written, self-stimulation is a symbol "of withdrawal from reality, of self-pitying loneliness . . . of fear to love, of anxiety with regard to other people, withdrawing from them and seeking to live without them."[8]

In the modern era, many people have come to consider self-stimulation a healthy behavior, or at least not a problem. Talk-radio hosts now openly joke about their masturbatory fantasies and pop psychologists enthusiastically endorse its supposed therapeutic effects. Popular sexologist Dr. Ruth Westheimer writes the following in her book, *Dr Ruth Talks to Kids About Sex.*

Sometimes boys like to look at sexy pictures in magazines when they masturbate. . . . If you have such magazines, make sure your parents understand that they're your
private, personal property.

There's absolutely nothing wrong with masturbating.
Most people do it, and it doesn't have any bad effects. . . .
One thing to remember, though, is that masturbation should
be done in private. Close your door if you do it in your
room, and make it clear to your family that they're not to
walk into your room without knocking. If you're afraid
they'll barge in, you can put a piece of heavy furniture in
front of the door.

Sometimes groups of boys will masturbate together.
There's nothing wrong with doing this in privacy.[9]

This is hardly the kind of advice to make parents cheer. Sexual
behavior should build intimacy. By severing the connection between
love and sex, self-stimulation creates obstacles to intimacy – in this
case, in the form of heavy furniture, between a child and his or her
family.

Though self-stimulation has historically been associated with
males, females are increasingly urged to participate. A segment of
the pornography industry is being directed specifically toward
women masturbators and sexologists express occasional frustration
at the continued disdain for the behavior among women. For example, the authors of a recent article in a sexological journal complain
that, "despite the effort in the past quarter century to encourage
women in our society to take greater responsibility for their own
bodies and their own sexuality and to engage in more sexual self-
exploration and self stimulation, results show that women continue
to masturbate much less than men."[10]

Self-stimulation is often defended with the disclaimer "as long as
it doesn't hurt anybody." Many people today consider it to be a benign manner of relieving oneself of sexual tension, and fail to appreciate its harmful influences. In contrast to the prevailing wisdom,
renowned essayist C. S. Lewis characterized the essence of masturbation:

For me the real evil of masturbation would be that it takes an appetite which, in lawful use, leads the individual out of himself to complete (and correct) his own personality in that of another (and finally in children and even grand-children) and turns it back into the prison of himself, there to keep a harem of imaginary brides. And this harem, once admitted, works against his ever getting out and really unit-ing with a real woman. For the harem is always accessible, always subservient, calls for no sacrifices or adjustments, and can be endowed with erotic and psychological attrac-tions which no real woman can rival.[11]

Perhaps the most difficult question about self-stimulation for par-ents is when to raise the issue with a child. It is best to wait until the child seems aware of the issue and then, initially, to broach the sub-ject in the most general terms, or perhaps with a question, and then evaluate the child's response. Though self-stimulation is a common behavior, and only asphyxophiliacs[12] die from it, as C. S. Lewis pointed out, it deflects people away from the fullness of life; this is the essential point to be made to all children who evidence interest in it.

Children should be advised that they have no need to relieve themselves through self-stimulation, but they do need to learn to cope with tension in healthy ways. Self-stimulation is often a re-sponse to feelings of emptiness, frustration, loneliness, self-pity, or other forms of discontentment. Parents should discuss practical ways to reduce these states, for example, by helping the child find interesting activities with others. Also, since pornography usually leads to self-stimulation, parents should discuss the pernicious effect of sexually stimulating materials on attitudes, and suggest ways in which these materials may be avoided. Wet dreams, too, should be explained lest they become a source of anxiety or guilt.

As with premarital sex and homosexual activity, the underlying drive to self-stimulate may prove untamable in the short run. Parents and teens may need to resign themselves to a long and arduous pro-cess to sexual control, with many failures and backslides along the way. Again, the initial goal is Level Two. Mistakes are an inevitable and natural part of the adventure. While mistakes should be duly noted, they should not be dwelt on. Rather, one must press forward under a spirit of forgiveness and with a resolute, earnest pledge to do better.

Parental Response to Physical Intimacy of Teenagers

This is perhaps the most challenging question in the area of sexuality. For sex to be an invariably positive experience, for unmarried couples to enjoy the fullest kind of life experience, they must avoid behavior which puts them at risk for "going too far." They must, therefore, restrain themselves from potentially arousing interactions. There is no evidence that sexual arousal prior to marriage benefits dating couples, but the documentation of the serious harm which has come from it, by people who went too far once aroused, would certainly fill many libraries.

The boundaries for arousal are different for each couple. Hugging and holding hands have little potential for stirring reckless passion, whereas prolonged kissing clearly does. There is no clear line as to how long a couple can kiss, or how far short of a prolonged kiss each couple may safely go. This ambiguity is part and parcel of dating life, and part of its intrigue.

Given the widespread addictive attitudes toward genital sexuality in our society, it would be no surprise if these recommendations meet, in some circles, with a clamor of disdain. Detractors will no doubt offer their stores of evidence as to the healthfulness of the new "liberated" approach to sex – barricading furniture up against the door and such. It may seem too much to ask for this level of restraint from today's teenagers, but the relevant question is: is it possible for adolescents to care enough about themselves and each other so as to enjoy the many benefits of sex but avoid unnecessary risks?

For many, these recommendations are the most challenging this book offers. But challenging or not, they are the manifest conclusions that follow the natural priorities and goals previously described.

Conclusion

Our Basis for Hope: Sexual Wisdom

There is a story about a newspaper reporter who is taking a survey at a busy downtown intersection, "What are the two greatest problems facing America today?" he asks a man who is striding rapidly along the street, "I don't know, and I don't care," the man shouts over his shoulder as he hurries on his way. "That's right," says the reporter, "Ignorance and apathy."

And we are still facing these same two problems in the wake of the sexual revolution: ignorance and apathy. The sexual revolution of the 1960s was based on ignorance – misconceptions and falsehoods, which people accepted because they didn't care enough about each other – and apathy.

On the other hand, much good has resulted from the sexual revolution: we enjoy a new openness today to discussing sexuality, which has great therapeutic value; many important issues are now "out of the closet" and no longer taboo; we talk openly about extramarital affairs, child molestation, incest, and date rape. And now that we are talking about them, we can do more to alleviate the suffering they cause.

Our society clearly needed a sexual revolution, but we got the wrong one. We needed a revolution based on love, but we got one based on uninhibited pursuit of freedom and pleasure. The net result is that we are not just "out of the closet," but awash in misunderstanding and misuse of our human sexuality. While some miscon-

ceptions and ignorance have always existed, the scientific and technological advances of the twentieth century have given us the illusion that we should be *free* to do anything we have the *power* to do.
Our society has become so obsessed with exceptions to rules that we
have lost sight of the rules themselves.

Now, as much as at any other time, our sexually challenged culture needs to seriously reconsider how to make sex a positive experience. Level 2 psychosexual functioning is not just wishful thinking. The more people who achieve Level 2, or even attempt to
achieve it, the better it will be for the rest of us. We are witnessing
increasing upheaval between the sexes, as evidenced by rising rates
of date rape, domestic abuse, and divorce. We may well ask if we,
as a society, are sophisticated enough to respond positively and constructively to the influences and forces now working to destroy relationships between men and women.

When we look back over the history of the past few decades, we
see that an enormous amount of suffering has been caused by uncontrolled and/or misdirected sexuality. The solution of the political
left was to free people from the natural ethic and practice a morality
so watered down that it hardly existed; in retrospect, we can see how
this course of action has catapulted us into the current morass. The
solution suggested by some of the political right, that all citizens
must accept a biblical foundation for morality, is not readily worka-
ble in a country which values religious freedom and depends on the
peaceful coexistence of many faiths.

There is no quick fix for our national dilemma today. Some of the
related ethical and psychosocial problems are enormously complex
and unwieldy, but others are more manageable than they may at first
have seemed. In the course of the preceding 18 chapters, we have
explored some realities and formulated some principles. On that
foundation, we can now make some concrete and specific suggestions for progress as we move into the twenty-first century.

1) Expose and reject "needs" and other misconceptions.

For decades, modern psychology has mistakenly embraced Dr.
Abraham Maslow's "hierarchy of needs," the fulfillment of which

supposedly leads to "self-actualization." Popular psychologists routinely refer to vague, contrived needs, such as those of one's "inner child." What they miss or ignore is the potential harm that can come to someone who stands in the way of another's attempts to meet these "needs." We must appreciate what Dr. Maslow himself eventually understood: it is dangerous to mislabel desires, drives, or interests as "needs" – because doing so creates endless opportunities for misbehavior, selfishness, and abuse.[1]

To live a life based on attempts to fulfill needs is enslaving. Take the religious counselor who called to inquire about natural family planning. His new bride was studying for an advanced degree and he predicted matter-of-factly that if she became pregnant their marriage would end and she would experience some kind of mental breakdown. He said that she was "dealing with some issues" and had a need to finish her schooling. Therefore, they needed a birth control method that was 100% effective (never mind that she was on the pill, which is not). Her supposed need meant that what is considered the greatest miracle of life for others would mean ruin for them. They felt they had no choice but to have her finish her degree. They had forsaken their freedom and were prisoners to a contrived circumstance.

The "needs" misconception is the most important falsehood about sex, because it directly contradicts the fundamental truth that all people are free to choose to "do good." If, in order to fulfill a "need," one would have to think or act in an unfeeling way, then one should reexamine whether it is truly a "need." It is by discrediting misconceptions and embracing our true nature that each person gains sexual wisdom and true sexual fulfillment.

2) Re-establish the priority of love and re-embrace its behavioral extension: natural morality.

The answer to our problems will come in the myriad applications of moral reason through our political and judicial systems, through activism, through our churches and, especially, in our daily lives. Acceptance of the natural priority of love means that we cannot always have as much fun or pleasure as we might like. It means that, when the stresses mount, we cannot simply escape life through the misuse of sex. It means consistently applying both the Golden and Silver Rules and making a genuine commitment to informing and following one's conscience.

3) Re-sensitize our society to the abuse of sex.

Exploitative, degrading forms of sexual expression are everywhere. We must reject the idea that there is any value in becoming desensitized to them. Because society has become callous to the consequences of the sexual revolution, it has failed to respond to them.

Many men in particular are desensitized; and many, as if to prove their masculinity, actually brag about their tolerance for sordid forms of sexual expression. In a newspaper editorial, a Hollywood screenwriter boasted, before watching a new, sex-oriented video made by a notoriously debased rock star, "I doubt it could offend me."[2] And a prominent Los Angeles movie reviewer who had forcefully criticized the violence in movies, casually remarked in the next breath that the sex in movies has never bothered him. The question here should be, why does it not bother him? The amazing thing is how he can be so acutely responsive to physical violence but inert when he confronts the psychological violence which results from the abuse of sex. Artists claim to be sensitive, yet some of the people who are the least sensitive to sexual degradation are found in the artistic community.

4) Emphasize the nurturing of children.

To strengthen relationships between couples, we must consciously reevaluate the various roles we play. In the course of a day, one man may play the roles of businessman, father, husband, consumer advocate, and peewee league coach. In the same space of time, one woman may play teacher, mother, wife, school board member, and amateur musician. At times, these roles will conflict in the same way priorities within relationships conflict, and so they, too, must be assigned relative values.

One tragedy of the social revolution we are experiencing is the acceptance of skewed values assigned to these roles. Husbands neglect their wives for the sake of their careers. Parents abandon their children while working extra jobs to secure material comforts and luxuries. Spouses use their children as an excuse for neglecting each other.

Divorce, the collapse of what at least once was a romance, is the consequence of one or both partners failing to maintain the natural first priority of the spousal role. Couples who are contemplating divorce should stop short and seriously consider what it would take for them to get along if they had to, how they would modify their behavior if cooperating with each other were the top priority. The marital contract is a solemn oath reflecting the reality that divorce entails serious, far-reaching consequences for the couple and others.

Modern society is suffering from the overwhelming consequences of prioritizing adult "needs" over the nurturing of children. Parents who have abandoned their offspring in so many ways can see the consequences of their own negligence in escalating crime, gang warfare, drug use, depression, and low self-esteem among youth. As more than one criminal justice worker has observed, when you hear about a serial killer or rapist, ask about his father. You will likely find his father was largely absent from his life. To re-establish cultural stability, both men and women must work to restore the priority of stable, two-parent families. Fortunately, in the past five years or so, our society has experienced a marked attitudinal shift toward acknowledging the far-reaching consequences of divorce.[3] We can hope that this sensitivity will soon extend to the equally important source of social instability: premarital sex.

5) More carefully evaluate modern technology and its implications for human relationships.

Artificial contraception is a striking example of our society's failure to look beyond the pleasure of the moment. People say, "We don't want to get pregnant, so we'll use a diaphragm," without considering the multitudinous ramifications such a decision can have. They ignore the big picture. This situation – and any use of artificial contraceptives – is analogous to the bathtub overflowing upstairs and everyone busying themselves cleaning up the watery mess downstairs. The more efficient people are at cleaning up the mess, the longer it will be before someone discovers that what they are doing isn't working. Someone needs to go upstairs and turn off the bathtub faucet. Far beyond the issue of contraceptive efficiency are questions about the consequences that using contraceptives will have on relationships. Regardless of their success rate in preventing pregnancy, their power to facilitate addictive and other injurious attitudes must count as failures.

Technological innovations have the power to alter dramatically our lives for the good. Medical science has produced many exciting benefits, but our rash acceptance of contraception, sterilization, abortion, and even infertility sciences is disturbing. Our society must reconsider whether these technologies are bringing people together or pulling them apart. We need to recognize the problems technology causes, and act effectively to solve them. In many ways, technology is producing ever-greater stress in our lives – we have lost control of it and are living in what Alvin Toffler glibly predicted in his bestseller *Future Shock*. We must learn to be discriminating so that we can discourage technological developments that increase our stress and support only those which relieve it.

I do not pretend that *Sexual Wisdom* can solve all of these problems, but I trust that this book will prompt its readers to become more aware of the complexities associated with sexuality and to reevaluate their attitudes and beliefs toward it. I sincerely hope that it will motivate them to question popular, simplistic assumptions and to strive for psychosexual maturity in their own lives.

Perhaps, too, *Sexual Wisdom* will induce some readers to consider the spiritual and religious dimensions of sexuality. According to tradition, human beings have three interconnected natures: physical, psychological, and spiritual – body, mind and soul. From the beginning, I have avoided any religious connections because of the great apprehension many people have about religion. We should, however, acknowledge that spiritual and religious issues are important for many people, including myself. They are areas in which many of us experience the greatest fulfillment in our lives and in our sexuality.

6) Challenge the common wisdom of our culture.

"Test everything; retain what is good," St. Paul recommended.[4] Through openness to both sides of the controversies, one necessarily comes to reconsider some of the premises about sex that are most widely accepted today. Without being reactionary, people must learn to question even the most basic popular principles. Individuals must learn to be wary of and test all authority: the authority of newspapers, the entertainment world, medical associations, government health agencies, Planned Parenthood, advice columnists, popular psychologists, the legal profession, sex educators and school personnel, religious leaders, and the fashion and advertising industries. These all speak with some authority on some issues but frequently offer biased, distorted or censored views about sex.

There is a wonderful place for sexual interactions within relationships. Sex truly can be one positive experience after another; and each individual can make the difference in his or her life by making good decisions. But those who are not willing to think for themselves or to be countercultural, those who are willing only to do as their neighbors do, will suffer the same pain as their neighbors. The reader is invited to challenge himself or herself to say "no" to this pain, and "yes" to sex on a higher level.

Appendix A

A Note To Health Professionals

Medical literature is essentially void of practical advice for physicians about how to discuss abstinence and related issues with patients. The following are my own observations. One example of what can happen in the physician's office was the case of a twenty-five-year-old woman who came to my office for a Pap smear. During the visit she mentioned that, until recently, she had been on the birth control pill and wished to renew her prescription. She and her boyfriend of three years had not been sexually active for a few months, but she expected they might resume sexual activity in the near future. I informed her that my practice included only natural methods of fertility regulation, and that I would therefore transfer her care to one of my partners. But before I could excuse myself, she expressed curiosity about my approach and so we discussed it.

I mentioned my concerns about the effect of contraception on relationships. I explained that one of my goals as a physician is to bring people together, that is, to encourage healthy relationships between the sexes, and that artificial forms of fertility regulation appeared to be incompatible with that objective.

We discussed what the goals of healthy sexual interactions should be. We discussed love, and how a man who loves a woman desires to protect her from serious, unnecessary risks, and would not expose her to them. We discussed how unloving premarital sex is, and also how unloving marital sex can be. She recounted her own experience with such risks when, some years earlier, she had become pregnant and then given up her child for adoption.

We discussed the misconception that people have specific, genital, sexual needs and how artificial birth control measures encourage this falsehood. I mentioned the benefits of using fertility awareness alone as a basis for decision-making, and how it is much more than one of many methods used to avoid pregnancy.

We discussed the fact that people are not bad, but their decisions and behaviors sometimes are. All of us make mistakes, and all of us need to work constantly to improve our attitudes about sex.

She left the office with some new, challenging ideas. She left without seeing any of my partners, and without receiving a prescription for birth control pills, but, hopefully, she left with something more. This woman is not the average patient. But there are many such women, and it is clear that she would have simply been prescribed the pill if she had seen perhaps any other gynecologist or family physician in my city.

Some people would argue that all family physicians should dispense contraceptives, that it is beyond the authority of the physician to restrict a patient's options. But such interactions as I have described could not have occurred if dispensing contraceptives upon request was the only option for clinicians. Those who dispense contraceptives and recommend sterilization must be held responsible for their management of this type of patient – a patient who will not express his or her reservations about these methods unless challenged.

More generally, if contraceptives entice people into accepting unhealthy attitudes and practices, how much responsibility does the dispensing physician bear for these widespread attitudes and practices? Are not physicians who dispense contraceptives responsible for maintenance or development of addictive and codependent attitudes among their patients? Not solely, perhaps, but dispensing physicians cannot realistically deny that they play a significant role.

Rarely do we find a physician endorsing in print any discussion of abstinence with patients, but Dr. Joseph Pastorek, writing in *Postgraduate Medicine,* employed analogy to propose this reasonable solution for the problems of human sexuality.

> Abstinence and monogamy have not been very popular ideas to some in today's society. But if these are the best answers, shouldn't the health care community attempt to promote them? At first, physicians may be reluctant to open the Pandora's box of patient sexuality. However, in the past decade or two, doctors have been taking greater interest in the private lives of their patients. Patients are being told what and how much to eat and when and where to exercise. They are being advised not to smoke, to abstain from alcohol, to avoid drugs, and to stay out of the sun . . . Considering the scope and severity of the problem, it seems only reasonable that the medical community take up the banner of responsible sexuality, promoting abstinence or strict monogamy.[1]

The more one discusses the heart of sexuality, including premarital abstinence, the more one respects how difficult such discussions are in a busy office setting. Further, identifying which patients might be most open to, or have the most to gain from, discussing these issues is next to impossible. My own predictions have often proven inaccurate.

Although it is preferable to raise these issues within a context relevant to the patient's chief complaint, I occasionally raise them out of context. My approach is to make a statement, often about premarital abstinence, in an authoritative but nonthreatening manner and await the reaction. Sensitivity to the patient's response is the most important aspect of such attempts at intervention and requires the most skill and concentration, especially if the challenge is unsolicited. If the patient appears disinterested, I drop the subject and refocus on more immediate concerns. Among such patients, I do not raise these issues at future office visits unless my views are solicited. At least for the near future, they may not be capable of challenging themselves on these issues and should not be antagonized.

Occasionally, a patient who I would never dream would be interested will display such enthusiasm that I will have difficulty ending a discussion once begun. Women over 25 years old, regardless of their background, tend to be especially excited to find a true advocate and will often have many questions. By this age, many women realize that, generally, they are the ones who pay the price for sexual "liberation."

Many teenagers and women younger than 25 years old, probably due to insecurities, react to these discussions by resorting instinctively to their defense mechanisms; and under these circumstances it is best not to provoke them. Men are generally less interested, but I am occasionally surprised at the sensitivity of some men, even those with relatively promiscuous backgrounds. Many men have earnestly thanked me − sometimes tearfully − for being candid and straightforward.

It is generally wise to address the issue of religion early on, so as to move beyond the concern about "imposing religion." I let patients know that religious issues need not concern us, only issues of love and morality. Of course, if the patient is open to religious aspects this can open up a whole new and potentially vital thread of conversation. I also explain that the primary reason I am so bold as to bring up these issues is because I aim aware that patients are unlikely to hear these opinions offered from other physicians. Patients readily concede this.

Physicians should not initiate discussions regarding the deeper issues of sexuality unless they are intellectually and psychologically primed. Not uncommonly, these discussions lead into issues such as alcoholism, drug abuse, eating disorders, and marital difficulties. It can be taxing to challenge multiple patients on any given day.

It is rewarding to discuss these issues with couples, especially those who have expressed an openness to them. However, it is most difficult to discuss them with couples for whom a physician-patient relationship has not already been established, especially if they have not requested such information.

Homosexuality is a potentially explosive issue, and a candid discussion of it requires that the homosexual have unusual confidence in the physician. Most homosexuals live in constant fear of how they are perceived. Therefore, to challenge the view of tolerance toward homosexual activity requires a doctor-patient relationship that is strong enough to allay their anxieties.

I have not researched the effectiveness of my office discussions about sexuality. However, the enthusiasm of so many patients for these ideas is striking, and leaves one with a sense of a serious obligation toward future opportunities. Physicians may initially feel unsure and timid about broaching these issues and so, as with other types of interventions, must gradually develop a consulting style. All primary care physicians are encouraged to be aggressive in discussing these significant issues with their patients, and thereby offer more truly comprehensive care in the area of sexuality.

Appendix B

The Swedish Card

We have discussed some of the barriers to constructive dialogue about sex. At least one more impediment is worth mentioning. No matter how forceful one's criticisms are of the sexual "liberation" which has occurred in the United States, there are those who insist that the sexual revolution is working well in other cultures. Sweden is the most commonly mentioned example. Swedes are well known to have permissive attitudes about sex. For example, they have had compulsory, contraceptive-based sex education since 1956.

Many Americans hold to the fantasy that Sweden is a model society in terms of its sexuality. This is a seriously inaccurate perception. For example, 49 percent of Swedish women have had sexual intercourse at the age of 16 years or younger.[1] Sweden has a 50 percent illegitimacy rate, the highest in the world.[2] In Sweden, the *majority* of teenage pregnancies end in abortion[3] and, despite extensive sex education, STDs have reached epidemic proportions.[4] For example, ten to twenty percent of sexually active Swedish adolescents are carriers of chlamydia.[5] Further; the rate of divorce and legal separation in Sweden tripled between 1963 and 1974. As one review article from Sweden puts it: "In light of the fact that Sweden is considered to have a well-established system for sex education and STD care, these figures are highly discouraging."[6]

Roland Utford, Scandinavian correspondent for the *London Observer,* notes in his book on Swedish life, *The New Totalitarians*[7]:

> "The new permissiveness has led to compulsive sexuality. There is among Swedish school children a pressure to have sexual intercourse, whether they want it or not. Even if a boy and a girl might prefer a platonic relationship, they will nevertheless usually force themselves into a sexual one."(p.322).

> "License to copulate has led to a sexual obsession pervading the whole of Swedish life." (p. 339)

> "In spite of themselves, the Swedes from time to time betray a yearning for something beyond the mechanics of sex. Maudlin cries for feeling appear in the correspondence columns of newspapers and in articles in women's magazines." (p. 338)

Sweden holds no edge on the United States in the area of sexuality. "Progressive" countries like Sweden are not the place to look for solutions to our own problems about sex.

Appendix C

Population Bombs

In this book we have discussed a number of misconceptions used to justify the use of contraceptives. Concern over world overpopulation is also used to justify their use (and in some countries to justify forced sterilizations and abortions). This is based on two assumptions. The first is that natural methods are ineffective and, therefore, are not a realistic answer to a world overpopulation crisis. As discussed in Chapter 8, this assumption is contradicted by the bulk of scientific literature.

The second assumption is that the world is, or will soon be, overpopulated. This, too, should be questioned. Consider the state of Texas in relationship to the entire globe. When asked how much elbow room each person would have if all 5.7 million earthlings lived within the borders of this one state most people answer two or three square feet. The statistical fact is that if all the people of the world were jammed into this relatively minuscule area, each person would have over 1,300 square feet to his or herself – the size of a small home.

Global issues of population, natural resource availability, and poverty are beyond the scope of this book and my expertise. But the following thought-provoking commentary by syndicated columnist Ben Wattenberg seems worth considering.

The Population Crisis That Wasn't

Finally, after all these years of demographic doom-saying, population proliferationism, and explosionism, comes a new report from the United Nations and a headline in *The New York Times:* "World Is Less Crowded Than Expected."

Really? Than expected by whom? Than expected by whom – when?

Apparently, not expected when it should have been expected by Joseph Chamie, director of the United Nations Population division, who is quoted thusly in the *Times* story: "we had some glimmer that this was occurring several years ago, but we weren't sure if it was simply a blip. Now we actually have concrete results showing this is a global trend."

Several years ago? A glimmer? A blip?

Actually, global fertility and birth rates have been declining – rapidly – beyond expectations – for more than a quarter of a century! The United Nation's own population data show that worldwide fertility rates were at a stratospheric 5.0-children-per-woman level in the 1950 to 1955 period. Fifteen years later, from 1965 to 1970, the level was still 4.9 children per woman. The cry of the Population Explosionists reached full throat. After all, it only takes a little over two children per women to merely "replace" a society at a long-term stable rate. Five children per woman would end up, it was said, yielding a global population of 10 billion, no, 12 billion, no, 15 billion people – even 20 billion people! (Such were the estimates, from establishment organizations and scare groups alike.)

Then fertility began falling like a heavy stone, and it has continued to fall right through the 1990 to 1995 period, as reported in the United Nations' new "World Population Prospects: The 1996 Revision." The current global total fertility rate is 2.96 children per woman. Consider what that means: In just the last 25 years, the world has gone from about five kids per woman to about three per woman, which is roughly two-thirds of the way to demographic stability! (Fertility in Bangladesh dropped from 6.2 children in 1980 to 1985, to 3.4 in 1990 to 1995.)

But there is no particular reason to think that global fertility will stop at the 2.1 child-per-woman "replacement rate." It is not a magic number. The new data in from Europe are somewhere between astounding and terrifying. From 1990 to 1995, from an already low below-replacement base, 37 of 39 European nations have seen further reductions in fertility rates. (The demographic behemoths of Luxembourg and Finland had minuscule increases, but remain in the 1.7 to 1.8 range, about 15 percent to 20 percent below the rate needed to maintain stability.)

Italy, Germany, and Spain have rates in the 1.2 to 1.3 range. At that level, according to one estimate, Italy's population would decrease from about 57 million today to about 37 million by the year 2030, and continue to fall rapidly.

Moreover, just about every developed country in the world has a below-replacement fertility rate (including the United States, with an estimated rate of 1.97 for 1996, having fallen for six straight years). There are already 27 countries officially designated as "developing" that have below-replacement rates.

Nothing like this has happened before in history.

But neither the United Nations nor the most important population and environmental organizations choose to stress this condition. The United Nations chooses a 2.1 global rate in the year 2050 and labels it "medium-variant," which is commonly interpreted to mean "most likely." That yields a population stabilizing at near 11 billion people, roughly doubling from the 5.7 billion people today. Forget it. It's not going to happen. The United Nation's "low-variant" assumption is closer to the mark and ends up with a population which tops out at about 7.7. billion in 2040, and then sinks.

Why such ongoing, systemic distortion? There are lots of answers bruited about. Popucrats need their budgets for legitimate family-planning services; apocalypse-mongering is seen as a way to get such budgets. Politics plays a role; proud nations do not want to be seen as shrinking. Environmentalists live off of crises; diminishing long-term population takes the air out of the panic balloon. Feminists don't like the whole idea of a birth dearth.

It's reached a point where most everyone believes in a population crisis. But you needn't.

[From the *Orange County Register*, 22 November 1996, Ben Wattenberg. Reprinted by permission of Newspaper Enterprise Association, Inc.]

Notes

Chapter 1

1. A. Kinsey, W. Pomeroy, C. Martin, *Sexual Behavior in the Human Male* (Philadelphia: WB. Saunders Company, 1948), 528.

2. E. O. Laumann, J. H. Gagnon, R. T. Michael, and S. Michaels, *The Social Organization of Sexuality: Sexual Practices in the United States* (Chicago: University of Chicago, 1994), 137. This most definitive sex survey to date comments that, contrary to a popular assumption, "most Americans do not use autoerotic activity to compensate for a lack of partnered sex. In fact, higher levels of autoeroticism are associated with higher levels of partnered sexual activity. Men do not masturbate to compensate for the lack of a partner, and women without partners are actually less likely to masturbate."

3. H. Harlow and M. Harlow, *The Effect of Rearing Conditions on Behavior* in J. F. Rosenblith and W. Allinsmith, *The Causes of Behavior* (Boston: Allyn and Bacon, Inc., 1969), 134-39.

4. For a discussion of the types of freedom see: M. Adler, *Six Great Ideas* (New York: Macmillan Publishing Company, 1981), 230-231.

5. T. Aquinas, *Summa Theologica* I-II, 94, 2.

6. Aristotle, *Rhetoric* ii, 4.

7. B. Schwartz, *The One Hour Orgasm* (Houston: Breathru Publishers, 1995).

8. C. Mast, *Sex Respect: The Option of True Sexual Freedom, A Public Health Workbook for Students* (Bradley, IL: Respect, Inc., 1986), 2.

9. V. C. Strasburger and R. Brown, *Adolescent Medicine: A Practical Guide* (Boston: Little, Brown, 1991), 168.

Chapter 2

1. F. L. Sonnenstein, J. H. Pleck, and L. C. Ku, "Sexual Activity, Condom Use, and AIDS Awareness among Adolescent Males," *Family Planning Perspectives*, 21 (1989), 152-58; B. Leigh, D. Morrison, K. Trocki and M. Temple, "Sexual Behavior of American Adolescents: Results from a U.S. National Survey," *Journal of Adolescent Health*,

15, no. 2 (1994): 117-125; Centers for Disease Control, "Premarital Sexual Experience among Adolescent Women - United States, 1970 - 1988, *Morbidity and Mortality Weekly Report*, 39, nos. 51 & 52 (1991): 929-32; S. Hofferth, J. Kahn, W Baldwin, "Premarital Sexual Activity among U.S. Teenage Women over the Past Three Decades," *Family Planning Perspectives*, 19, no. 2 (1987): 46-53; M. Zelnik, J. Kantner, "Sexual Activity, Contraceptive Use and Pregnancy among Metropolitan-Area Teenagers: 1971-1979," *Family Planning Perspectives* 12, no. 5 (1980): 230-238.

    2. H. Alzate, "Sexual Behavior of Unmarried Colombian University Students: a Follow-Up," *Archives of Sexual Behavior*, 18, no. 3 (1989): 239-50.

    3. Laumann, 198, 202.

    4. "Letters to the *Times*-Abortion Controversy," *Los Angeles Times*, 29 December 1991.

    5. For example: W. R. Mattox, "What's Marriage Got to Do with It? Good Sex Comes to Those Who Wait," *Family Policy*, 6, no. 6 (1994): 1-8.

    6. S. S. Janus and C. L. Janus, *The Janus Report on Sexual Behavior* (New York: John Wiley and Sons, 1993), 176; Laumann, 507.

    7. According to a University of Wisconsin study, 38 percent of couples who lived together before marriage had separated within 10 years; in significant contrast, only 27 percent of couples who had not lived together before marriage had separated within 10 years. *Medical Aspects of Human Sexuality*, (January 1990): 23. A study from the National Bureau of Economic Research at Cambridge, MA, reported that "Couples who lived together before marriage have nearly an 80 percent higher divorce rate than those who did not and they seem to have less regard for the institution." *New York Times*, 7 December 1987. See also: J. D. Teachman, J. Thomas, and K. Paasch, "Legal Status and the Stability of Coresidential Unions," *Demography*, 28 (1991): 571-586; D. Scott, "Living Together: Education for Marriage?" *Journal of Pastoral Counseling*, (Spring-Summer 1983): 47; D. Popenoe, *Disturbing the Nest* (Hawthorne, New York: Aldine de Gruyter, 1988), 173. This last study reported the "dissolution rate of cohabiting couples with one child was, on average, three times the dissolution rate of comparable married couples."

8. "There Is No Safe Sex," *Newsweek*, 1 April 1991: 8.

Chapter 3

1. National Center for Health Statistics reported in *American Family Physician* 48, no. 8 (1993): 1351.

2. Division of STD/HIV Prevention, "An Update on Sexually Transmitted Diseases (STDs)," *Fact Sheet*, (Atlanta: U.S. Department of Health and Human Services, CDC, 1992); S.O. Aral and M. E. Guinan, "Women and Sexually Transmitted Diseases" Chapter 8 in K. K. Holmes et al., eds., *Sexually Transmitted Diseases*, (New York: McGraw-Hill, 1984), 85-89.

3. R. Hatcher et al., *Contraceptive Technology* (New York: Irvington Publishers, 1994), 78.

4. For example: Laumann, 329; M. Oliver; J. Hyde, "Gender Differences in Sexuality: a Meta-Analysis," *Psychological Bulletin*, 114, no. 1 (1993): 29-51; S. Sprecher, "Premarital Sexual Standards for Different Categories of Individuals," *The Journal of Sex Research*, 26, no. 2 (1989): 232-248; J. Carroll, K. Volk, J. Hyde, "Differences Between Males and Females in Motives for Engaging in Sexual Intercourse," *Archives of Sexual Behavior*, 14, no. 2 (1985): 131-9.

5. *"Cosmopolitan's* Bachelor of the Month…the Lust Hurrah," *Los Angeles Times*, 10 November 1988.

6. G. Steinem, "The Way We Were – and Will Be," *Ms.*, (December 1979), 77-78.

7. Boston Women's Health Book Collective, *The New Our Bodies Ourselves: A Book By and For Women* (New York: Touchstone/Simon and Schuster; 1992), 213.

8. "No Fear of Flying," *Los Angeles Times*, 22 January 1990.

9. Jacqueline Jackson Kikuchi, Rhode Island Rape Crisis Center, Providence, R.I. (quoted from "Harper's Index," *Harper's*, July 1988: 15.

10. "Rapes Vastly Undercounted Study Finds," *Los Angeles Times*, 24 April 1992; Laumann, 336.

11. "New View of Women Who Are Abused," *Los Angeles Times*, 20 August 1991.

12. *Kiplinger Washington Letter* reported in *The American Family Physician* 43, no. 4 (April 1991): 1121. In 1970, 40 percent of Ameri-

can households consisted of two parents with children, in contrast to the 25 percent figure 20 years later.

13. "Choice with Few Options: Some Find Abortion the Pragmatic Decision," *Los Angeles Times*, 14 June 1992. Between 1959 and 1986 the percentage of families falling below the poverty line that were maintained by a woman with no husband present increased from 23 to 51. Divorce and premarital sex are major contributing factors to this "feminization of poverty."

14. D. Blankenhorn, "Let's Hear It for Fatherhood," *Los Angeles Times*, 22 November 1995.

15. S. McLanahan, G. Sandefur, *Growing Up With a Single Parent: What Hurts, What Helps* (Cambridge, Massachusetts: Harvard University Press, 1994). This, according to the *Los Angeles Times*, is the most comprehensive study on the subject. The *Times* also reported on a 1988 study by the National Center for Health Statistics which "found that children in single-parent families (including those whose parents never married) are more likely to drop out of high school, become pregnant as teenagers, abuse drugs and get into trouble with the law than those living with both parents." "Signs indicate shift in stance toward divorce," *Los Angeles Times*, 27 May 1996. See also: "Honor thy Children," *Newsweek*, 27 February 1995: 39-49.

16. R. Whitley et al., "Predictors of Morbidity and Mortality in Neonates with Herpes Simplex Virus Infections," *New England Journal of Medicine*, 324, no. 7 (1991): 450.

17. J. L. Fletcher, "Perinatal Transmission of Human Papillomavirus," *American Family Physician*, 43, no. 1 (January 1991): 145.

18. U.S. Preventive Services Task Force, "Counseling to Prevent HIV Infections and Other Sexually Transmitted Diseases," *Guide to Clinical Preventive Services* (Baltimore: Williams and Wilkens, 1989), excerpted in *American Family Physician*, 41, no. 4 (April 1990): 1180.

19. Centers for Disease Control, "Syphilis and Congenital Syphilis-United States, 1985-1988," *Morbidity and Mortality Weekly Report*, 37 (1988): 486-489.

20. Centers for Disease Control, *Special Report: HIV/AIDS Prevention*, (July 1991): 2.

21. Centers for Disease Control, *Monthly Vital Statistics Report*, 43, no. 6 (S) (1995): 23.

22. "Ancestral Shelter," *Los Angeles Times*, 15 December 1996.

23. W. Kelley, *Textbook of Internal Medicine*, (Philadelphia: Lippincott, 1992), 512-3; G.L. Mandell, J.E. Bennett, R. Polin, *Principles and Practice of Infectious Diseases* (New York: Churchill Livingstone, 1995), see individual diseases.

Chapter 4

1. "Who's Had Who," *Harper's*, November 1987: 28.

2. "A Silent Epidemic in America," *Los Angeles Times*, 26 October 1994.

3. P. Donovan, *Testing Positive: Sexually Transmitted Disease and the Public Health Response* (New York: Alan Guttmacher Institute, 1993), 4.

4. Division of STD/HIV Prevention, *1991 Annual Report* (Atlanta: Centers for Diseases Control, 1992).

5. G. Pantaleo et al., "Studies in Subjects with Long-standing Nonprogressive Human Immunodeficiency Virus Infection," *New England Journal of Medicine*, 332, no. 4 (1995): 209.

6. E. McAnarney et al., *Textbook of Adolescent Medicine*, (Philadelphia: W.B. Saunders, 1992), 701-02.

7. G. Hart, "Factors Associated with Trichomoniasis, Candidiasis and Bacterial Vaginosis," *International Journal of STD and AIDS*, 4, no. 1 (1993): 21-25.

8. F. Oski, *Principles and Practice of Pediatrics* (Philadelphia: J.B. Lippincott, 1994), 786; J. Last and R. Wallace, *Public Health and Preventive Medicine* (East Norwalk, CT: Appleton and Lange, 1992), 105.

9. J. Pastorek, *Obstetrics and Gynecologic Infectious Disease* (New York: Raven Press, 1994), 111.

10. A. Washington and P. Katz, "Cost of and Payment Source for Pelvic Inflammatory Disease: Trends and Projections, 1983 through 2000," *Journal of the American Medical Association*, 266, no. 18 (1991): 2565-69.

11. See note 6 above: 705.

12. See note 9 above: 240.

13. See note 6 above: 703.

14. See note 8 above, Oski: 787.

15. See note 8 above, Last: 104; Centers for Disease Control, *Morbidity and Mortality Weekly Report*, 44, no. 41 (1995): 761-64.

16. See note 9 above: 479.

17. See note 9 above: 459.

18. D. Hewlett, "Congenital Syphilis: An Emerging Health Problem," *Hospital Physician* (April 1990): 15.

19. See note 8 above, Oski: 549.

20. D. Fleming et al., "Herpes simplex virus type 2 in the United States, 1976 to 1994," *The New England Journal of Medicine*, 337, no. 16 (1997): 1105-11.

21. See note 9 above: 457.

22. See note 20 above.

23. R. Whitley, "Neonatal Herpes Simplex Virus Infections: Is there a Role for Immunoglobulin in Disease Prevention and Therapy?" *Pediatric Infectious Disease Journal*, 13, no. 5 (1994): 432-39.

24. See note 8 above, Last: 105.

25. See note 8 above, Last: 107.

26. See note 6 above: 708.

27. See note 9 above: 458.

28. See note 8 above, Last: 107.

29. See note 8 above, Last: 107.

30. See note 2 above.

31. P. Elliott et al., "Changing Character of Cervical Cancer in Young Women," *British Medical Journal*, 298 (4 February 1989): 288-90.

32. G. Mandell, J. Bennett, and R. Dolin, *Principles and Practice of Infectious Diseases* (New York: Churchill Livingstone, Inc., 1995), 1394.

33. See note 32 above: 1393.

34. See note 6 above: 709.

35. See note 9 above: 495.

36. See note 6 above: 697.

37. See note 9 above: 123.

38. Boston Women's Health Book Collective, *The New Our Bodies Ourselves: A Book By and For Women* (New York: Touchstone/ Simon and Schuster; 1992), 268.

39. T. H. Green, *Gynecology: Essentials of Clinical Practice* (Boston: Little, Brown and Company Inc., 1990), 280.

40. See note 9 above: 99.

41. "A Patient Guide: Genital Herpes," *Medical Aspects of Human Sexuality* (New York: Cahners Publishing Co., 1990).

42. L. Madaras, *The What's Happening to My Body Book for Girls* (New York: Newmarket Press, 1988), 200-201.

43. See note 6 above: 703.

44. See note 6 above: 706.

45. See note 8 above, Last: 110.

46. See note 9 above: 485.

47. L. Koutsky et al., "Underdiagnosis of Genital Herpes by Current Clinical and Viral-Isolation Procedures," *New England Journal of Medicine*, 327, no. 15 (1992): 1098-99.

48. P. Field, D. Ho, and A. Cunningham, "The Diagnosis of Recent Herpes Simplex Virus Type 2 Genital Infections by the Simplex-2 Test," *Pathology*, 24, no. 4 (1992): 302-06.

49. See note 6 above: 709.

50. A. Campbell and N. McIntosh, *Textbook of Paediatrics* (New York: Churchill Livingstone, Inc., 1992): 1501.

Chapter 5

1. G. Meyers, "Tenth Anniversary Perspectives on AIDS," *AIDS Research and Human Retroviruses*, 10, no. 11 (1994): 1317.

2. "Estimate of HIV Infection Rises to 30.6 Globally," *Washington Post*, 26 November 1997.

3. Centers for Disease Control, "Annual summary of births, marriages, divorces, and deaths: United States, 1994," *Monthly Vital Statistics Report*, 43, no. 13 (1995): 7.

4. "Seeking a Cure: Faith, Frustration," *Los Angeles Times*, 7 August 1994.

5. Early HIV Infection Guideline Panel, Rockville, Maryland, "Managing Early HIV Infection," *American Family Physician*, 49, no. 4 (1994): 801.

6. Centers for Disease Control, "Women and AIDS: the growing crisis," *HIV/AIDS Prevention*, 2, no. 1 (1991): 1.

7. E. McAnarney, R. Kreipe, D. Orr, and G. Comerci, *Textbook of Adolescent Medicine* (Philadelphia: W.B. Saunders, 1992), 711.

8. American Association of Sex Educators, Counselors and Therapists, *Newsletter*, 29, no. 8 (1995): 9.

9. "Outlook is Pessimistic at AIDS Conclave," *Los Angeles Times*, 8 August 1994.

10. "AIDS Continues to Rise in Adolescents and Young Adults," *Family Practice News*, 15 March 1997.

11. "Gonorrhea Rise Stirs AIDS Concerns," *Los Angeles Times*, 26 September 1997.

12. "AIDS: Getting More than Its Share," *Time*, 25 June 1990: 80.

13. "Who Decides?" *Forbes*, 27 January 1997.

14. "AIDS Vaccine Proving to be Elusive Goal," *Los Angeles Times*, 11 May 1997.

15. "Let Half a Billion Condoms Bloom: Thailand's Mechai Thrives as the Barnum of Birth Control and Safe Sex," *People*, 24 September 1990: 90.

16. For example: Taylor was pictured holding a condom on the cover of *Vanity Fair*, November 1992 issue.

17. "Finds Safe Sex Still a Rarity at Colleges," *Family Practice News*, 1-14 May 1990: 1.

18. "Elders is an Insult to People of Faith." *Los Angeles Times*, 25 July 1993.

19. "AIDS - You and Those You Care For: Information for AIDS Patients and Their Families" (Wilmington, Delaware: Stuart Pharmaceutical Company, 1987), 3.

20. H. Barber, "Condoms (Not Diamonds) Are a Girl's Best Friend," *The Female Patient*, 15 (1990): 14-16.

21. Centers for Disease Control, *Morbidity and Mortality Weekly Report* (1988): 37 (S-2): 7.

22. "What About Living with HIV?" *STD Bulletin* 10, no. 2 (1990): 5.

23. L. Bresolin, "Winning the Battle against the HIV Epidemic," *American Family Physician*, 43, no. 4 (1991): 1434.

24. Centers for Disease *Control HIV/AIDS Prevention*, 4, no. 1 (1993): 2. See also: M. Jewell and G. Jewell, "How to Assess the Risk of HIV Exposure." *American Family Physician*, 40, no. 1 (1989): 158;

J. Trussell, D. Warner, and R. Hatcher, "Condom Slippage and Breakage Rates," *Family Planning Perspectives*, 24 (1992): 20-23; Fischl MA et al., "Evaluation of Heterosexual Partners, Children, and Household Contacts of Adults with AIDS," *Journal of the American Medical Association*, 257, no. 5 (1987): 640; Wegersna and Oud., "Safety and Acceptability of Condoms for Use by Homosexual Men as a Prophylactic Against Transmission of HIV During Anogenital Sexual Intercourse," *British Medical Journal*, 295 (1987): 94; F. Pollner, "Experts Hedge on Condom Value," *Medical World News*, 28 August 1988, 60; J. Goedert, Sounding Board: What Is Safe Sex? *New England Journal of Medicine*, 316, no. 21 (1987): 1339-42; Y. Laurian, J. Paynet, and F. Verroust, "HIV Infection in Sexual Partners of HIV-Seropositive Patients with Hemophilia," *New England Journal of Medicine*, 320 (1989): 183; M. Musicco, For the Italian Partners' Study, "Oral Contraception, IUD, Condom Use and Man to Woman Transmission of HIV Infection," Presented at the Sixth International Conference on AIDS, 21 June 1990, San Francisco, Calif. Abstract ThC 584; European Study Group on Heterosexual Transmission of HIV, "Comparison of Female to Male and Male to Female Transmission of HIV in 563 Stable Couples," *British Medical Journal*, 304 (1992): 809-813; S. Weller; "A Meta-Analysis of Condom Effectiveness in Reducing Sexually Transmitted HIV," *Social Science and Medicine*, 36, no. 12 (1993): 1635-1644; Centers for Disease Control, *Morbidity and Mortality Weekly Report*, 42, no. 30 (1993): 589-591; I. De Vincenzi for the European Study Group on Heterosexual Transmission of HIV, "A Longitudinal Study of Human Immunodeficiency Virus Transmission by Heterosexual Partners," *The New England Journal of Medicine*, 331,no, 6 (1994): 341-6; D. Celentano et al., "Risk Factors for HIV-1 Seroconversion among Young Men in Northern Thailand," *Journal of the American Medical Association*, 275, no. 2 (1996): 122-7.

25. Planned Parenthood Federation of America, Inc., New York, 1988.

26. S. Cochran and V. Mays, "Sex, Lies, and HIV," Letter to Editor, *New England Journal of Medicine*, 322, no. 11 (1990): 774.

27. G. Marks, J. Richardson, and N. Maldonado, "Self-Disclosure of HIV Infection to Sexual Partners," *American Journal of Public Health*, 81, no. 10 (1991): 1321-1332.

28. S. Landis et al., "Results of a Randomized Trial of Partner Notification in Cases of HIV Infection in North Carolina," *New England Journal of Medicine*, 326 (1992): 101-106.

29. "There Is No Safe Sex," *Newsweek*, 1 April 1991: 8.

30. Planned Parenthood Federation of America, *A Five-Year Plan:1976-1980* (1975), 5.

31. Centers for Disease Control, *Morbidity and Mortality Weekly Report*, 24, no. 46 (1995): 849.

32. K. Siegel, L. Bauman, G. Christ, and S. Krown, "Patterns of Change in Sexual Behavior among Gay Men in New York City," *Archives of Sexual* Behavior, 17, no. 6 (1988): 481-497.

33. "Gay Black Men Slow to Practice Safe Sex, Survey Finds," *Los Angeles Times*, 14 June 1990.

34. "Stopping Pattern of Unsafe Sex," *Los Angeles Times*, 18 June 1992. See also: T. Myers et al., "Sexual Risk and HIV-Testing Behavior by Gay and Bisexual Men in Canada, *AIDS Care*, 8, no. 3 (1996): 297-309. Results of this study of 4,803 gay men showed that, nationally, 22.9% of respondents reported at least one episode of unprotected anal intercourse in the three months prior.

35. J. Martin, L. Dean, M. Garcia, and W. Hall, "The Impact of AIDS on a Gay Community: Changes in Sexual Behavior; Substance Use, and Mental Health," *American Journal of Community Psychology*, 17 (1989): 269-293.

36. K. Siegel, B. Drauss, and D. Karus, "Reporting Recent Sexual Practices: Gay Men's Disclosure of HIV Risk by Questionnaire and Interview," *Archives of Sexual Behavior*, 23, no. 2 (1994): 217-230. See also: R. Hays, S. Kegeles, and T. Coates, "High HIV Risk-Taking among Young Gay Men," *AIDS*, 4, no. 9 (1990): 901-7.

37. M. Ekstrand and T. Coates, "Maintenance of Safer Sexual Behaviors and Predictors of Risky Sex: The San Francisco Men's Health Study," *American Journal of Public Health*, 80 (1990): 973-977; R. Stall, M. Ekstrand, L. Pollack, L. McKusick, and T. Coates, "Relapse from Safer Sex: The Next Challenge for AIDS Prevention Efforts," *Journal of Acquired Immune Deficiency Syndrome*, 3 (1990): 1181-1187; K. O'Reilly et al., "Relapse from Safer Sex among Homosexual Men: Evidence from Four Cohorts in the AIDS Community Demonstration Projects," Poster presented at the VI International Conference

on AIDS, San Francisco, California, June 20-24, 1990; S. Adib, J. Joseph, D. Ostrow, M. Tal, and S. Schwartz, "Relapse in Sexual Behavior among Homosexual Men: A 2-year Follow-Up from the Chicago MACS/CCS," *AIDS*, 5 (1991): 757-760; J. Kelly, J. St. Lawrence, and T. Brasfield, "Predictors of Vulnerability to AIDS Risk Behavior Relapse," *Journal of Consulting and Clinical Psychology*, 59 (1991): 163-166.

38. Centers for Disease Control, *Morbidity and Mortality Weekly Report*, 42 (1993): 883.

39. See note 11 above: 1. See also: M. Pepe, D. Sanders, and C. Symons, "Sexual Behavior of University Freshman and the Implications for Sexuality Educators," *Journal of Sex Education and Therapy*, 19, no. 1 (1993): 20-30; S. Caron, C. Davis, W. Halteman, and M. Stickle, "Predictors of Condom-Related Behaviors among First-Year College Students," *The Journal of Sex Research*, 30, no. 3 (1993): 252-259.

40. R. Keeling, "Time to Move Forward: An Agenda for Campus Sexual Health Promotion in the Next Decade, *Journal of American College Health*, 40 (1991): 51-53.

41. W. Geringer, S. Marks, W. Allen, and K. Armstrong, "Knowledge, Attitudes, and Behavior Related to Condom Use and STDs in High Risk Population," *Journal of Sex Research*, 30, no. 1 (1993): 77-83; J. Ickovics et al., "Limited Effects of HIV Counseling and Testing for Women," *Journal of the American Medical Association*, 272, no. 6 (1994): 443-448.

42. Centers for Disease Control, "Continued Sexual Risk Behavior among HIV-Seropositive, Drug-Using Men-Atlanta; Washington, D.C.; and San Juan, Puerto Rico," *Morbidity and Mortality Weekly Report*, 45, no. 7 (1996): 151-2. E. Parra, M. Shapiro, C. Moreno, and L. Linn, "AIDS-Related Behavior; Knowledge, and Beliefs among Women and Their Mexican-American Sexual Partners Who Used Intravenous Drugs," *Archives of Family Medicine*, 2 (1993): 603-610.

43. Y. Laurian, J. Peynet, and F. Verroust, Letter: "HIV Infection in Sexual Partners of HIV-Seropositive Patients with Hemophilia," *The New England Journal of Medicine*, 320, no. 3 (1989): 183; I. De Vincenzi for the European Study Group on Heterosexual Transmission of HIV, "A Longitudinal Study of Human Immunodeficiency Virus

Transmission by Heterosexual Partners," *The New England Journal of Medicine*, 331, no. 6 (1994): 341-6. This second study showed that fewer than half of the couples with one partner known to be infected with HIV used condoms consistently despite counseling sessions held every 6 months to reinforce the couples' knowledge about the transmission of HIV.

44. This is the consistent finding of the many studies done on the subject. For example, Planned Parenthood's *Family Planning Perspectives*, 25, no. 6 (1993): 252-72, reported four studies which examined the sexual behavior of women, Hispanics, blacks, and young adults in high-risk cities. All four of the studies concluded that those persons who are at the highest risk to contract HIV were the least likely to use condoms.

45. M. Becker and J. Joseph, "AIDS and Behavioral Change to Reduce Risk: A Review," *American Journal of Public Health*, 78, no. 4 (1988): 408. In the same vein, the highly publicized comprehensive study on American sexual practices from the University of Chicago found that "(a)lthough adults know about the effectiveness of condoms and monogamy in avoiding the risk of HIV/AIDS, the question remains whether they put that knowledge into practice. Table 11.26 and a few other statistics that we discuss next suggest that the answer is that they do, but insufficiently." E. Laumann et al., *The Social Organization of Sexuality: Sexual Practices in the United States* (Chicago: University of Chicago Press, 1994), 428.

46. For a highly publicized, similar case see: "Man Infects 9 with AIDS Virus in Pastoral New York," *Los Angeles Times*, 28 October 1997. In this episode it was eventually discovered that the 20-year-old man had directly infected 28 women and may have infected another 53 persons indirectly (people who had sex with the original 28).

47. S. Monteith, *AIDS: The Unnecessary Epidemic* (Sevierville, TN: Covenant House, 1991), 90.

48. Centers for Disease Control, *Morbidity and Mortality Weekly Report*, 41, no. 15 (1992): 245.

49. "Treating HIV Like Any Epidemic: Improved Therapies Bolster Arguments for Public Health Strategies," *American Medical* News, 24 March 1997.

50. R. Janssen et al., "HIV Infection among Patients in U.S. Acute Care Hospitals," *New England Journal of Medicine*, 327, no. 7 (1992): 327.

51. Centers for Disease Control, *Morbidity and Mortality Weekly Report*, 42, no. RR-14 (1993): 7.

52. Centers for Disease Control, *Morbidity and Mortality Weekly Report*, 36, no. 11 (1987): 157; E. Cortes et al., "HIV-1, HIV-2, and HTLV- 1 Infection in High-Risk Groups in Brazil," *New England Journal of Medicine*, 320 (1989): 953; Centers for Disease Control, *Morbidity and Mortality Weekly Report*, 38, no. 24 (1989): 430.

53. E. Morse P. Simon, P. Balson, and H. Osofsky, "Sexual Behavior Patterns of Customers of Male Street Prostitutes," *Archives of Sexual* Behavior, 21, no. 4 (1992): 347-357; J. Boles and K. Elifson, "Sexual Identity and HIV: The Male Prostitute," *The Journal of Sex Research*, 31, no. 1 (1994): 39-46.

54. "Stories from the Front: Lesbians Seeking HIV Education," *SIECUS Report*, 19, no. 2 (1991): 22.

55. According to the National Gay and Lesbian Task Force: "7000 Hate Crimes on Gays Reported in '89," *Los Angeles Times*, 8 June 1990.

56. "Using Rage to Fight the Plague," *Time*, 5 February 1990: 7.

57. J. Reisman and E. Eichel, *Kinsey, Sex and Fraud* (Lafayette, LA: Huntington House, 1990), 106.

Chapter 6

1. "Today They're Trying to Censor Rap, Tomorrow...," *Los Angeles Times*, 5 November 1990.

2. *Reuters*, 12 December 1996.

3. *Merriam-Webster's Collegiate Dictionary*, 10th ed. 1994.

4. "Hef: Taming of a Playboy," *Los Angeles Times*, 11 November 1992.

5. *Orange Coast*, October 1994: 25.

6. *Canon USA* billboard advertisement campaign, 1993.

7. *1994 Plastic Surgery Statistics*, (Arlington, IL: American Society of Plastic and Reconstructive Surgery, 1993).

8. Abby [Van Buren], "Getting to the Bottom of his Need to Look," *Los Angeles Times*, 9 January 1990.

9. "What I Did for Love," *Life* (April 1990): 70.

10. "Charity Muscles," *Los Angeles Times*, 25 October 1990.

11. "Grass Roots Tactics in the Drug War;" *Los Angeles Times*, 17 July 1989.

12. "Is Hollywood Ruining America?" *Los Angeles Times*, 21 June 1992.

13. G. Steinem, *Outrageous Acts and Everyday Rebellions* (New York: Holt, Rinehart and Winston, 1983), 223.

14. E. Grimmsley, "Men Must Come to Grips with Sexual Harassment," *Orange County Register*, 21 October 1991.

15. "Scrubbing 'Indecency' from the Air," *Los Angeles Times*, 5 June 1992.

16. "MTV Was, Like, Totally Right to Relocate Show," *Los Angeles Times*, 20 October 1993.

Chapter 7

1. National Center for Health Statistics, U.S. Department of Health and Human Services, *Family Practice News*, 15-31 December 1990; Association of Reproductive Health, *American Family Physician*, 48, no. 5 (1994): 711.

2. Census Bureau, "Report," *Contemporary Sexuality*, 28, no. 9 (1994): 12.

3. "Sex Education for Bureaucrats," *Scotsman*, 29 June 1981.

4. C. Tietze, "Abortion and Contraception," *Abortion: Readings and Research (Toronto:* Butterworths, 1981), 54-60.

5. M. Calderone, ed., *Abortion in the United States, A Conference Sponsored by the PPFA and the New York Academy of Medicine* (New York: Harper and Row, 1958): 157.

6. "Report," *Cambridge Evening News*, 7 February 1973.

7. International Symposium of Contraception, 28 October 1986, Singapore; *American Journal of Obstetrics and Gynecology*, 157, no. 4 (1987): 1019.

8. American Medical Association, *Family Medical Guide* (New York: Random House, 1982), 608.

9. L. Potter, "How Effective Are Contraceptives? The Determination and Measurement of Pregnancy Rates," *Obstetrics and Gynecology*, 88, no. 3 (1996): 135-235.

10. R. Hatcher et al., *Contraceptive Technology, 16th Edition* (New York: Irvington, 1994), 113; G. Farr et al., "Contraceptive Efficacy and Acceptability of the Female Condom," *American Journal of Public Health*, 84 (1994): 1960-1964; Centers for Disease Control, "Update: Barrier Protection Against HIV Infection and Other Sexually Transmitted Diseases," *Morbidity and Mortality Weekly Report*, 42, no. 30 (1993): 590.

11. See: J. Roberts, "Women in U.S. Sue Makers of Norplant," *British Medical Journal*, 309 (1994): 145.

12. Among adolescents, compliance with Norplant is less than 40 percent at one year. D. Rainey et al., "Compliance with Return Appointments for Reproductive Health Care among Adolescent Norplant Users," *Journal of Adolescent Health*, 16, no. 5 (1995): 385-388.

13. J. Westfall, D Main, and L. Barnard, "Continuation Rates among Injectable Contraceptive Users," *Family Planning Perspectives*, 28, no. 6 (1996): 275-7; H. Sangi-Haghpeykar et al., "Experiences of Injectable Contraceptive Users in an Urban Setting," *Obstetrics and Gynecology*, 88 (1996): 227-33; M. Polaneczky, M. Guarnaccia, J. Alon and J. Wiley. "Early Experience with the Contraceptive Use of Depot Medroxyprogesterone Acetate in an Inner-City Clinic Population,"*Family Planning Perspectives*, 28, no. 4 (1996): 174-8.

14. A. Davidson et al., "Injectable Contraceptive Discontinuation and Subsequent Unintended Pregnancy among Low-Income Women," *American Journal of Public Health*, 87, no. 9 (1997): 1532-1534.

15. C. Musham, E. Dan, and M. Strossner. "A Qualitative Study of the Perceptions of Dissatisfied Norplant Users," *The Journal of Family Practice*, 40, no. 5 (1995): 465-470; M. Miller, Letter: "Depot Levonorgestrel (Norplant) Use in Teenagers," *The Western Journal of Medicine*, 158, no. 2 (1993): 183; K. Kalmuss et al., "Determinants of Early Implant Discontinuation among Low-Income Women," *Family Planning Perspectives*, 28, no. 6 (1996): 256-60.

16. J. Ross, "Contraception: Short-term vs. Long-term Rates," *Family Planning Perspectives*, 21, no. 6 (1989): 275-277. According to the article, "The 10-year risk of one or more failures over the years is the probability of surviving one month without pregnancy taken to the 120th power (120 months), and then subtracted from 1.0. Thus, a one percent probability of failure is a 99 percent probability of success.

Taking 0.99 to the 120th power gives 0.299 as the probability of going 10 years without a pregnancy, or a 70 percent chance of one (or more) failures."

17. "California Academy in Action: Family Health Month Off to Healthy Start," *California Family Physician* (November/December 1994): 20.

18. United States Public Health Service, "Counseling to Prevent Unintended Pregnancy," *American Family Physician*, 50, no. 5 (1994): 97 1-74.

19. Institute of Medicine, *The Best Intentions* (Washington, D.C.: National Academy Press, 1995), 99.

20. "Birth Control Access Could Halve Abortions," Letter to the Editor; *Wall St. Journal*, 26 April 1991.

21. S. Henshaw and K. Kost, "Abortion Patients in 1994-1995: Characteristics and Contraceptive Use," *Family Planning Perspectives*, 28, no. 4 (1996): 140.

22. Ross, see note 9.

23. G. Chamberlain, ed., *Contemporary Obstetrics and Gynecology* (London: Butterworths, 1988), 315; C. Hamilton and H. Hoogland, "Longitudinal Ultrasonographic Study of the Ovarian Suppressive Activity of a Low-dose Triphasic Oral Contraceptive during Correct and Incorrect Pill Intake, *American Journal of Obstetrics and Gynecology*, 161, no. 5 (1990): 1159-62.

24. "Contraceptive Advances, Part II: IUDs and Barrier Methods," *The Female Patient*, 15 (1990): 25.

25. P. Kramer, *The Dynamics of Relationships* (Kensington, MD: Equal Partners).

26. "Morning After" Use of Pill Found Safe by FDA Panel," *Los Angeles Times*, 29 June 1996.

27. R. Hatcher et al., *Contraceptive Technology* (New York: Irvington Publishers, 1989), 71.

28. Supreme Court document.

29. "Everett Koop: The Former Surgeon General Examines the Nation's Health," *Los Angeles Times*, 23 February 1992.

30. "Pregnancy Is Still Surprising a Lot of Us," *Los Angeles Times*, 8 June 1995.

31. "Psychic' Barrier to Birth Control," *Los Angeles Times*, 1 June 1993.

Chapter 8
1. A. Ghosh, S. Saha, and G. Chattergee, "Symptothermia vis-à-vis Fertility Control," *Journal of Obstetrics and Gynaecology of India*, 32 (1982): 443-47.
2. J. Doud, "Use-Effectiveness of the Creighton Model of NFP," *International Review of Natural Family Planning*, 9 (1985): 54; T. Hilgers, "The Effectiveness of the Ovulation Method as a Means of Achieving and Avoiding Pregnancy. Presented at Education Phase III Continuing Education conference for Natural Family Planning Practitioners, 24 July 1980, Mercy Fontenelle Center, Omaha, Nebraska; M. Howard, "Use-Effectiveness of the Ovulation Method of Natural Family Planning." Presented at the Ninth Annual Meeting of the American Academy of Natural Family Planning, Milwaukee, Wisconsin, July 26, 1990; F. Rice and C. Lanctot, "Results of a Recent Study *on* the Sympto-thermal Method of Natural Family Planning," *Linacre Quarterly*, 45, no. 4 (1978): 388-39 1, J. Roetzer, "The Sympto-Thermal Method: Ten Years of Change," *Linacre Quarterly*, 45, no. 4 (1978): 370; J. Trussell and L. Grummer-Strawn, "Contraceptive Failure of the Ovulation Method of Periodic Abstinence," *Family Planning Perspectives*, 22, no. 2 (1990): 65-75; World Health Organization, "A Prospective Multicenter Trial of the Ovulation Method of Natural Family Planning. II. The Effectiveness Phase," *Fertility and Sterility*, 36, no. 5 (1981): 591-598; R. Kambic, "Natural Family Planning Use-Effectiveness and Continuation," *American Journal of Obstetrics and Gynecology*, 165 (1991): 2046-2048. This article reviews eleven studies; K. Dorairaj, "The Modified Mucus Method in India," *American Journal of Obstetrics and Gynecology*, 165 (1991): 2066-7; J. Medina, A. Cifuentes, J. Abernathy, J. Spieler; and M. Wade, "Comparative Evaluation of Two Methods of Natural Family Planning in Columbia," *American Journal of Obstetrics and Gynecology*, 138 (1980): 1142-7; P. Frank-Herrmann, G. Freundl, S. Baur, M. Bremme, G. Doring, E. Godehardt, and U. Sottong, "Effectiveness and Acceptability of the Symptothermal Method of Natural Family Planning in Germany," *American Journal of Obstetrics and Gynecology*, 165 (1991): 2052-4; R. Rice, C. Lanctot, and C. Garcia-

Devesa, "Effectiveness of the Symptothermal Method of Natural Family Planning: an International Study," *International Journal of Fertility*, 26, no. 3 (1981): 222-230; R. Ryder, "Natural Family Planning: Effective Birth Control Supported by the Catholic Church," *British Medical Journal* 307 (1993): 723-6; B. Ryder and H. Campbell, "Natural Family Planning in the 1990s," *Lancet*, 346 (1995): 233-4.

3. It is interesting that studies on the effectiveness of condoms in preventing HIV transmission typically emphasize method failure rate. This emphasis is in contrast to studies on condoms as contraceptives (and contraceptive efficacy studies in general) which highlight the user failure rate. This unique bias is used to promote a political agenda, i.e. method failure rates make condoms appear to be a far more effective weapon in the war against HIV than they actually are.

4. *Basics of Birth Control* (Planned Parenthood Federation of America, Inc. 1984). In contrast to this view, see: A. Bitto *et* al., "Adverse Outcomes of Planned and Unplanned Pregnancies among Users of Natural Family Planning: A Prospective Study," *American Journal of Public Health*, 87, no. 3 (1997): 338-43.

5. FDA Standards

6. Making Choices: Evaluating the Health Risks and Benefits of Birth Control Methods (New York: Alan Guttmacher Institute, 1983): 8.

7. *The Medical Letter*, 30, no. 779 (1988): 108.

8. Dr. Joyce Brothers, "Wife Refusing to Have Unsafe Sex with Him," *Los Angeles Times*, 15 April 1993.

9. R. Slacks and T. Hilgers, "Advertising Trends in Major Journals of Obstetrics and Gynecology," *Natural Family Planning*, 9, no. 4 (1985): 292-305.

10. T. Sollom, R. Benson Gold, and R. Saul. "Public Funding for Contraceptive, Sterilization and Abortion Services, 1994, *Family Planning Perspectives*, 28, no. 4 (1996): 166-73.

11. J. Frost, "Family Planning Clinic Services in the United States, 1994," *Family Planning Perspectives*, 28, no. 3 (1996): 92-100.

12. *Washington Post*, 22 March 1931. Reference from J. Kippley, *Sex and the Marriage Covenant: A Basis for Morality*, (Cincinnati, Ohio: The Couple to Couple League, 1991), 325.

13. R. Jackson, *Human Ecology* (Petersham, MA: St. Bede's Publications, 1990), 92.

14. M. McCusker, *Couples' Perceptions of the Use of Fertility Awareness Methods of Natural Family Planning on Their Marriage Relationship*, (Washington, D.C.: Catholic University of America) A master's degree thesis, June, 1976; J. Tortorici, "Conception Regulation, Self Esteem, and Marital Satisfaction among Catholic Couples: Michigan State University Study," *International Review of Natural Family Planning*, 3, no. 3 (1979): 191-205.

15. "Harper's Index," *Harper's* (February 1989): 13. See also: E. Laumann, J. Gagnon, R. Michael, and S. Michaels. *The Social Organization of Sexuality: Sexual Practices in the United States* (Chicago: University of Chicago Press, 1994), 499.

Chapter 9

1. K. Henshaw, "Abortion Trends in 1987 and 1988: Age and Race," *Family Planning Perspectives* 24, no. 2 (1992): 85-86.

2. M. K. Zimmerman, *Passage Through Abortion: The Personal and Social Reality of Women's Experiences* (New York: Praeger, 1977), 189-90 [Note that this book is decidedly pro-choice in perspective.]; H. Cvejic, I. Lipper; R. Kinch, and P. Benjamin, "Follow-up of 50 Adolescent Girls Two Years After Abortions," *Canadian Medical Journal*, 116 (1977): 44-46.

3. B. Shostak and G. McLouth, *Men and Abortion: Lessons, Losses, and Love* (New York: Praeger, 1984), 34 [This book offers a consistent pro-choice bias].

4. Zimmerman, 122.

5. *Abortion and Women's Health*, Alan Guttmacher Institute, 1990, 20.

6. H. Gow, "True Feminism Is Anti-Abortion," *Wanderer*, 11 April 1991.

7. B. N. Nathanson and R. N. Osting, *Aborting America* (Garden City, NY: Doubleday, 1979), 193.

8. Centers for Disease Control, *Morbidity and Mortality Weekly Report*, 46, no. SS-4 (1997): 96, Table 35.

9. Commission on Professional Hospital Activities (Ann Arbor; MI) and IMS America, Ltd., (Ambler, PA), *Hospital Record Study* (1969-1977).

10. See forward: D. C. Reardon, *Aborted Women: Silent No More* (Chicago: Loyola University Press, 1987), xxii.

Chapter 10

1. A. W. Schaef, *When Society Becomes an Addict* (San Francisco: Harper SF, 1987), 4.

2. *Merriam- Webster's Collegiate Dictionary*, 10th ed.

3. C. Cloninger, M. Bohman, S. Sigvardsson, "Inheritance of Alcoholism: Cross Fostering Analysis of Adopted Men," *Archives of General Psychiatry*, 38 (1981): 861-66; R. J. Cadoret and A. Gath. "Inheritance of Alcoholism in Adoptees," British Journal of Psychiatry, 132 (1978): 252-58; R. J. Cadoret, C.A. Cain, and W. M. Grove, "Development of Alcoholism in Adoptees Raised Apart from Alcoholic Biologic Relatives," *Archives of General Psychiatry*, 37 (1980): 561-563; C. R. Cloninger, "Genetic and Environmental Factors in the Development of Alcoholism," *Journal of Psychiatric Treatment and Evaluation*, 5 (1983): 487-496; D. W. Goodwin et al., "Alcohol Problems in Adoptees Raised Apart from Alcoholic Biological Parents," *Archives of General Psychiatry*, 28 (1973): 238-243; M. A. Schuckit, D. *A.* Goodwin, and G. Winoker, "A Study *of* Alcoholism in Half-Siblings," *American Journal of Psychiatry*, 129 (1972): 1132-1136.

4. D. Barry, "Any Questions: Ronald K. Siegel," *California Magazine*, December 1989: 14.

5. Workshops on Adult Children of Alcoholics with Sharon Wegscheider-Cruse and Rokelle Lerner, Rocky Mountain Council on Alcoholism, Denver, Colorado, January 1984 (unpublished report). Referenced from: A. Schaef *When Society Becomes an Addict* (San Francisco: Harper and Row, 1987).

6. P. Boyer, "The Intimate Steve Garvey," *Los Angeles Times Magazine*, 24 September 1989.

7. "Playing Rough in a Custody Fight, Steve Garvey has Cyndy, His Ex, Tossed into Jail," *People*, 16 October 1989: 93.

8. Sex Addiction as Devastating as Alcoholism, *Family Practice News*, 15 January 1990.

9. B. Darrach, "The Father; the Director and the Holy Terror," *Life* (September 1990): 66-75.

10. Front page news item, *Los AngelesTimes*, 16 May 1990.

Chapter 11

1. A. Kinsey, W. Pomeroy, and C. Martin, *Sexual Behavior in the Human Male* (Philadelphia: W. B. Saunders, 1948): 638.

2. W. Masters and V. Johnson. *Homosexuality in Perspective* (Boston: Little, Brown and Company, 1979), 182.

3. E. 0. Laumann, J. H. Gagnon, R. T. Michael, and S. Michaels, *The Social Organization of Sexuality: Sexual Practices in the United States* (Chicago: University of Chicago, 1994), 297; "Homosexuals and the 10% Fallacy," *The Wall Street Journal*, 31 March 1993. This article summarizes the results of numerous research papers.

4. *Orange*, (San Francisco: Multi-Focus, Inc. 1970).

5. *New York Times*, 4 April 1988. Referenced from: J. Riesman and E. Eichel, *Kinsey, Sex and Fraud* (Lafayette, LA. Huntington House, 1990): 152.

6. For example, the U.S. Department of Health and Human Services 1989 *Report of the Secretary s' Task Force on Youth Suicide*, states that "All youth need to be provided with positive information about homosexuality that presents it as a viable adaptation. We must accept a homosexual orientation in young people in the same manner that we accept a heterosexual orientation," (Vol. 3, p. 134).

7. For example, the Episcopal Church donated $10,000 to *Parents and Friends of Lesbians and Gays* for a program whose primary message is. "that homosexuality is natural and healthy." "Tolerance of Gays Tied to Prevention of Youths' Suicides, *Orange County Register*, 13 October 1990. Also, the Central Conference of American Rabbis, representing 1,750 rabbis, has voted to support civil marriage for homosexuals and to oppose governmental attempts to bar such unions. "Rabbis Endorse Gay Marriage," *San Francisco Chronicle*, 29 March 1996.

8. L. Barker et al., *Principles of Ambulatory Medicine*, 4th ed. (Baltimore: William & Wilkins, 1995), 1360.

9. J.C. Bennett and F. Blum. *Cecil Textbook of Medicine*, 20th ed. (Philadelphia: W.B. Saunders, 1996), 764.

10. K. Isselbacher et al., *Harrison's Principles of Internal Medicine, 13th ed.* (New York: McGraw-Hill, 1994), 760; J. Levy, C. Stegman, E. Katz, and S. Wagner, "An 18-Year-Old with Acute Testicular Pain," *The Western Journal of Medicine*, 154 (1991): 201-2.

11. M. Corman, *Colon and Rectal Surgery* (Philadelphia: J.B. Lippincott, 1993), 131.

12. Council of Scientific Affairs, American Medical Association, "Health Care Needs of Gay Men and Lesbians in the United States," *The Journal of the American Medical Association*, 275, no. 17 (1996): 1355. See also: G. Mandell, J. Bennett, *and* R. Dolin. *Principles and Practice of Infectious Diseases* (New York: Churchill Livingstone 1995), 1393.

13. J. Harvey, *The Homosexual Person* (San Francisco: Ignatius, 1987): 68.

14. "Luther Campbell Draws the Line," *Harper's*, January 1991: 34.

15. Many heterosexuals are openly hostile toward homosexuals, some, no doubt, due to insecurities about their own homosexual feelings. This hostility is referred to as "homophobia." Extremists use the term to denote anyone who questions the validity of homosexual behavior.

16. A. Bell and M. Weinberg, *Homosexualities: A Study of Diversity among Men and Women* (New York: Simon & Schuster; 1978), 82.

17. W. Aaron, *Straight* (New York: Bantam Books, 1972), 208.

18. A.A. Deenen, M.A. Gijis, and *A.* X. van Naerssen. "Intimacy and Sexually in Gay Male Couples," *Archives of Sexual Behavior*, vol. 23, no. 4 (1994): 421-43 1.

19. D. McWhirter and A. Mattison, *The Male Couple: How Relationships Develop* (Englewood Cliffs, NJ: Prentice-Hall,1984), 252.

20. K. Jay and A. Young, *The Gay Report: Lesbians and Gay Men Speak Out About Sexual Experiences and Lifestyles* (New York: Summit, 1979), 247.

21. "The Future of Gay America," Newsweek 12 March 1990: 22.

22. Dangerous Liaisons, *Los Angeles Times Magazine*, 25 July 1993: 10.

23. "High-Risk Sex on the Rise, Conference Told," *Los Angeles Times*, 9 July 1996.

24. "Fund and Fear on Gay Party Circuit," *Los Angeles Times*, 13 October 1997.

25. A. Landers, "Mom Is in Love with Daughter's Boyfriend," *Los Angeles Times*, 17 November 1992.

26. For a review of 19 studies that have demonstrated successful treatment of homosexuality see: J. Nicolosi, *Reparative Therapy of Male Homosexuality* (Northvale, NJ: Jason Aronson, 1991), 17-19. See also: J. Harvey, *The Truth About Homosexuality* (San Francisco: Ignatius, 1996), 69-114.

27. "Psychologists Reconsider Gay 'Conversion' Therapy." *The Washington Post*, 14 August 1997.

28. E. Siegel, *Female Homosexuality, Choice Without Volition: A Psychoanalytic Study* (Hillside, NJ: Analytic Press, 1988), xi-xii.

29. W. Byne and B. Parsons, "Human Sexual Orientation: The Biological Theories Reappraised," *Archives of General Psychiatry*, 50 (1993): 228-239. See also: "Gay Genes Revisited," *Scientific American*, November 1995: 26.

30. See: J. Bailey and R. Pillard, "A Genetic Study of Male Sexual Orientation," *Archives of General Psychiatry*, 48 (1991): 1089-96; L. Heston and J. Shields, "Homosexuality in Twins: A Family Study and a Registry Study," *Archives of General Psychiatry*, 18 (1968): 149-160; M. King and E. McDonald, "Homosexuals Who Are Twins. A Study of 46 Probands," *British Journal of Psychiatry*, 160 (1992): 407-9. Another study, which reportedly lent credence to a genetic basis for homosexuality actually supported the opposite conclusion. The study found that homosexuals tend to have more older brothers than heterosexuals. The number of brothers one has strongly affects ones environment, but has no effect on one's genetic makeup. R. Blanchard and A. Bogaert. "Homosexuality in Men and Number of Older Brothers," *American Journal of Psychiatry*, 153 (1996): 27-31.

31. G. Cowley, "The Biology of Beauty, "*Newsweek*, 3 June 1996: 66.

32. E. Moberly, *Homosexuality: A New Christian Ethic* (Cambridge: James Clarke, 1983); G. van den Aardweg, *On the Origins and Treatment of Homosexuality, A Psychoanalytic Reinterpretation* (Westport, CN: Praeger, 1986).

Chapter 12

1. M. Mead, *Coming of Age in Samoa* (New York: W. Morrow, 1928).

2. D. Freeman, *Margaret Mead and Samoa: The Making and Unmaking of an Anthropological Myth* (Cambridge, MA: Harvard University Press, 1983).

3. "Letters to the Editor," *Los Angeles Times*, 10 January 1992.

4. L. Smith, "Best Wishes from Liz to Liz," *Los Angeles Times*, 30 July 1991.

5. "Playboy Interview: Dr. Mary Calderone," *Playboy*, April 1970: 78.

6. Kinsey, 238.

7. "Genetic Component Found in Lesbianism, Study Says," *Los Angeles Times*, 12 March 1993.

8. "Study Strongly Links Genetics, Homosexuality," *Los Angeles Times*, 16 July 1993.

9. "Survey of Identical Twins Links Biological Factors with Being Gay," *Los Angeles Times*, 15 December 1991.

10. "Many Cheer a Second Study Suggesting that Homosexuality Has Physical Causes," *Los Angeles Times*, 12 August 1992.

11. "In Gay Rights Debate, Concern about Children Is Never Far Away," *Los Angeles Times*, 6 June 1993.

12. *Diagnostic and Statistical Manual of Mental Disorders, 4th ed.* (Washington, D.C.: American Psychiatric Association, 1994), 525-532.

13. *Diagnostic and Statistical Manual of Mental Disorders, 3rd ed. and revised* (Washington, D.C.: American Psychiatric Association, 1987), 282-290.

14. *Diagnostic and Statistical Manual of Mental Disorders, 2nd ed.* (Washington, D.C.: American Psychiatric Association, 1968), 44.

15. *Diagnostic and Statistical Manual of Mental Disorders: 3rd ed.* (Washington, D.C.: American Psychiatric Association, 1980), 281.

16. M. S. Peck, *The Road Less Traveled* (New York: Touchstone/Simon and Schuster, 1978), 151.

17. "The Joy of What?" *Wall Street Journal*, 12 December 1991.

Chapter 13

1. D. von Hildebrand, *Man and Woman* (Manchester; NH: Sophia Institute Press, 1992): 59.

2. J. Kippley, *Sex and the Marriage Covenant* (Cincinnati, OH: Couple *to* Couple League, 1992), 7-8.

3. Available from: ETR Associates, Santa Cruz, CA 95061-1830. Phone: (800) 321-4407. Request item #063 (1991). For a similar list: "50 Creative Dating Ideas," *Focus on the Family Magazine*, February 1992. Available from: Focus on the Family, P.O. Box 35500, Colorado Springs CO, 80935-3550.

Chapter 14

1. W. Fassbender; *You and Your Health* (New York: John Wiley and Sons, 1977), 156.

2. "An Introduction to World Religions," *Christopher News Notes*, (New York: The Christophers, November 1992).

3. I. Reiss, *Premarital Sexual Standards*, Study Guide #5 (New York: SIECUS, 1967).

4. "In May, 1973 . . . Dr. James D. Watson, Nobel Prize-winning scientist (for physiology and medicine), stated that consideration should be given to withholding legal status from an infant until three days after his birth. Parents who suspect fetal abnormalities may now legally obtain an abortion, he pointed out; but most birth defects are not discovered until birth: 'If a child were not declared alive until three days after birth, then all parents could be allowed a choice that only a few are given under the present system. . . . The doctor could allow the child to die if the parents so chose and save a lot of misery and suffering. I believe this view is the only rational, compassionate attitude to have." Excerpts from: P. Marx, *The Mercy Killers* (Front Royal, VA: Human Life International).

5. "Thai Monks Help Wean Addicts From Drugs," *Los Angeles Times*, 31 December 1991.

6. D. Reardon, *Aborted Women: Silent No More* (Westchester, IL: Crossway Books, 1987), 319.

7. R. Bolt, *A Man for All Seasons* (New York: Random House, 1962), 13.

8. The first amendment to the United States Constitution reads:

"Congress shall make no law respecting an establishment of religion, or prohibiting the free exercise thereof or abridging the freedom of speech, or of the press; or the right of the people peaceably to assemble, and to petition the Government for a redress of grievances."

9. "Letters to the Editor," *Los Angeles Times*, 17 April 1991.

Chapter 15

1. A. Huxley, *Brave New World* (London: Chatto & Wyndus, 1932).

2. I. Reiss, Sexual Pluralism: Ending America's Sexual Crisis, *SIECUS Report*, February/March 1991: 5.

3. A. Ellis, "Rationality in Sexual Morality," *The Humanist*, September/October 1969: 18.

4. *India Today*, 31 January 1988.

5. *The Serious Reader's Guide* (Harrison, NY: Ignatius, 1989).

6. "A New Bill of Sexual Rights and Responsibilities," *The Humanist*, January/February 1976.

7. Editorial: "The Real Issue Is Life – and Who Controls It," *Los Angeles Times*, 6 November 1989.

8. St. Augustine, *Confessions* ii.

9. Editors of Conan Press, *Random Acts of Kindness* (Emoryville, CA: Conan Press, 1993), 3-4.

10. A. Bloom, ed., *The Republic of Plato* (HarperCollins, 1991) 184.

11. "Pure Gore," *Los Angeles Times Magazine*, 28 January 1990: 16.

12. A. Bloom, *The Closing of the American Mind* (New York: Simon and Schuster, 1987), 38.

13. "Bisexuality," *Newsweek*, 17 July 1995: 44-50.

14. Fullerton, CA Police Department. Based on interview data compiled for the 1988 Conference of Educators and Law Enforcement Officers (San Francisco, CA), sponsored by the California State Department of Education. Reference from: W. Kilpatrick, *Why Johnny Can't Tell Right From Wrong* (New York: Simon and Schuster, 1992), 100.

15. *From the Wall Street Journal*, quoted *in Reader's Digest*, May, 1992: 71.

16. In response to my own letter to *The Female Patient*, 14 (1989): 17.

17. "The Marriage Counselor," *Family Foundations*, Couple to Couple League, Cincinnati Ohio. (May/June 1989): 11.

Chapter 16

1. Centers for Disease Control, "Premarital Sexual Experience among Adolescent Women," *Morbidity and Mortality Weekly Report*, 39 (1991): 929-32.

2. "Teen Sex-Education Campaign Launched," *Los Angeles Times*, 17 October 1986.

3. P. Cutright, "Illegitimacy: Myths, Causes and Cures," *Family Planning Perspectives*, 3, no. 1 (1971): 47.

4. "Understanding Adolescent Sexuality: Helping Teens to Use Contraception," *Contraceptive Technology* Conference, Anaheim, CA, 21 March 1990.

5. R. Cross, "Helping Adolescents Learn about Sexuality," *SIECUS Report* 19, no. 4 (1991): 11.

6. Centers for Disease Control, *Morbidity and Mortality Weekly Report*, 34, no. 19 (1985): 277; 5. K. Henshaw and J. Van Vort, "Teenage Abortion, Birth and Pregnancy Statistics: An Update," *Family Planning Perspectives*, 21, no. 2 (1989): 85-88.

7. Teenagers account for 30 percent of all cases of sexually transmitted diseases, E. McAnarney, R. Kreipe, D. Orr, and G. Comerci, *Textbook of Adolescent Medicine* (Philadelphia: W.B. Saunders, 1992): 696. Forty-five percent of sexually active teenagers using birth control have chlamydial infections. J. Maurice, "Ubiquitous Parasite: Chlamydial Infections Now Commonest Sex-Transmitted Disease," *International Health Magazine*, 3 (1983): 19-20. Rates of venereal wart virus infection among teenage girls is reported to be as high as 40 percent. J. Martinez et al., "High Prevalence of Genital Tract Papilloma-Virus Infection in Female Adolescents, *Pediatrics*, 82 (1989): 604.

8. "Number of Sex Partners Not Increased by Giving Contraceptives to Teens," *Family Planning Perspectives*, 10, no. 6 (1978): 368. It is worth noting that this article title is misleading. Within the article the statement actually is that teens given contraceptives "were found to be 'moderately' more sexually active, and not involved with a larger num-

ber of sexual partners, than they had been before they began to practice contraception." See also: L. Zabin and S. Clark, "Why They Delay: A Study of Teenage Family Planning Clinic Patients, *Family Planning Perspectives*, 13, no. 5 (1981): 213, Table 8. J. Olsen and S. Weed. "Effects of Family Planning Programs for Teenagers on Adolescent Birth and Pregnancy Rates," *Family Perspectives*, 20 (1986): 133. P. A. Reichelt, "Changes in Sexual Behavior among Unmarried Teenage Women Utilizing Oral Contraception," *Journal of Population*, 1 (1978): 57.

9. According to Dr. Robert Kirsner of Harvard Medical School, a developer of the oral contraceptive, "About 10 years ago I declared that the pill would not lead to promiscuity. Well I was wrong....introduction of the birth control pill has been a major causal factor in the rapid increase in both VD and cervical cancer among adolescents by stimulating higher levels of promiscuity." *Family Practice News*, 15 December 1977. Dr. Min-Chueh Chang, another codeveloper of the birth control pill, once remarked that he was sorry the pill had "spoiled young people. It's made them more permissive." *Fidelity* 10, no. 8 (1991): 18.

10. K. McCleary, "Sex, Morals, and AIDS," *USA Today Weekend*, 27-29 December 1991: 4; L. Wolk and R. Rosenbaum, "The Benefits of School-Based Condom Availability: Cross-Sectional Analysis of a Comprehensive High School-Based Program," *Journal of Adolescent Health*, 17 (1995): 186. In this second study, teenagers reported "that having condoms made it easier to have intercourse more often."

11. A 1983 study found that the majority of physicians believed that the increased availability of contraceptives has led to increased sexual activity among teenagers. A. Pietropinto, "Survey Analysis," *Medical Aspects of Human Sexuality*, 21, no. 5 (1987): 150.

12. *Teenage Pregnancy: the Problem That Hasn't Gone Away* (Washington, DC: Alan Guttmacher Institute, 1981), 5.

13. John Kantner and Marvin Zelnik, from Johns Hopkins, performed large national surveys on adolescents from 1971-1979. Their results were published in the following four articles: "Sexual and Contraceptive Experience of Young Unmarried Women in the United States, 1976 and 1971," *Family Planning Perspectives*, 9, no. 2 (1977): 55-71; "First Pregnancies to Women Aged 15-19: 1976 and 1971," *Family Planning Perspectives*, 10, no. 1 (1978): 11-20; "Contraceptive

Patterns and Premarital Pregnancy among Women Aged 15-19 in 1976," *Family Planning Perspectives*, 10, no. 3 (1978): 135-143; "Sexual Activity, Contraceptive Use and Pregnancy among Metropolitan-Area Teenagers: 1971-1979," *Family Planning Perspectives*, 12, no. 5 (1980): 230-238.

14. See Olson, note 8 above; L. Edwards, M. Steinman, and E. Hakanson, "An Experimental Comprehensive High School Clinic," *American Journal of Public Health*, 67, no. 8 (1977): 765-766; A. Kenney, "School-Based Clinics: A National Conference," *Family Planning Perspectives*, 18 (1986): 45; L. Edwards, M. Steinman, K. Arnold, and E. Hakanson, "Adolescent Pregnancy Prevention Services in High School Clinics," *Family Planning Perspectives*, 12, no. 1 (1980): 6-14; D. Kirby et al., "The Effects of School-Based Health Clinics in St. Paul on School-Wide Birthrates," *Family Planning Perspectives*, 25, no. 1 (1993): 12-16. These studies report on a school-based clinic program in St. Paul, Minnesota. The data from these clinics is the most widely referenced data used to justify the promotion of contraception to teenagers through school-based clinics. The clinic reported that, following increased utilization of the clinics, there was a significant reduction in the fertility rate of the students. This statistic deserves several comments. First, pregnancy and abortion rates were not reported. By definition, the fertility rate is the *birth rate*, and this is reduced by either a reduction in the pregnancy rate or an increase in the abortion rate. The lack of forthrightness with regard to this data is very suspicious, especially in light of other evidence which indicates contraception promotion leads to higher rates of abortions among teens. Higher abortion rates in response to the promotion of contraception is indirect evidence that contraceptives encourage promiscuity and risk-taking behavior (the antecedents to "unwanted" pregnancies). Second, it should be noted that this clinic made monthly follow up calls to ensure compliance with contraceptives. This is extremely cost-ineffective and impractical for most clinical facilities. Third, recent reports from Planned Parenthood have questioned the validity of the data reported in this study.

In an article entitled "Six School-Based Clinics: Their Reproductive Health Services and Impact on Sexual Behavior," Planned Parenthood states: ". . . none of the clinics had a statistically significant effect on school-wide pregnancy rates." D. Kirby, C. Waszak, and J.

Ziegler, "Six School-Based Clinics: Their Reproductive Health Services and Impact on Sexual Behavior;" *Family Planning Perspectives*, 23, no. 1 (1991): 6-16.

L. S. Zabin et al., "Evaluation of a Pregnancy Prevention Program for Urban Teenagers," *Family Planning Perspectives*, 18 (1986): 119-126. This study, from Baltimore Maryland, reported a reduction in pregnancy rates in response to utilization of school-based clinics, but inexplicably bent the statistics by reporting only pregnancy rates of those who were sexually active. The pregnancy rates of the entire student population were not reported. Again, this is indirect evidence that the promotion of contraceptives leads to promiscuity. For the pregnancy rate to remain stable while the rate among those who were sexually active decreased, more students must have been sexually active, i.e., the promotion of contraceptives led to greater rates of sexual activity.

F. Earls, L. Robins, A. Stiffman and J. Powell, "Comprehensive Health Care for High-Risk Adolescents: An Evaluation Study," *American Journal of Public Health*, 79, no. 8 (1989): 999-1005. This study found that "the funded clinics were not able to alter the propensity of their patients to continue their adverse life-styles and to accumulate additional problems."

E. Brann et al., "Strategies for the Prevention of Pregnancy in Adolescents," *Advances in Planned Parenthood*, 14, no. 2 (1979): 69-76. This article reviewed seven school-based clinics and, again, failed to mention the effect of any clinic on the pregnancy rate but only discussed fertility rates.

See also: M. Hughs, F. Furstenberg and J. Teitler, "The Impact of an Increase in Family Planning Services on the Teenage Population of Philadelphia," *Family Planning Perspectives*, 27, no. 2 (1995): 60-65,78; L. Wolk and R. Rosenbaum, "The Benefits of School-Based Condom Availability: Cross-Sectional Analysis of a Comprehensive High School-Based Program," *Journal of Adolescent Health*, 17 (1995): 186. In this last study, teenagers reported "that having condoms made it easier to have intercourse more often."

15. J. Dryfoos, "School-based Health Clinics: Three Years of Experience," *Family Planning Perspectives*, 20, no. 4 (1988): 196. See also: R. Maynard and A. Rangarajan, "Contraceptive Use and Repeat

Pregnancies among Welfare-Dependent Teenage Mothers," *Family Planning Perspectives*, 20, no. 5 (1994): 198-205. This article by Planned Parenthood reports that a program of contraceptive promotion to teenaged mothers on welfare "did little or nothing to delay subsequent pregnancies," See also: E. Kisker and R. Brown, "Do School-Based Health Centers Improve Adolescents' Access to Health Care, Health Status, and Risk Taking Behavior?" *Journal of Adolescent Health*, 18, no. 5 (1996): 335-343. This article states that the effect of school-based health centers on risky behaviors was "inconsistent" and "not statistically significant."

16. P. Cutright, "Illegitimacy in the United States: 1920-1968," Research Reports, U.S. Commission on Population Growth and the American Future, Vol. 1, *Demographic and Social Aspects of Population Growth* (Washington, DC: United States Government Printing Office, 1972), 421.

17. K. Davis, "The American Family in Relation *to* Demographic Change," Research Reports, U.S. Commission on Population Growth *and the* American Future Research Reports, Vol. 1, *Demographic and Social Aspects of Population Growth* (Washington, DC: US Government Printing Office, 1972), 253.

18. B. Mosbacker, *Special Report: Teenage Pregnancy and School-Based Clinics* (1986): 13.

19. M. Zelnik and J. Kantner, "Contraceptive Patterns and Premarital Pregnancy among Women Aged 15-19 in 1976," *Family Planning Perspectives*, 10, no. 3 (1978): 140.

20. See Olsen, note 9 above.

21. D. Mishell, "Medical Progress: Contraception," *New England Journal of Medicine*, 320, no. 12 (1989): 779.

22. "Some Teens Still Having Risky Sex," *Los Angeles Times*, 5 March 1992.

23. G. Remafedi, "Predictors of Unprotected Intercourse among Gay and Bisexual Youth: Knowledge, Beliefs, and Behavior," *Pediatrics*, 94, no. 2 (1994): 163-68. M. Rotheram et al., "Sexual and Substance Use Acts of Gay and Bisexual Male Adolescents in New York City," *The Journal of Sex Research*, 31, no. 1 (1994): 47-57.

24. E. Persson and G. Jarlbro, "Sexual Behavior among Youth Clinic Visitors in Sweden: Knowledge and Experiences in an HIV Perspective, *Genitourinary Medicine*, 68, no. 1 (1992): 26-31.

25. 5. Kegeles, N. Adler, and C. Irwin, "Adolescents and Condoms," *American Journal of Diseases of Children*, 143 (1989): 911-15; R. DiClemente, L. Brown, N. Beusoleil, and M. Lodico, "Comparison of AIDS Knowledge and HIV-Related Sexual Risk Behaviors among Adolescents in Low and High AIDS Prevalence Communities," *Journal of Adolescent Health*, 14, no. 3 (1993): 23 1-236.

26. "Adolescents and AIDS: Females' Attitudes and Behaviors toward Condom Purchase and Use," *Journal of Adolescent Health Care*, 10 (1989): 313.

27. "The Truth about Latex Condoms," *SIECUS Report: Fact Sheet*, 24, no. 1 (1995): 22.

28. C. Weisman et al., "Consistency of Condom Use for Disease Prevention among Adolescent Users of Oral Contraceptives," *Family Planning Perspectives*, 23, no. 2 (1991): 71-74.

29. R. DiClemente et al., "Determinants of Condom Use among Junior High School Students in a Minority, Inner-City School District," *Pediatrics*, 89, no. 2 (1992): 197-02; L. Ku, F. L. Sonenstein, and J. H. Pleck, "Patterns of HIV Risk and Preventive Behaviors Among Teenage Men," *Public Health Reports*, 107 (1992): 131; D. Orr and C. Langefeld, "Factors Associated with Condom Use by Sexually Active Male Adolescents at Risk for Sexually Transmitted Disease," *Pediatrics*, 91, no. 5 (1993): 873-79; F. Sonenstein, J. Pleck, and L. Ku, "Sexual Activity, Condom Use and AIDS Awareness among Adolescent Males," *Family Planning Perspectives*, 21 (1989): 152- 58.

R. DiClemente et al., "Determinants of Condom Use among Junior High School Students in a Minority, Inner-City School District," *Pediatrics*, 89, no. 2 (1992): 197-202; This study found that the "number of sexual partners was inversely related to frequency of condom use."

M. Durbin et al., "Factors Associated with Multiple Sex Partners among Junior High School Students," *Journal of Adolescent Health*, 14 (1993): 202-07; J. H. Pleck, F. L. Sonenstein, and L. Ku, "Changes in Adolescent Males' Use of and Attitudes toward Condoms, 1988-1991," *Family Planning Perspectives*, 25, no. 3 (1993): 106-10. This study found that "as the respondents grew older; their condom use declined" and, of course, older adolescents also tend to be more sexually active."

See also: Centers for Disease Control, "Health-Risk Behaviors among Persons Aged 12-21 Years - United States, 1992," *Morbidity and Mortality Weekly Report*, 43, no. 13 (1994): 232; K. Hem et al., "Comparison of HIV+ and HIV- Adolescents: Risk Factors and Psychosocial Determinants, *Pediatrics*, 95, no. 1 *(1995):* 96-104; 5. Magura, J. Shapiro, and S. Kang, "Condom Use among Criminally-Involved Adolescents," *AIDS Care*, 6, no. 5 (1994): 595-603; S. Millstein, A. Moscicki and J. Broering, "Female Adolescents at High, Moderate, and Low Risk of Exposure to HIV: Differences in Knowledge, Beliefs and Behavior," *Journal of Adolescent Health*, 15, no. 2 (1993): 133-142; G. Remafedi, "Predictors of Unprotected Intercourse among Gay and Bisexual Youth: Knowledge, Beliefs, and Behavior," *Pediatrics*, 94, no. 2 (1994): 163-168; L. Ku, F. Sonenstein, and J. Pleck, "Young Men's Risk Behaviors for HIV Infection and Sexually Transmitted Diseases, 1988 through 1991," *American Journal of Public Health*, 83, no. 11 (1993): 1609-1615; M. Donald et al., "Determinants of Condom Use by Australian Secondary School Students," *Journal of Adolescent Health*, 15, no. 6 (1994): 503-510; G. Remafedi, "Cognitive and Behavioral Adaptations to HIV/AIDS among Gay and Bisexual Adolescents," *Journal of Adolescent Health*, 15, no. 2 (1994): 147; R. DiClemente et al., "African-American Adolescents Residing in High-Risk Urban Environments Do Use Condoms: Correlates and Predictors of Condom Use among Adolescents in Public Housing Developments," *Pediatrics*, 98, no. 2 (1996): 269-278.

30. Letters to the Editor, *The Female Patient*, 14 (1989): 17. See also: A. Sikand, M. Fisher and S. Friedman. "AIDS Knowledge, Concerns, and Behavioral Changes among Inner-City High School Students," *Journal of Adolescent Health*, 18, no. 5 (1996): 327.

31. "Risky Business," *People*, 5 November 1990: 54.

32. See note 31 above.

33. I. Litt, "Through the Looking Glass: Self-Esteem in Adolescents," *Journal of Adolescent Health*, 19 (1996): 1. A. Faulkner and L. Cranston, "Correlates of Same-Sexual Behavior in a Random Sample of Massachusetts High School Students," *American Journal of Public Health*, 88, no. 2 (1998): 262-266.

34. American Academy of Pediatrics, Committee on Adolescence, "Suicide and Suicide Attempts in Adolescents and Young Adults," *Pediatrics*, 81, no. 2 (1988): 322.

35. Project Reality. Golf, Illinois.

36. "Abortion Battle is Concern," *Washington Star*, 3 May 1979.

37. L. Ku, F. Sonenstein, and J. Pleck. "Association of AIDS Education and Sex Education with Sexual Behavior and Condom Use among Teenage Men," *Family Planning Perspectives*, 24, no. 3 (1992): 100.

38. *How to Help Your Kids Say "No" to Sex* (Colorado Springs, CO: Focus on the Family, 1992).

39. L. Ku, F. Sonenstein, and J. Pleck, "The Association of AIDS Education and Sex Education with Sexual Behavior and Condom Use among Teenage Men" *Family Planning Perspectives*, 24, no, 3 (1992): 103, Table 3; W. Marsiglio and F. Mott, "The Impact of Sex Education on Sexual Activity, Contraceptive Use and Premarital Pregnancy among American Teenagers," *Family Planning Perspectives*, 18, no 4 (1986): 151-61. L. Ku, F. Sonenstein and J. Pleck. "Factors Influencing First Intercourse for Teenage Men," *Public Health Reports*, 108, no. 6 (1993): 680-694.

40. J. Stout and F. Rivera, "Schools and Sex Education: Does It Work? *Pediatrics*, 83, no. 3 (1989): 3 75-79; P. Kilmann et al., Sex Education: A Review of its Effects," *Archives of Sexual Behavior*, 10, no. 2 (1981): 177-205; D. Kirby, "Sexuality Education: A More Realistic View of Its Effects," *Journal of School Health*, 55, no. 10 (1985): 421-24. One article states: "Major reviews of sexuality education programs in the American educational system consistently conclude that these programs have minimal impact on our adolescents." D. Greydanus, H. Pratt, and L. Dannison, "Sexuality Education Programs for Youth: Current State of Affairs and Strategies for the Future," *Journal of Sex Education and Therapy*, 21, no. 4 (1995): 244.

41. L. Muraskin, "Sex Education Mandates: Are They the Answer?" *Family Planning Perspectives*, 18, no. 4 (1986): 171.

42. Regular condom use was found among 34.4 percent of those who received AIDS education as opposed to 33.4 percent of those who did not. J. Anderson et al., "HIV/AIDS Knowledge and Sexual Behavior among High School Students," *Family Planning Perspectives*, 22,

no. 6 (1990): 252; L. Brown, G. Fritz, and V. Barone, "The Impact of AIDS Education on Junior and Senior High School Students," *Journal of Adolescent Health Care*, 10 (1989): 3 86-392. This last article begins with the comment: "Prevention, through school-based education campaigns, has been suggested as a response to the AIDS crisis although the impact of such education is unproven." In this study it was found that "change in knowledge was independent of change in tolerance, attitudes regarding high-risk behaviors, or coping strategies."

See also: V. Rickert, A. Gottlieb, and M. Jay, "A Comparison of Three Clinic-Based AIDS Education Programs on Female Adolescents' Knowledge, Attitudes, and Behavior;" *Journal of Adolescent Health Care*, 11 (1990): 298-303. The authors note: "No statistical differences were noted across groups regarding attitudes, or condom acquisition.

See also: V Rickert, M. Jay, A. Gottlieb, and C. Bridges, "Female's Attitudes and Behaviors Toward Condom Purchase and Use," *Journal of Adolescent Health Care*, 10 (1989): 3 13-316. The authors conclude that *"(*t)hese findings suggest that although adolescent females have an awareness about AIDS, their behavior remains unchanged" and "(i)t appears from our data, as well as others, that the media has sensitized this adolescent generation about the threat of AIDS, but most teens are not effecting changes that will optimally preclude transmission." This study also quotes a study by Kastinaki et al., which found that "those who were more knowledgeable were no more likely to use a condom."

See also: M. Durbin et al., "Factors Associated with Multiple Sex Partners among Junior High School Students, *Journal of Adolescent Health*, 14 (1993): 202-207; H. Huszti, "Acquired Immunodeficiency Syndrome Educational Program: Effects on Adolescents' Knowledge and Attitudes," *Pediatrics*, 84, no. 6 (1989): 986-94; J. Johnson et al., "A Program Using Medical Students to Teach high School Students about AIDS," *Journal of Medical Education*, 63 (1988): 522-530; R. DiClementi et al., "Evaluation of School-Based AIDS Curricula in San Francisco," *Journal of Sex Research*, 26 (1989): 188-198; A. Ruder, R. Flaim, D. Flatto, and A. Curran, "AIDS Education: Evaluation of School and Worksite Based Presentations," *New York State Medical Journal*, 90 (1990): 129-133; M. Nguyen, J. Saucier and L. Pica, "Influence of Attitudes on the Intention to Use Condoms in Quebec Sexually Active Male Adolescents," *Journal of Adolescent Health*, 15 (1994): 269-274.

43. 5. Kegeles, N. Adler and C. Irwin, "Sexually Active Adolescents and Condoms: Changes over One Year in Knowledge, Attitudes and Use," *American Journal of Public Health*, 78, no. 4 (1988): 460-61.

44. J. Jemmott, L. Jemmott, and G. Fong, "Reductions in HIV Risk-Associated Sexual Behaviors among Black Male Adolescents: Effects of an AIDS Prevention Intervention," *American Journal of Public Health*, 82 (1992): 372-377; H. Walter and R. Vaughan, "AIDS Risk Reduction among a Multiethnic Sample of Urban High School Students," *Journal of the American Medical Association*, 270, no. 6 (1993): 725-730; L. Ku, F. Sonenstein, and J. Pleck, "The Association of AIDS Education and Sex Education with Sexual Behavior and Condom Use among Teenage Men," *Family Planning Perspectives*, 24, no. 3 (1992): 100-106; J. Anderson et al., "HIV/AJD5 Knowledge and Sexual Behavior among High School Students," *Family Planning Perspectives*, 22, no. 6 (1990): 252-255.

45. "How California Can Fight Teen Pregnancy," an advertisement in the *Los Angeles Times*, 25 June 1996, placed by The Family Connection, A Partnership for Responsible Parenting.

46. How to Talk to Your Children about AIDS (New York: SIECUS, 1989), 8.

47. National Guidelines Task Force, "Guidelines for Sexuality Education: Kindergarten-12th Grade" (New York: SIECUS, 1991).

48. G. Kelly, *Learning About Sex: The Contemporary Guide for Young Adults* (New York: Barron's, 1986), 61.

49. T. Zanzig, *Sharing the Christian Message II* (Winona, MN: St. Mary's Press, 1985), 86.

50. S. Sheehan, "Another Kind of Sex Ed: Commitment, Not Condoms, Should Be the Lesson to Learn," *Newsweek*, 13 July 1992.

51. P. Kramer, *The Dynamics of Relationships*, Teacher Manual, Book 2 (Silver Spring, MD: Equal Partners, 1994), 14.

52. A. Landers, *Sex and the Teenager* (Creators Syndicate, Inc., 1987), 19.

53. "Rich and Judy" (San Francisco: Multifocus).

54. S. Montauk and M. Clasen, "Sex Education in Primary Care: Infancy to Puberty," *Medical Aspects of Human Sexuality*, January 1989: 27.

55. "Letters to the Editor;" *American Family Physician*, 46, no. 1 (1992): 45.

56. D. Kirby et al., "Reducing the Risk: Impact of a New Curriculum on Sexual Risk-Taking, *Family Planning Perspectives*, 23, no. 6 (1991): 253-63.

57. "Policy Statement: Contraception and Adolescents," *American Academy of Pediatrics News*, May 1990.

58. *Adolescent Medicine: State of the Art Reviews* (Philadelphia: Janley, Janley and Belfus, Inc., 1990): 43.

59. M. Howard and J McCabe, "Helping Teenagers Postpone Sexual Involvement," *Family Planning Perspectives*, 22, no. 1 (1990): 21.

60. L. Ku, F. Sonenstein, and J. Pleck, "The Association of AIDS Education and Sex Education with Sexual Behavior and Condom Use among Teenage Men," *Family Planning Perspectives*, 24, no. 3 (1992): 103, Table 3.

61. Community of Caring, Washington, D.C.

62. TEEN STAR, Natural Family Planning Center of Washington, D.C.

63. Best Friends Foundation, Washington, D.C.

64. Teen Choice, Educational Resource Center; Falls Church, VA.

65. Teen-Aid, Spokane, WA.

66. M. Young, P. Core-Gebhart, and D. Marx. "Abstinence-Oriented Sexuality Education: Initial Field Test Results of the Living Smart Curriculum," *FLEducator*, Summer 1992: 4-8.

67. S. Jorgensen, "Project Taking Charge: An Evaluation of an Adolescent Pregnancy Prevention Program," *Family Relations*, 40 (1991): 373-80.

68. J. Frost and J. Forrest, "Understanding the Impact of Effective Teenage Pregnancy Prevention Programs," *Family Planning Perspectives*, 27, no. 5 (1995): 188-195; D. Kirby et al:, "School-based Programs to Reduce Sexual Risk Behaviors: A Review of Effectiveness, *Public Health Reports*, 109, no. 3 (1994): 339-60; A. Mellanby et al., "School Sex Education: An Experimental Programme with Educational and Medical Benefit," *British Medical Journal*, 311 (1995): 414-7.

69. J. F. Masterson, *The Search for the Real Self: Unmasking the Personality Disorders of Our Age* (New York: The Free Press, 1988), 156.

70. A. Keyes, "The Condom Craze," *Orange County Register*, 9 March 1992.

71. H. V Sattler, *Challenging Children to Chastity* (St. Louis, MO: Central Bureau of the Catholic Central Verein of America, 1991): 47.

72. D. Haffner, "Sexual Backlash," *SIECUS Report*, April/May 1992: 20.

73. A. Ginsberg. S. Hanson, and D. Myers, *Responsibility and Knowledge: Their Role in Reducing Out-of- Wedlock Childbearing*, Washington D.C.: Department of Education. From: "In Defense of a Little Virginity," an advertisement placed by Focus on the Family in the *Los Angeles Times*, 9 September 1993.

74. R. Day, "Transition to First Intercourse among Racially and Culturally Diverse Youth," *Journal of Marriage and the Family*, 541 (1992): 749-62. For a study demonstrating higher rates of premarital sex among girls with poor relationships with their mother see: J. Jaccard, P. Dittus, and V Gordon. "Maternal Correlates of Adolescent Sexual and Contraceptive Behavior," *Family Planning Perspectives*, 28, no. 4 (1996): 159-65. Public discourse on the problem of absent fathers is increasing, yet one often finds its inexplicable absence in some of the most ostensibly authoritative articles on the subject. A recent editorial in the *Journal of the American Medical Association* listed the multiple factors thought responsible for the high rates of adolescent pregnancy in the United States. The author's best guess was that the problem is due to failure to provide education, limits to access for contraceptives, the irresponsible presentation of sex in the media, poverty, poor self-image, depression, and substance abuse with no mention of the obvious association of fatherlessness. I. Litt. "Pregnancy and Adolescence," *Journal of the American Medical Association*, 275, no. 13 (1996): 1030.

Chapter 17
1. "The Myth of Quality Time," *Newsweek*, 12 May 1997: 62-69.

2. "Letters in View," *Los Angeles Times*, 29 July 1991.

3. Self-Esteem Movement Gains Mainstream Respect, *Los Angeles Times*, 12 February 1996.

4. Zanzig, 84.

5. J. Coughlin, author of two chastity programs: *Facing Reality* and *Choosing the Best.*

6. J. Brothers, "Time for Parents to Do Some Soul-Searching," *Los Angeles Times*, 11 April 1991.

7. "Young and the Randy: Networks Build Plots around Teenage Sex," *Los Angeles Times*, 18 September 1991.

8. P. M. Quay, *The Christian Meaning of Human Sexuality* (San Francisco: Ignatius Press, 1985), 68.

9. R. Westheimer; *Dr. Ruth Talks to Kids About Sex* (New York: Macmillan Publishing Co., 1993), 52-53.

10. H. Letenberg, M. Detzer, and D. Srebnik, "Gender Differences in Masturbation and the Relation of Masturbation Experience in Pre-adolescence and/or Early Adolescence to Sexual Behavior and Sexual Adjustment in Young Adulthood, *Archives of Sexual Behavior*, 22, no. 2 (1992): 87-98.

11. J. Harvey, "The Pastoral Problem of Masturbation," *Linacre Quarterly*, 60, no. 2 (1993): 26. As noted in this reference, the complete text is found in "Letter to a Mr. Masson (March 6, 1956)," Wade Collection, Wheaton College, Wheaton, IL.

12. Asphyxophilia, or autoerotic strangulation, is most commonly performed by teenage boys. The participant stimulates himself, while applying a tight noose around his neck. The state of oxygen deficiency thus created enhances sexual stimulation. An estimated 500-1000 people die annually in the U.S. from misjudging the tightness of the noose. V Geberth, "Sexual Asphyxia: The Phenomenon of Autoerotic Fatalities," *Law and Order*, 37, no. 8 (1989): 79-85.

Conclusion

1. Personal communication: William Coulson, Ph.D., 9 September 1993.

2. "Don't Tell Me What to Read, See, or Think," *Los Angeles Times*, 14 January 1991.

3. D. Blankenhorn, *Fatherless in America: Confronting our Most Urgent Social Problem* (New York: Basic Books, 1995); B. Whitehead, *The Divorce Culture* (New York: Alfred A. Knopfe, 1997).

4. 1 Thessalonians 5, 21.

Appendix A

1. J. Pastorek, "Sexually Transmitted Diseases: Should Physicians More Strongly Advocate Abstinence and Monogamy?" *Postgraduate Medicine*, 91 (1992): 302.

Appendix B

1. "Swedish Women Prefer Reversible Methods; Few Choose to be Sterilized," *Family Planning Perspectives*, 22, no. 1 (1990): 43.

2. *Public Sex Education: A Report.* (Tupelo, MS: American Family Association, 1991).

3. E. Jones et al., "Teenage Pregnancy in Developed Countries: Determinants and Policy Implications," *Family Planning Perspectives*, 17 (1985): 56.

4. E. Persson and G. Jarlbro, "Sexual Behavior among Youth Clinic Visitors in Sweden: Knowledge and Experiences in an HIV Perspective," *Genitourinary Medicine*, 26 (1992): 5 14-24.

5. A. Andersson-Ellstrom and L. Forssman, "Sexually Transmitted Diseases-Knowledge and Attitudes among Young People, Developments in Sweden Between 1986 and 1988," *Journal of Adolescent Medicine*, 12 (1991): 72-6.

6. C. Anagrius, A. Hallén, H. Moi, and E. Persson, "Prevention of Sexually Transmitted Diseases and Abortions - The Present Situation for Medical Care of Sexually Transmitted Diseases in Sweden," *Seminars in Dermatology*, 9, no. 2 (1990): 190-3.

7. R. Utford, *The New Totalitarians* (New York: Stein and Day, 1972).

Glossary

Note: Definitions marked * are quoted from *Merriam Webster's Collegiate Dictionary*, 10th edition, 1994.

abortion. The intentional killing of a human embryo or fetus. This may be done through surgical or chemical means. Spontaneous abortion is the medical term for miscarriage, in which case the developing embryo or fetus dies spontaneously within the womb, without artificial, external influence. Spontaneous abortions often occur in association with birth defects, abnormalities of the uterus, and maternal illnesses.

abortifacient. A device or hormone, often considered a "contraceptive," but which has as its primary mechanism of action killing of a developing embryo, not creation of a barrier to fertilization.

addiction. Habitual behavior primarily used to reduce, avoid or escape stress that entails likely subsequent, serious harm to the addict and/or others.

AIDS. The Acquired Immunodeficiency Syndrome. The last stage of HIV infection characterized by unusual infections and cancers.

arousal. A state of excitement.

barrier methods of contraception. Methods of contraception which prevent sperm from coming into contact with an egg, e.g., condom, diaphragm, and cervical cap.

bisexual. A person whose gender orientation is roughly equal toward males and females.

birth control pill/"the pill". A potent steroid hormone pill which artificially regulates a woman's menstrual cycles and which is commonly prescribed for use as a contraceptive. Its primary mode of action is to reduce the likelihood of conception but it can also act to abort a developing embryo.

cervix. The lowest part of the uterus (womb). A common location for cancer to develop.

codependency. *"A psychological condition or a relationship in which a person is controlled or manipulated by another who is affected with a pathological condition (as an addiction to alcohol or heroin)."

colposcopy. The clinical examination of a woman's vagina and cervix incorporating a special magnifying instrument (colposcope) and dyes for better visualization and evaluation of the tissues.

conception/fertilization. The union of sperm and egg which occurs in the fallopian tube approximately one week after ovulation. This union forms the one-celled zygote.

contraceptives. Medications or devices used to prevent the union of egg and sperm.

dysfunctional. Unhealthy, abnormal, or otherwise impaired.

ectopic or tubal pregnancy. Occurs when an embryo becomes lodged in the fallopian tube during its travel toward the uterus. Such embryos eventually die and may threaten the life of the mother by causing internal bleeding.

embryo. The developing human person from conception through the second month of life.

exhibitionist. A person who indecently exposes parts of his on her body to unsuspecting strangers.

extramarital sex. Sexual intercourse between a married person and someone other than his or her spouse.

fallopian tube. *"Either of the pair of tubes conducting the egg from the ovary to the uterus."

fertile. Capable of reproducing.

Fertility Awareness. A method by which a couple achieves greater awareness of the woman's natural, biological rhythms and uses this knowledge to attempt to achieve or avoid pregnancy.

fertility rate. Birth rate, i.e., number of births per one thousand women per year.

fertility regulation. Any attempt to increase or decrease a sexually active couple's chances of reproducing.

fetus. The developing organism inside the uterus during the period from the end of the second month of life until birth.

frustration. Disappointment or dissatisfaction arising from unfulfilled desires.

gay. A synonym for "homosexual" which supposedly connotes other characteristics, the specifics of which no one can agree.

health. * "Sound in body, mind, or spirit." That state which allows one to live a full and content life.

heterosexual. A person whose predominant gender orientation is toward the opposite sex.

HIV. The Human Immunodeficiency Virus, the causal organism of HIV disease and AIDS.

holistic (approach to sex). To view sexuality in the greater sense as it relates to each person as a whole or each couple as a unit; in contrast to arbitrarily distinguishing between genital and non-genital sexual interactions, isolating a person's sexuality from himself or herself, or isolating a couple's sexuality from the totality of their relationship.

homophobia. *"Irrational fear of, aversion to, or discrimination against homosexuality or homosexuals."

homosexual. A person whose predominant gender orientation is toward the same sex.

implantation/nidation. The attachment of a developing embryo to the uterine wall. The placenta develops at this site of attachment.

I.U.D. Intrauterine device. A birth control device which is placed in the uterus. Most I.U.D.s work primarily by inhibiting implantation of the developing embryo onto the wall of the uterus, thereby causing an abortion.

masturbation. Sexual self-stimulation of the genitals.

ménage à trois. An intimate sexual interaction or relationship involving three people, not all of the same sex.

menstruation. The monthly evacuation of the inner lining of the uterus following the demise of the unfertilized ovum (egg). Often associated with uncomfortable, lower abdominal cramps.

method failure rates. As applied to efforts to avoid pregnancy, the optimal estimated failure rate that may be achieved by a method of fertility regulation under ideal conditions. It is an unrealistic expectation when considering any population of imperfect humans.

miscarriage. *"Spontaneous expulsion of a human fetus before it is viable and esp. between the 12th and 28th weeks of gestation."

modesty. The moral virtue which moderates how one dresses, moves and speaks so as to avoid undue attention to one's sexual nature. An excess of modesty is prudishness, a lack of it is immodesty.

Morality. of, or relating to, the goodness of behavior.

Natural Family Planning. See "Fertility Awareness."

nonsurgical. Not involving surgery. The desired therapeutic effect is brought about without resorting to surgery, e.g., through medications alone.

objective. *"Reality independent of the mind."

oral contraceptive. See "birth control pill."

outercourse. Intimate sexual activity between two people that leads to climax for one or both of them but does not involve genital penetration.

ovum. *"The female gamete"; an egg prior to fertilization (conception).

ovulation. The release of the ovum (egg) from the ovary.

Pap smear. A screening test for cancer of the cervix that is performed during a gynecological exam. A sample of cervical cells are obtained using a swab, small spatula or brush and are then sent to the laboratory for evaluation.

pelvic inflammatory disease. An infection of the fallopian tubes in the female. It is always considered to be sexually transmitted and is most commonly caused by chlamydia or gonorrhea.

PID. See "pelvic inflammatory disease."

"The Pill." See "birth control pill."

Planned Parenthood Federation of America. A private national organization which actively promotes access to abortion, contraception, and comprehensive sex education. Planned Parenthood clinics perform 134,000 abortions annually, making it the foremost provider of abortion services in the United States, (See: Planned Parenthood Federation of America 1993-1994 Annual Report [New York: Planned Parenthood Federation of America, 1994]). It receives large sums of money from the United States government and from many national foundations and corporations.

pornography. *"The depiction of erotic behavior (as in pictures or writing) intended to cause sexual excitement." Or, to paraphrase Supreme Court Justice Potter Stewart: I don't know how to define it, but I know it when I see it.

pregnancy. The state of carrying a developing embryo or fetus.

premarital abstinence. Refraining from premarital sex.

premarital sex. Sexual intercourse between two single people.

procreate. To bring forth offspring, to have children.

psychosexual. Mental processes related to sex.

psychosexual dysfunction. Unhealthy attitudes about sex.

religion. A faith, an institutionalized set of teachings, or ritualized activities with which an individual affiliates because it or they most accurately reflect the individual's understanding about the nature of God and humankind, and the relationship of the two to each other.

screening tests for STDs. Tests that are used to identify patients who harbor a sexually transmitted disease despite having no symptoms.

secondary virginity. When one who has previously engaged in premarital sex resolves not to do so again.

self-esteem. One's value of oneself. Self-confidence, self-respect, self-love.

self-stimulation. See "masturbation."

sequela. Aftereffects, results, or consequences.

sexual. *"of relating to, on associated with sex or the sexes."

sexuality. *"The quality or state of being sexual."

sexual revolution. The current period of dramatic change in the attitudes and behaviors related to sex and family life which began in the 1960s.

SIECUS. The Sex Information and Education Council of the United States. A private, national organization committed to promoting comprehensive sex education to all children, starting in kindergarten. It actively promotes the use of contraceptives and abortion services, the use of sexually explicit videos, and self-stimulation. It does not consider premarital or homosexual sex acts to be unhealthy or immoral.

situational ethics. An ethical system which states that no act is objectively or certainly immoral, that the morality of all behaviors must be considered in the light of the circumstances involved.

sperm. *"A male gamete." As the egg is to the female, the sperm is to the male. Both contain half of the genetic material needed to create new life. Sperm are contained in semen.

spiritual nature. An indomitable inner force that leads people to aspire to greatness, whether or not they ascribe to a particular religious belief system. It imparts an instinctual sense of purpose in life, of the existence of a transcendental realm, and thereby summons all persons to selflessness and to do good and avoid evil.

sterilization. A surgical procedure performed on a male or female for the purpose of making that person incapable of reproducing.

subjective. *"Characteristic of or belonging to reality as perceived rather than as independent of mind."

symptom. *"Subjective evidence of disease or physical disturbance."

transsexual. *"A person with a psychological urge to belong to the opposite sex that may be carried to the point of undergoing surgery to modify the sex organs to mimic the opposite sex."

transvestite. *"A person and especially a male who adopts the dress and often the behavior typical of the opposite sex especially for purposes of emotional or sexual gratification."

user failure rates. As applied to efforts to avoid pregnancy, the realistic failure rate for a particular method of fertility regulation under typical conditions.

virgin. *"A person who has not had sexual intercourse."

virtue. A good habit. Those character traits that are most admired and that lead to the most genuine freedom, love and self-fulfillment. The greatest virtue, the one toward which all others are directed, is charity.

voyeur. *"One who habitually seeks sexual stimulation by visual means."

zygote. The single-celled organism formed by the union of sperm and egg. Through cell division the zygote becomes an embryo.

Resources

These resources are of particular value for those who are interested in further reading but unsure where to start. Appearance in this list does not guarantee that any of these resources coincide entirely with the author's position.

General

Dr. James Dobson's Focus On The Family organization is the best single resource for practical information of which I am aware. It is Protestant and most of its resources are religious oriented, but it is a remarkable source of practical information for everyone. Focus on the Family produces a daily syndicated radio program and publishes numerous books, magazines, and videos geared toward intact and single parent families, teenagers, physicians, etc. Write to:

Focus on the Family, P.O. Box 35500, Colorado Springs, CO 80935-3550. (800) 232-6459 or (800) A-FAMILY.

Pornography and Censorship

Michael Medved, *Hollywood vs. America* (New York: Zondervan, 1992).

A Guide to What One Person Can Do About Pornography. A report published by the American Family Association, Post Office Drawer 2440, Tupelo, MS 38803. (601) 844-5036.

Fertility Awareness/Natural Family Planning

For more information about the Ovulation Method:
Pope Paul VI Institute, 6901 Mercy Road, Omaha, NE 68106. (402) 390-9168. This is a Catholic organization.

For more information about the Symptothermal Method:
The Couple to Couple League, P.O. Box 111184, Cincinnati, OH 45211-1184. (513) 471-2000. This is an interfaith organization.

For more information about the Billing's Ovulation Method:
Natural Family Planning Center of Washington, D.C. Inc., P.O. Box 30239, Bethesda, MD 20817-0239. (301) 897-9323.

To contact a physician sympathetic to natural family planning: *NFP – Only Physicians Directory: A listing of physicians and other medical professionals who do not prescribe, perform, or refer for contraception, sterilization, abortion, or in-vitro fertilization.* Published by: One More Soul, 616 Five Oaks Avenue, Dayton, OH 45406. (800) 307-7685.

Thomas Hilgers, MD. *The Medical & Surgical Practice of NaProTechnolog* (Pope Paul VI Institute Press, Omaha Nebraska, 2004). This is an extraordinary, 1,200 page medical text representing a lifetime of work by the leading NFP physician in the United States.

Abortion

Reardon, *David. Aborted Women Silent No More* (Westchester, IL: Crossway Books, 1987).

Willke, John C. *Abortion: Questions & Answers* (Cincinnati, OH: Hays Publishing Co., Inc., 1988).

Sexual Addiction

Focus on the Family. Ask for information about sexual addiction.
P.O. Box 35500, Colorado Springs, CO 80935-3550
(800) 232-6459

Arterburn, Stephen. *Addicted to "Love." Understanding Dependencies of the Heart: Romance, Relationships and Sex* (Ann Arbor, MI: Servant, 1996).

Carnes, Patrick. *Out of the Shadows: Understanding Sexual Addiction* (Minneapolis, MN: CompCare, 1992). (800) 328-3330.

Self-help Organizations

Sexaholics Anonymous
P.O. Box 111910, Nashville TN, 37222
(615) 331-6230

Sex and Love Addicts Anonymous
P.O. Box 650010, West Newton, MA 02165-0010

(617) 332-1845

Sex Addicts Anonymous
National Service Organization for S.A.A. Inc.
P.O. Box 70949, Houston TX 77270
(713) 869-4902

Sexual Compulsives Anonymous
(800) 977-4325

Sex Offenders Anonymous (SOANON)
P.O. Box 8287, Van Nuys, CA 91409
(818) 244-6331

Homosexuality

Books:

Harvey, John. *The Homosexual Person (San* Francisco: Ignatius, 1987). The author, a Catholic priest, addresses a general audience.

Nicolosi, *Joseph. Healing Homosexuality: Case Stories of Reparative Therapy* (Northvale, NJ: Jason Aronsen, 1993).

Worthen, Anita and Davies, Bob. *Someone I Love is Gay: How Family & Friends Can Respond,* (Downers Grove, *IL: Intervarsity,* 1996). A sensitive and useful book written from a Christian perspective.

Siegel, Elaine V. *Female Homosexuality: Choice without Volition* (Hillsdale, NJ: Analytic, 1988; Distributed *by* Lawrence Erlbaum Associates, Inc., 365 Broadway, Hillsdale, NJ 07642).

Dr. Siegel writes for mental health professionals, is quite academic, and, therefore, is recommended only for those with a serious interest in lesbianism.

Self-help Organizations

Homosexuals Anonymous
P.O. Box 7881, Reading, PA 19603.
(215) 376-1146

Courage (Catholic)
Fr. John Harvey, St. Michael's Rectory,
424 West 34th St., New York, NY 10001.
(212) 421-0426

Exodus International (Protestant/Evangelical)
P.O. Box 2121, San Rafael, CA 94912.
(415) 454-1017

Teaching Morality to Children

Kilpatrick, William. *Why Johnny Can't Tell Right From Wrong: Moral Illiteracy and the Case for Character Education* (New York: Simon and Schuster, 1992). Kilpatrick writes with particular relevance for parents and teachers.

Sex Education

Sexual Wisdom for Catholic Adolescents. This 18 lesson course, written by Dr. Richard Wetzel, the author of *Sexual Wisdom*, is available as a free download from sexual-wisdom.com. It was written specifically for late-adolescent Catholic students but is recommended to any parent who takes seriously his or her role as the primary sex educator of his or her children. It was written to compliment this book with more specific guidance to parents on sex educating their children. It is the course that makes good on the promise: "I'll tell you when you get older!" We expect to publish it in book form very soon.

National Guidelines for Sexuality and Character Education by the Medical Institute for Sexual Health, P.O. Box 4919, Austin, TX 78765-4919. (800) 892-9484.

Whitehead, Margaret and Onalee McGraw. *Foundations for Family Life Education: A Guidebook for Professionals and Parents* by the Educational Guidance Institute, 188 Berbusse Lane, Front Royal, VA 22630. (540) 635-4420. Or obtain through Project Reality at P.O Box 97, Golf, IL 60029-0097, (708) 729-3298.

Public School Sex Education: A Report. Published by the American Family Association, Post Office Drawer 2440, Tupelo, MS 38803.

Sedlak, James. Parent Power!! – How Parents Can Gain Control of the School Systems that Educate their Children (1992). To obtain this book write: James W. Sedlak at STOPP International, P.O. Box 1350, Stafford, VA 22555-9986.

Newman, Anne and Dinah Richard. *Healthy Sex Education In Your Schools.* Available through Texas Family Research Center at (210) 681-4311. This practical book for parents describes how to evaluate school sex education courses.

School-based Clinics

Mosbacker, Barret L. *School Based Clinics* (Westchester IL: Crossway Books, 1988).

Parenting

Norris, C. and J. Waibel Owen. *Know Your Body* (Huntington, IN: Our Sunday Visitor, 1982). Written from a Catholic perspective. Other Catholic material may be obtained from the Alliance for Chastity Education. P.O. Box 11297, Cincinnati, OH 45211-0297.

Dobson, James. *Preparing for Adolescence* (Ventura, CA: Gospel Light Publishers, Regal Books Division, 1989). Written from a Protestant perspective. Other Protestant literature is obtainable from Focus on the Family (listed above).

World Population

Kasun, Jacqueline. *The War Against Population* (San Francisco: Ignatius, 1988).

Sanera, Michael and Jane Shaw. *Facts Not Fear: A Parent's Guide to Teaching Children About the Environment* (Washington, D.C.: Regnary, 1996).